♠ ♡ ♣

Play More Bridge With OMAR SHARIF

♠ ♡ ♣ ♢

♠ ♡ ♣ ♢

Play More Bridge

WITH

OMAR SHARIF

♠ ♡ ♣ ♢

In association with the

First published 1994 by Pan Macmillan Limited

Cavaye Place London SW10 9PG
and Basingstoke

Associated companies throughout the world

ISBN 0 333 61416 X

Copyright © Express Newspapers plc 1994

The right of Omar Sharif to be identified as the
author of this work has been asserted by him in accordance
with the Copyright, Designs and Patents Act 1988.

All rights reserved. No reproduction, copy or transmission
of this publication may be made without written permission.
No paragraph of this publication may be reproduced, copied or
transmitted save with written permission or in accordance with
the provisions of the Copyright Act 1956 (as amended). Any
person who does any unauthorised act in relation to
this publication may be liable to criminal prosecution
and civil claims for damages.

1 3 5 7 9 8 6 4 2

A CIP catalogue record for this book is available from
the British Library

Typeset by CentraCet Limited, Cambridge
Printed and bound in Great Britain by
Cox & Wyman Ltd, Reading, Berks

This book is sold subject to the condition that it shall not,
by way of trade or otherwise, be lent, re-sold, hired out,
or otherwise circulated without the publisher's prior consent
in any form of binding or cover other than that in which
it is published and without a similar condition including this
condition being imposed on the subsequent purchaser

Contents

Preface

It is perhaps odd that, for although not usually at a loss for words, I found it difficult to write this preface. The trouble is that this book – based on hands used in my weekly articles published in the *Sunday Express* – is a sequel to *Play Bridge with Omar Sharif* which was also based on these articles. Although I say it myself, the first book was well reviewed, seemed successful, and the translations into Italian and Spanish read equally pleasantly. However, the preface to the first book encapsulated my introduction to and career in bridge and leaves me little to say now.

The solution, as I saw it, was to introduce myself to new readers with a précis of the previous preface (with the recommendation that they read the first book for further details!) and compensate by reflecting and reminiscing a little before leading into each chapter.

I started taking an interest in bridge when I picked up a Charles Goren primer in a Cairo bookshop during a break in filming. As a lot of film work consists of simply waiting, I had plenty of time to get completely hooked on the game. I spent a great many evenings (and nights!) playing in Cairo and, later, in the middle of *Lawrence of Arabia*, a two month break in London meant that I could widen my bridge experience and, more important, widen my circle of friendship with many of the leading players of the day.

High points in my bridge career included playing in my own Bridge Circus; sponsoring a world tour with Garozzo, Belladonna, Delmouly and Yallouze; joining the Lancia team, again with members of the famous Italian Blue Team; and representing the United Arab Republic in the 1964 and 1968 World Team Olympiads. I should mention, with due modesty, that I was already a double sporting international. This all stemmed from when, at the age of ten, I was transferred from a French school in Cairo, where there was no sport, to an English school where I was positively encouraged to work at cricket (yes, cricket!) and football. Subsequently I toured England with an Egyptian cricket team and also played football for the Egyptian national side. I played against Pele and also the famous Hungarian side of 1963.

I experienced considerable difficulty in classifying the hands that I finally selected for this book. Into which chapter should I put an optimistically bid slam hand that met a good defence and ended with a memorably funny remark? Then, again, I decided on a neat and descriptive chapter heading that fitted a couple of hands beautifully. Unfortunately I found no other hands that matched and so the proposed chapter had to be scrapped and its two solitary constituents despatched to other homes. This explains, to some extent, why each chapter has a wide ranging title. Indeed, at one point I was seriously considering entitling them Bridge Hands I, Bridge Hands II, etc.

My final worry was that, especially after 15 years, I am not quite sure of the provenance of all the deals. Sometimes I may have picked up an idea from a magazine and modified the hand to illustrate a particular point. Much more often the hands are from my personal experience and I think that it would be fitting to dedicate this book to all those partners (and opponents!) who I have telephoned late at night to ask, for example, 'What were your Hearts on the hand where you led the Jack of Diamonds against Three No-trumps?' Without their willing help, a number of the weekly articles would never have seen the light of day.

CHAPTER ONE

Slams

For many people slams are the high point of this game. At high-stake rubber bridge their success or failure can make all the difference between a good or bad session. Even in a pairs competition, where the financial interest may be lacking, it is a well-established fact that on hands with twelve top winners (no more, no less) the side bidding and making the apparently obvious small slam will score comfortably over average. Inevitably, especially in a large and mixed field, some pairs will have stopped in game, some will have hazarded an impossible grand, and some will end in a strange part score!

There is always an air of increased tension when a slam has been reached. The player on lead seems to deliberate longer before making his selection. Declarer waits anxiously to see if his partner has the right cards. Perhaps dummy has the most nerve-racking task – first of all waiting to see if declarer beams or scowls when his hand is exposed and, later, watching the tempo at which his partner plays. Is it brisk and confident, with an early claim in mind? Is it slow and laborious with longer and longer intervals between each play (often a prelude to failure)?

There is the delightful but possibly apocryphal

story of two of my old friends of the famous Italian Blue Team – Giorgio Belladonna and Benito Garozzo – having the innocuous arrangement that when dummy appeared declarer was supposed to say 'Thank you' if everything had gone according to plan and '*Grazie*' if he thought that his partner had made the wrong bid. You can visualise the situation – an extremely complex artificial auction had led to an extremely reasonable grand slam. After the opening lead, declarer, already immersed in percentage calculations, absent-mindedly murmured '*Grazie*'. Convinced that he had made exactly the right responses to all of the elaborate asking bids, dummy rose to his feet in indignation. '*Grazie*?' he stormed. 'What do you mean, "*Grazie*"?'

Justifiable Excitement

'I only made an overcall!' complained South as the bidding ended. 'You didn't have to get so excited!' But he brightened up when he saw dummy . . .

With North-South vulnerable, East dealt and opened Three Hearts. South, with little excuse, over-called with Three Spades. North launched immediately into Blackwood but South was so ashamed of his vulnerable intervention at the Three level that he replied Five Clubs denying an Ace. (This is neither unethical nor illegal, but it totally destroys partnership confidence.)

Reluctantly North bid only Six Spades and West led the two of Hearts (clearly a singleton). A successful

Diamond finesse would give him all 13 tricks but, if it failed, he would lose two tricks.

There was no rush, so declarer started by playing the King, Ace and another Club which ruffled in hand. When East showed out, it was clear that he had started with seven Hearts, singletons in both black suits, and hence four Diamonds.

South could see daylight now – he played off his remaining trumps, throwing a Heart and a Diamond from dummy. East had to keep the King of Hearts and his guarded Queen of Diamonds. Declarer exited with a Heart to the King and the enforced Diamond return gave dummy the last three tricks.

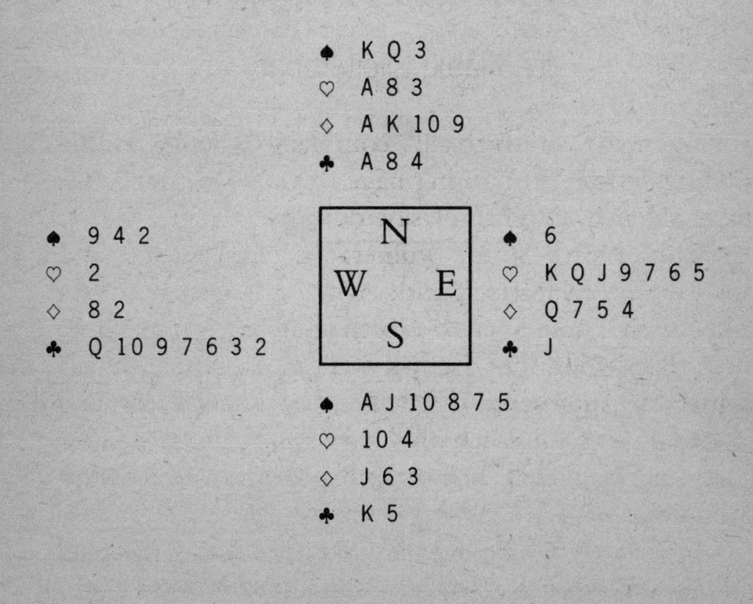

What was the Problem?

Do you, like me, find hands (not always with the bidding or the final contract) written down on the backs of old score-cards and then waste considerable time trying to puzzle out what the problem could have been? At least the following deal had 'Seven Diamonds' scrawled beneath it.

It looks cut and dried. In Seven Diamonds declarer can draw trumps in three rounds, test the Hearts – just in case either defender has started with Q10 doubleton – and, when this fails, fall back on the winning ruffing finesse in Spades.

What *could* have been the problem? At last the penny dropped. At some stage, after Diamonds had been

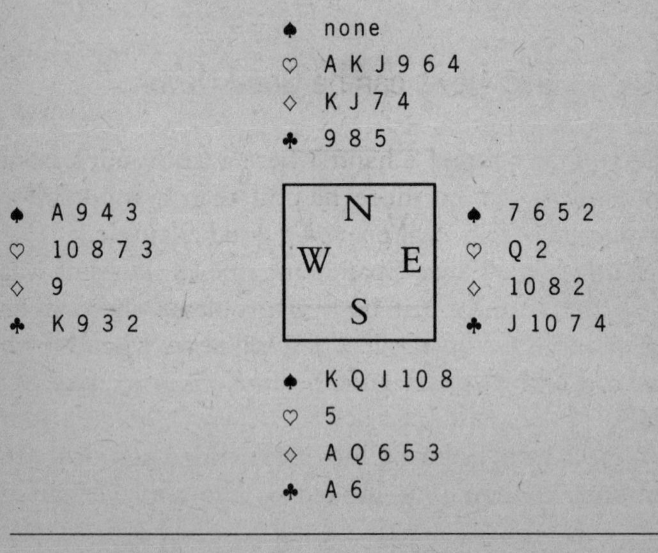

North: ♠ none; ♡ A K J 9 6 4; ◇ K J 7 4; ♣ 9 8 5

West: ♠ A 9 4 3; ♡ 10 8 7 3; ◇ 9; ♣ K 9 3 2

East: ♠ 7 6 5 2; ♡ Q 2; ◇ 10 8 2; ♣ J 10 7 4

South: ♠ K Q J 10 8; ♡ 5; ◇ A Q 6 5 3; ♣ A 6

agreed as trumps, North must have made a bid that guaranteed first-round control in Spades, his partner's first suit. West, knowing this must be a void – for he held the Ace himself – imaginatively led a low Spade against the grand slam!

A likely sequel would have been that, as East was 'marked' with the Ace of Spades, declarer ruffed on the table and started on trumps. The 3-1 break would have meant that there was no chance of establishing Hearts with a ruff – that would have led to 12 tricks at most.

Apparently needing six tricks from the Heart suit, declarer finessed the Jack on the first round . . .

Did it actually happen? A successful underlead of an Ace against a grand slam? I am sure that in that case it would have been widely reported. Alas, it was probably just a might-have-been.

Bad News can be Good News

Have you ever found a hand where a really unpleasant trump break can be more helpful than a moderately irritating one? This deal proved a good example.

South opened Two Spades at game all. His suit was not all that strong, but he saw problems ahead if he opened only One Spade. It was good news when North raised to Three Spades and the final contract was Six Spades.

West led the Jack of Clubs and, with a sure loser in Diamonds to come, it looked as though everything would depend on a kindly trump position. With commendable foresight declarer, after winning, began with the Ace of Hearts and a Heart ruff in hand.

Now a Spade to the Ace revealed the bad news, but gave declarer an intriguing chance. He ruffed another Heart in hand and followed with three rounds of Clubs, ruffing his Queen on the table – the key play.

A third Heart ruff in hand was followed by his remaining top Diamond and another Diamond. With nothing but trumps left, West was forced to ruff and lead a Spade into South's King-Jack.

And if West had held only **S** Q 10 9? Then declarer would have been faced with two sure losers, for West would not have been on lead at the critical stage.

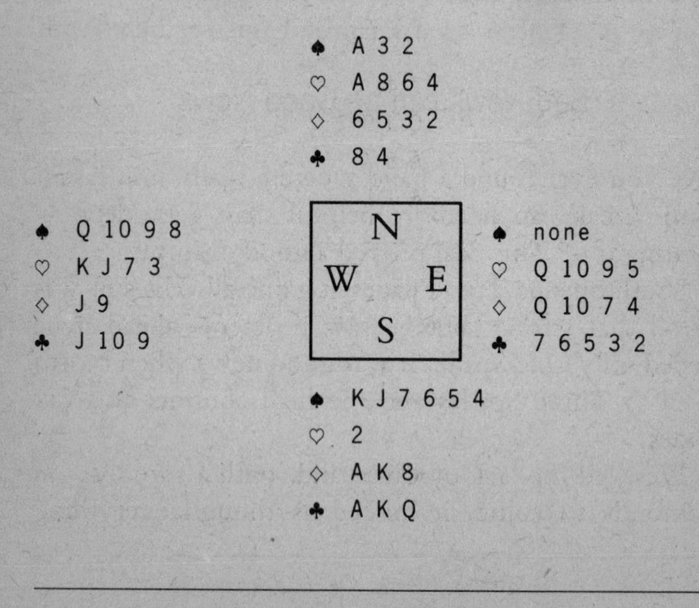

Rediscovery

The play of this hand may not be a completely new idea – but it was nevertheless a delight to watch my partner discover the tactic for himself during this slam contract.

As North at love-all I opened One Club. Partner responded One Heart, West overcalled with One Spade and I supported the Hearts. With my rather feeble opening bid I was slightly alarmed when partner leapt to Six Hearts without investigation – I assumed he knew what he was doing.

West led the Queen of Spades, and declarer won. He laid down the Ace of Hearts and looked hurt when East showed out.

With a sure trump loser it looked as though the slam would depend on a Diamond finesse, but South

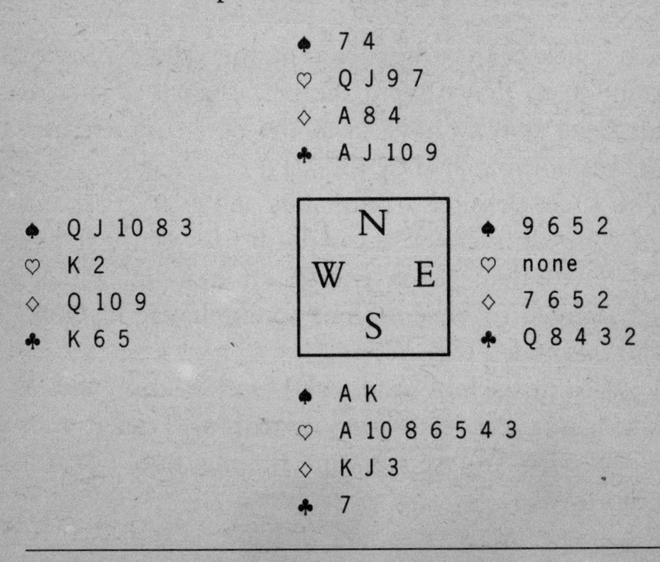

found a neat way to improve his chances. He played off his second top Spade and cashed the Ace of Clubs – the key play – before giving West the lead with the King of trumps.

As either a Spade (conceding a ruff and discard) or a Diamond would be fatal, West was reduced to leading a Club. But which one? If he led the King, declarer would ruff and take a ruffing finesse against East's Queen to discard his losing Diamond.

So West tried the six of Clubs. South ruffed East's Queen, crossed to dummy with a trump and, judging the position perfectly, trumped another Club to bring down West's King, so establishing dummy's Jack.

Very neat! And partner was justifiably proud.

The Operation was a Success, But . . .

More by luck than judgement, partner and I reached the grand slam that offered the best chance of success on this deal. It may have been the best contract but, alas, it was not matched by the play.

With three possible trump suits and every first and second control in the pack, we both had plenty to say for no fewer than seven rounds of bidding. Finally partner jumped to Seven Clubs to emphasise his solid suit and this ended the auction.

West led the Jack of Spades and, with 12 top winners in sight, it was automatic to draw trumps. Four rounds were necessary and this meant finding two discards from dummy.

Arguing that the Diamonds, where there were only four cards missing, were more likely to behave than the Hearts (where five were missing), declarer threw two Hearts from the table. This proved fatal and eventually a trick had to be lost in Diamonds. The point that South overlooked was that he needed only four Diamond tricks, not five.

If he throws two Diamonds from the table, he can test the Diamonds. As long as they are not 4–0 he can claim. If, as the cards lie, West shows out, there is time to play the Ace, Queen and King of Hearts, then ruff a Heart. This establishes dummy's long Heart for the 13th trick. It was an expensive mistake.

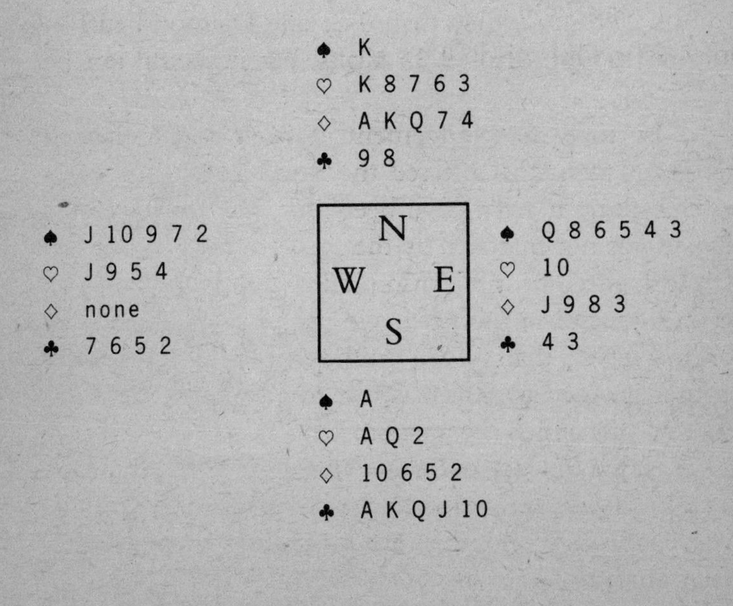

Keeping Control

Players often fail to find the best line when dealing with a high-level contract with only a 4–3 fit in trumps. Consider this example.

At love-all South opened One Diamond. North responded One Heart and South rebid One Spade. North explored with Two Clubs (fourth suit) and South stretched a little when he jumped to Three Diamonds. North's next move of Blackwood, with no suit agreed, was ill-advised and the partnership ended uneasily in Six Spades.

West led the Queen of Clubs and declarer won in dummy. If the Diamonds divided evenly and the trumps were no worse than 4-2, one Diamond ruff in dummy would yield all 13 tricks; but it would not be

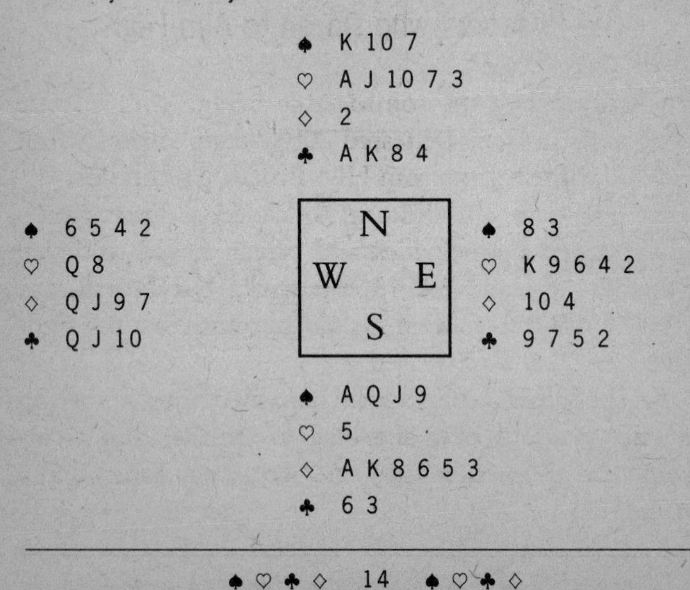

possible to trump two Diamonds (in the event of a bad break) unless the trumps divided 3-3.

Rather than establish his long suit, declarer pinned his hopes on a cross-ruff – with five side-suit winners he could score all of his trumps separately provided he could ruff the third round of Diamonds with dummy's seven of trumps. But East over-ruffed that seven with the eight and returned a Club.

Perhaps the best way to tackle the hand, so as to cater for 4-2 breaks in both critical suits, is to concede a Diamond at trick two. After winning a Club or Heart return on the table, South can come to hand with a trump, ruff a low Diamond and overtake dummy's King of Spades to draw trumps and enjoy the established Diamonds.

The Prisoners who Dared to Aim High

Not for everyone the comfortable bridge club – some recent rubbers were contested 20,000ft up Everest! And this hand came to me from HM Prison, Highpoint.

At one table the bidding followed a direct route. South opened Four Spades and North raised to Seven (!) Spades. There were 13 top tricks but North was distinctly lucky in finding his partner with just the right cards.

At the other table South launched into a forcing sequence without ever showing his Spades and ascertained that his partner held one Ace, two Kings and a Queen.

The final plunge to Seven Spades again worked well, for partner turned up with the right Ace and right Kings. Both North–South pairs relaxed, only to find neither had gained.

How could the grand slam have been reached accurately? A popular idea is to open Four Diamonds with the South hand (South African Texas), showing a very good bid of Four Spades without the high cards to open Two, with Spades as the agreed trump suit.

North makes a gentle move with Five Clubs, South co-operates with Five Diamonds and, with no Heart control, North signs off in Five Spades. Now, when South shows his first round control with Six Hearts, North may take the plunge.

I am not sure if I'd have got it right – but they certainly did at Highpoint.

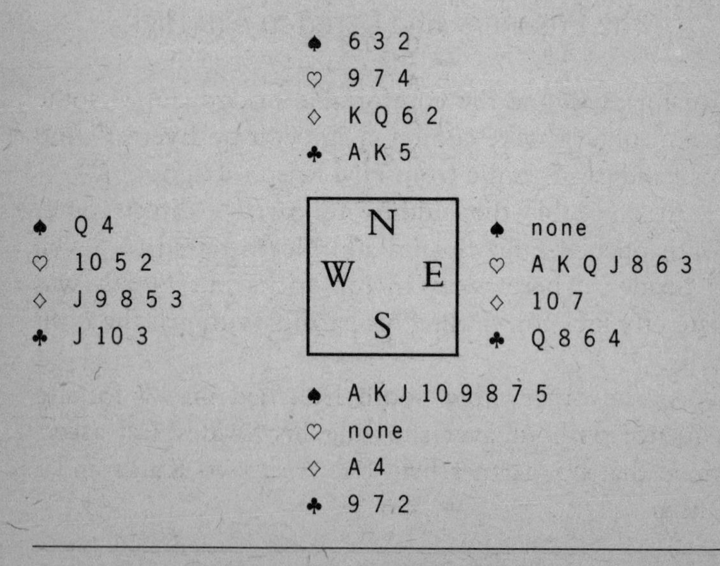

It's a Pleasure . . .

One of the pleasures in this game comes when you recognise a standard situation. Even more fun is finding a winning play from first principles.

With East–West vulnerable, South dealt and opened Four Spades. Lacking any delicate machinery to explore the possibilities of a grand slam, North raised directly to Six Spades.

West led the King of Diamonds and a glance at dummy showed South that, if the Clubs divided 4-1, even the small slam required careful play.

After winning the lead and drawing the missing trumps with his Ace, declarer played off the two top Clubs. A 3-2 division would have allowed an immediate claim and, if West had shown up with four Clubs, a straightforward Heart finesse would have end-played

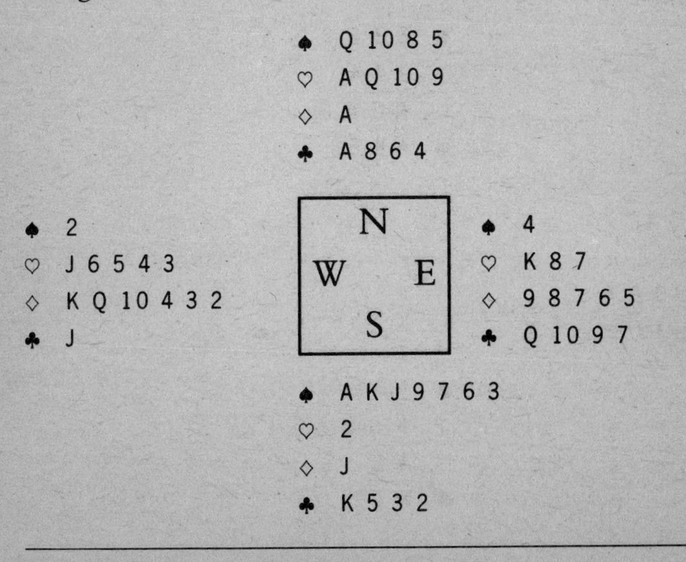

East. But this was not the case. Declarer played off the Ace of Hearts and followed with the Queen. If West had played low South planned to discard a Club, leaving West on lead with the choice of conceding a ruff and discard or establishing dummy's ten of Hearts.

As the cards lay, East covered with the King, South ruffed, crossed to dummy with a trump and triumphantly discarded a losing Club on the ten of Hearts. West won but the nine of Hearts was established and provided declarer's 12th trick.

Camrose Carelessness

The difference between the expert and the competent player lies less in sheer technique than in the avoidance of mistakes.

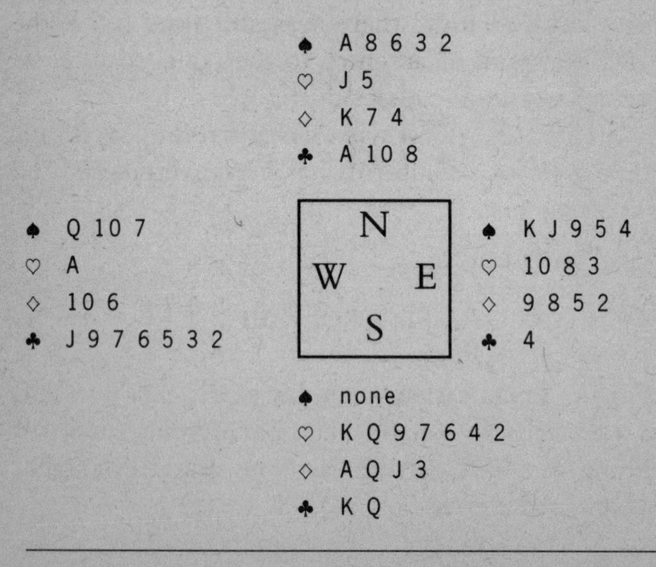

Take this deal from a Camrose match (one of the home internationals) – the trouble was that it all looked too simple with about 14 possible winners in sight and only the Ace of trumps to lose . . .

South played in Six Hearts after a straightforward auction and West led the three of Clubs – a slightly deceptive choice! You can guess how declarer played: in a completely routine fashion, he won in hand and led a trump towards dummy's Jack. West won, gave his partner a Club ruff and that was the end of the slam.

How might a more suspicious declarer have tackled matters? By winning the opening lead with dummy's Ace, discarding the Queen of Clubs on the Ace of Spades and, only then, starting on trumps by leading the Jack from the table.

If West had started with all four of the missing trumps, there was never anything to be done. But if East had held all four, there was still time (with the King of Diamonds as an entry to the table) to pick up the ten and restrict the losses to the Ace of trumps.

As the cards lie, West wins the first round of trumps but the danger of a Club ruff has been averted and the slam becomes safe.

A Change of Plan

South made a plan early in the play of the deal overleaf. It was a perfectly reasonable plan, but after he had learnt something of the lie of the cards he might profitably have reassessed matters.

North opened One Diamond at love all and South forced to game with Two Spades. North judged that he held suitable cards and, after several rounds of bidding, the final contract was Six Spades.

West led the Queen of Hearts and it became clear to declarer that the slam was no certainty. The best chance seemed to lie in finding West with Jack of Clubs. South won the Heart lead on the table and immediately led a Club to his Queen, which held.

He continued with the Ace of Hearts and a Heart ruff, then drew trumps in four rounds, discarding two Diamonds from dummy. Then, following his plan, he led a Club to the ten.

It was no good; East won with the Jack, got off lead with the Ace of Clubs (trumped by South) and waited for a trick in Diamonds. But declarer had missed his chance earlier in the hand. Once the Queen of Clubs

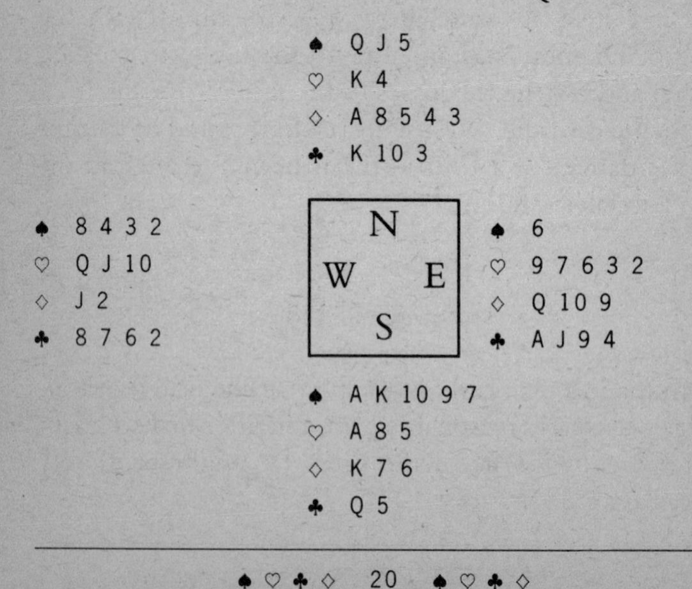

had held (thus placing the Ace), an alternative line was at least as good.

After ruffing his Heart loser, suppose South plays off all five of his trumps, discarding Diamonds from dummy? As the cards lie, East will be reduced to finding a discard from **D** Q 10 9 **C** A J.

To release a Diamond would be immediately fatal; but after East has parted with the Jack of Clubs, declarer simply leads a Club to establish his 12th trick.

'It Might Confuse . . .'

East found a very subtle defence on this deal. Everybody congratulated him, but he spoiled the effect by asking why his ploy had worked. He would have enhanced his reputation considerably if he had not explained that he 'thought he might confuse declarer'.

	♠ 10 8 3 ♡ 7 4 2 ◇ A Q 2 ♣ K Q 7 6	
♠ Q J ♡ K J 9 6 3 ◇ 5 4 3 ♣ 10 9 3	N W E S	♠ 9 5 4 ♡ Q 10 8 5 ◇ K 7 6 ♣ 8 5 2
	♠ A K 7 6 2 ♡ A ◇ J 10 9 8 ♣ A J 4	

South opened One Spade, North responded Two No-trumps and perhaps they both did a little too much after that to end in Six Spades. It was not a great contract, superficially depending on the Diamond finesse and a 3-2 break in trumps.

West led the ten of Clubs, declarer won in hand and started by playing off the Ace of trumps. He viewed the fall of West's Jack with mixed feelings. Could it be from Queen-Jack doubleton, or was it a singleton? In the latter case he could lead low to the ten and then pick up East's remaining trumps, but then he would need to find the Diamond finesse right.

South, a thoughtful player, finessed in Diamonds at trick three. If West held the King, he reasoned, he could now afford the safety play in trumps – perhaps losing an unnecessary trick but making his contract. If, however, the Diamond finesse lost, he would be reduced to hoping for the drop of the Queen and Jack of trumps.

Can you foresee the sequel? East unblinkingly let the Diamond finesse win! Now a low Spade lost to the Queen – and the subsequent Diamond finesse lost too.

Many Years Ago . . .

After a space of many years an old theme suddenly becomes fresh again. Having gone down, somewhat unluckily, in his slam on this deal, South remembered an article of some 30 years ago. If only he had followed its advice . . .

South dealt at game all and some efficient bidding

led to the excellent contract of Six Hearts. West led the Jack of Diamonds and it looked as though nothing could go wrong, until a low trump to dummy's Jack found East discarding a Spade.

Abandoning trumps, declarer drove out the Ace of Clubs but East returned a Diamond, forcing South to ruff and leaving him with fewer trumps than West.

There still seemed to be chances and declarer played off his winning Clubs. If at any time West had ruffed, an over-ruff and dummy's ten would have let declarer draws the remaining trumps and claim. However, West simply threw away his two Spades. Sooner or later he was bound to come to a trump trick and defeat the contract.

To succeed, South needed to play off just one top Spade before running his Clubs. Now all three of dummy's remaining Spades can be discarded and, when finally the Jack of Spades is led, West has to ruff. Then

West	North	East
	♠ A K 6 4 ♡ J 10 4 ◇ 9 6 5 4 ♣ K J	
♠ Q 2 ♡ 9 8 7 3 2 ◇ J 10 2 ♣ 8 4 2	N / W E / S	♠ 10 9 8 7 3 ♡ none ◇ K Q 8 7 3 ♣ A 7 3
	♠ J 5 ♡ A K Q 6 5 ◇ A ♣ Q 10 9 6 5	

the over-ruff in dummy provides the 12th trick and neutralises West's extra trump length.

Double Embarrassment

South found himself in the embarrassing position of playing in the wrong slam (in which he appeared to have 12 top winners) and ending with only 11 tricks. The winning play, although simple, was curiously elusive.

At game-all South opened One Spade and North responded Two Diamonds. It was not easy for them to determine that they held all the key cards necessary for a grand slam in Diamonds and they ended, reasonably enough, in Six Spades. West led his singleton Diamond and, after winning in dummy, declarer drew trumps in three rounds.

	North	
	♠ 6 5 3	
	♡ K J	
	◇ A K Q 3 2	
	♣ 10 7 4	
West		**East**
♠ 8 4 2	N	♠ 10
♡ Q 10 7 6 5	W E	♡ A 9 8 4 3 2
◇ 6	S	◇ J 7 5
♣ Q 8 6 5		♣ K 9 2
	South	
	♠ A K Q J 9 7	
	♡ none	
	◇ 10 9 8 4	
	♣ A J 3	

A second top Diamond revealed that the suit was blocked. Ducking a Diamond, to restore communications, would lead to two sure losers; so declarer decided to pin his hopes on finding East with both the King and Queen of Clubs. This brought no joy and South ended by losing two tricks.

A rather unusual 'loser-on-loser' play would have solved South's problems. When the second top Diamond fails to drop the Jack, he should lead a Heart from dummy and, whether it is covered or not, discard a blocking Diamond.

Then he comes to six Spades, five Diamonds and the Ace of Clubs for his contract, losing only an apparently unnecessary Heart trick.

The Agonies of Dummy

One of the most nerve-racking moments in bridge comes when you are dummy and, even from your side of the table, it seems clear your partner has lost his way. Then he recovers right at the end to leave you feeling it would have been better not to have watched . . .

East dealt with North-South vulnerable and opened Three Clubs, South passed and West raised defensively to Five Clubs. North doubled, South bid Five Hearts and North decided to go on to the small slam. A sacrifice by East-West would have been cheap but all passed.

West led **C** 3 against Six Hearts and declarer started on the wrong foot when he threw a Spade from hand.

He drew trumps and led a Diamond, allowing West's nine to win.

West continued the suit and, after discovering the bad break, declarer played off **S** A K and ruffed a Spade. Then he followed with his remaining trumps. Discarding in front of dummy West was forced to unguard either Spades or Diamonds and the slam came home – rather luckily.

Can you see a simpler route to success? If South discards a Diamond on the Ace of Clubs and, in the fullness of time, loses a Spade to the Queen he has 12 top tricks.

West		East
	♠ A K 3 2 ♡ K J 8 6 ◇ A K 8 5 ♣ A	
♠ Q 9 8 5 ♡ none ◇ Q J 10 9 ♣ 10 8 5 3 2	N W E S	♠ 7 6 ♡ 5 4 2 ◇ 3 ♣ K Q J 9 7 6 4
	♠ J 10 4 ♡ A Q 10 9 7 3 ◇ 7 6 4 2 ♣ none	

Not Easy to See

Squeezes can be very dull to read about and are often difficult to follow but – as someone once said – if you play your cards in the right order they often work.

North opened One Spade at love-all and South forced with Three Hearts. North jumped to Four Spades – conventionally showing a solid suit, for the partnership was in a game-forcing situation – and South, after checking on Aces, went on to the grand slam. He chose to bid it in No-trumps in case either long suit broke badly.

West led the ten of Diamonds to the Queen and Ace. This was the last entry to declarer's hand so it was now or never with the Hearts. Seven rounds of the suit left dummy with **S** A K Q 10 **C** A but when declarer

West	North	East
	♠ A K Q 10 8 6 3	
	♡ none	
	♢ 8 6 4	
	♣ A 5 2	
♠ 7	N	♠ J 9 5 2
♡ 10 8 7 2	W E	♡ 5 4
♢ 10 9 7	S	♢ K Q 5
♣ J 9 7 4 3		♣ K 10 8 6
	♠ 4	
	♡ A K Q J 9 6 3	
	♢ A J 3 2	
	♣ Q	

tested the Spades he discovered the bad news and had to concede the last trick.

There was a curious extra chance that South could have given himself. Clearly if the Spades had broken better he would not have needed dummy's Ace of Clubs.

Suppose that he throws it away and keeps five Spades in dummy? On the last Heart East has to discard from **S** J 9 5 2 **D** K **C** K – a Spade is immediately fatal and if he throws either minor suit King declarer cashes the appropriate winner and squeezes East again.

Benefit of the Doubt

I like to think that East planned his deceptive defence on this deal very carefully but I do not know for sure.

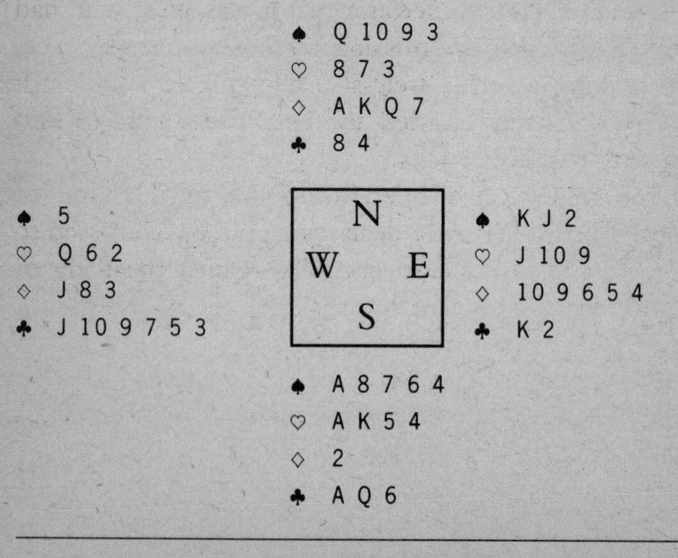

His partner took me on one side afterwards and said, 'You think he actually *planned* something? Why, he just forgot what trumps were!' West, however, is a well-known joker at the bridge table – shall we give East the benefit of the doubt?

South dealt at love-all and opened One Spade which North raised to Three Spades. Both of them did a little too much bidding after that and the final contract was Six Spades. (We have all been in worse slams.)

West led the Jack of Clubs and South won with the Queen. It was a good start and it looked as though he would be able to ruff his losing Club on the table and discard his losing Hearts on the top Diamonds.

The only problem lay in avoiding the loss of two trump tricks. Declarer started by playing off his Ace of Clubs and (after the fall of East's King) trumping his last Club with dummy's nine of Spades.

It seemed clear to declarer that it was West who had started with both the missing trump honours so, perhaps playing a little carelessly, he came to hand with the Ace of Spades and led another Spade, only to find East with two sure tricks.

And if East had over-ruffed the third round of Clubs? Almost certainly declarer would have crossed to the table and finessed successfully against the King of trumps to make his slam.

Charm of the Game

Have you ever noticed how weaker players are ever ready to criticise their stronger partners, quite apart from always wanting to play the hand? It is one of the charms of the game, I suppose.

South dealt at love-all and the bidding, I would say, was excellent. Without interference it went Two Clubs, Two Diamonds; Two Spades, Three Spades; Four Clubs, Four Diamonds; Four Hearts, Four Spades; Five Clubs, Six Spades.

Both players had done enough but it did not stop South launching into the attack as soon as he saw dummy.

'If you had shown your third-round Club control over my five Clubs, we might have reached the grand

West	North	East
	♠ Q 5 2 ♡ 8 7 3 2 ◇ A 8 6 4 ♣ 6 5	
♠ J ♡ Q J 10 9 ◇ K J ♣ Q 10 9 4 3 2	N / W E / S	♠ 10 9 7 ♡ 6 5 4 ◇ Q 10 9 7 3 2 ♣ J
	♠ A K 8 6 4 3 ♡ A K ◇ 5 ♣ A K 8 7	

slam!' he complained. North nodded gravely, and impassively watched his partner end up with only 11 tricks.

The Queen of Hearts was led to declarer's Ace. The Queen and Ace of trumps revealed the 3-1 break but, after the second top Club had been ruffed by East, there was still another unavoidable loser in the suit.

The correct timing in the small slam is quite delicate. Best, after winning the Heart lead, is to cash one top trump from hand and just one top Club; then cross to the Ace of Diamonds and lead another Club. If East trumps, he is only ruffing a loser. So suppose he discards.

After winning, declarer ruffs a Club with the Queen of trumps, comes to hand with a Diamond ruff and ruffs his last Club with the five of Spades. East can over-ruff – but this is his side's last trick.

Stampede!

South found himself stampeded into a slam on this deal. He might well have got there anyhow, he might well have made his contract, but it was East-West who ended with a plus score.

West dealt with North-South vulnerable and after three passes South opened One Club, hardly imagining that this next decision would be at the six level.

West overcalled with Three Spades, North raised to Four Clubs and East, to put on the pressure, made an advance sacrifice by bidding Five Spades. (This would have cost 500 points, a reasonable save against a certain game.)

South could have taken the money by doubling but, not unreasonably, he pushed on to Six Clubs and all passed. West led a top Spade, declarer ruffed and drew trumps. There were two main chances – a finesse in Diamonds or an end-play.

South started by eliminating the Hearts – three top winners and a ruff in dummy. Next came **D** 4 and, if East had played low, declarer planned to cover with the seven to end-play West, who would have to lead a Diamond or concede a ruff and discard.

East was awake however and, seeing the danger, covered **D** 4 with the eight. South fell back on his second chance and finessed **D** Q but West won and returned a Diamond and there was another loser in the suit.

When East followed with **D** 8 there was no rush to

	♠ 7 ♡ A 9 3 ◇ 10 6 5 4 ♣ A 10 8 7 4	
♠ K Q 10 9 6 3 ♡ 10 8 6 4 ◇ K 3 ♣ 5	N W E S	♠ A J 8 5 4 2 ♡ J 7 ◇ J 9 8 2 ♣ 2
	♠ none ♡ K Q 5 2 ◇ A Q 7 ♣ K Q J 9 6 3	

play him for the King. If South had won with the Ace and crossed to dummy with a trump before leading another Diamond, he could still make his contract if East held **D** K.

As the cards lay, his Queen would lose to the King but, with no Diamonds left, West's compulsory ruff and discard would give the trick.

A Minus Score in Spite of 37 Points

How do you feel if you are dealt 26 points? It is obviously good news but if, in addition, your partner opens the bidding your natural reaction is to start adding up the score even before seeing dummy. Yet it is on just these hands that a moment's inattention can be so costly.

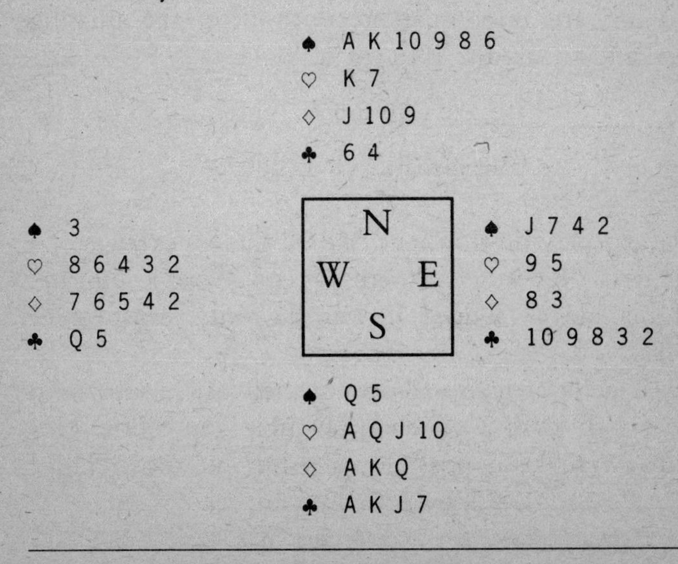

North dealt at love-all and opened One Spade. After reassuring himself (twice) that his partner had opened it was not long before South became declarer in Seven No-trumps.

West led the seven of Diamonds to declarer's Queen and, without too much concern, South started on Spades.

The second round revealed the bad news that there were only 12 top tricks and there seemed little opposition but to try a Club finesse. Its failure left South seething quietly – it was infuriating to end up with a minus score despite a combined holding of 37 points.

Declarer played too hastily. Suppose he cashes his seven red suit winners before testing the Spades? Can you see what happens? When, after taking three Spades, a Club is led from the table, East is marked with the Jack of Spades and therefore only two remaining Clubs.

West must have only two Clubs as well and the Ace and King are now guaranteed to drop the missing Queen and ensure the 13th trick.

Guesswork? Or Logic?

Declarer's play on this hand had all the appearance of a wild guess. Nevertheless there was considerable logic behind his idea – indeed it was his only prospect of success.

East dealt at game-all and opened Three Hearts to leave South with a problem. Double and Three No-trumps were both possible calls but he chose Three

Spades. Now North became excited and Blackwood led to a contract of Six Spades.

West led the King of Clubs and, after winning in dummy, declarer drew two rounds of trumps to leave West with the Queen. There seemed no hope of avoiding a Club loser as well for, if the Diamonds divided 3-2, West would be able to ruff the fourth round and cash the Queen of Clubs.

Declarer spotted a slender chance. If West had to follow to four rounds of Diamonds and his partner held the singleton nine, ten or Jack, the losing Clubs would go away before West could ruff.

At trick four South played off Ace of Diamonds and was encouraged by the fall of East's nine. A finesse of **D** 8 followed (there was nothing that West could do

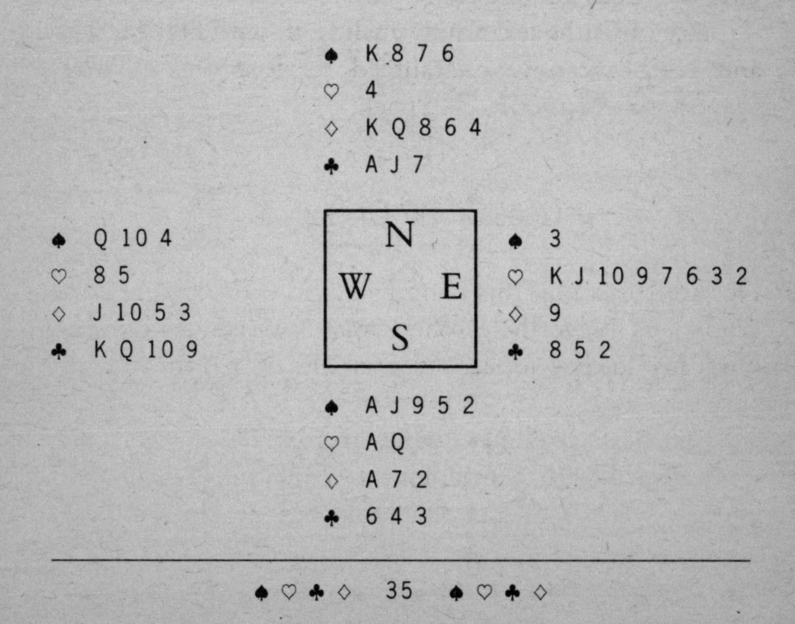

about it) and by the time that West ruffed the last Diamond, all of South's losing Clubs had gone away.

Lucky? Yes, but the only chance.

An Odd Finesse

Finesses are curious things – if you look at a suit of **Q** 10 9 8 in hand facing **A** 2 in the dummy (and you can afford to lose one trick in the suit), your first thought is to play Ace and another. Sometimes, though, one discard does not help.

South dealt at game all, and opened Two Spades. North raised to Three Spades, conventionally showing Spade support and at least one Ace.

South cue-bid his Ace of Diamonds, North showed his Ace of Clubs and South pushed on with Five Hearts.

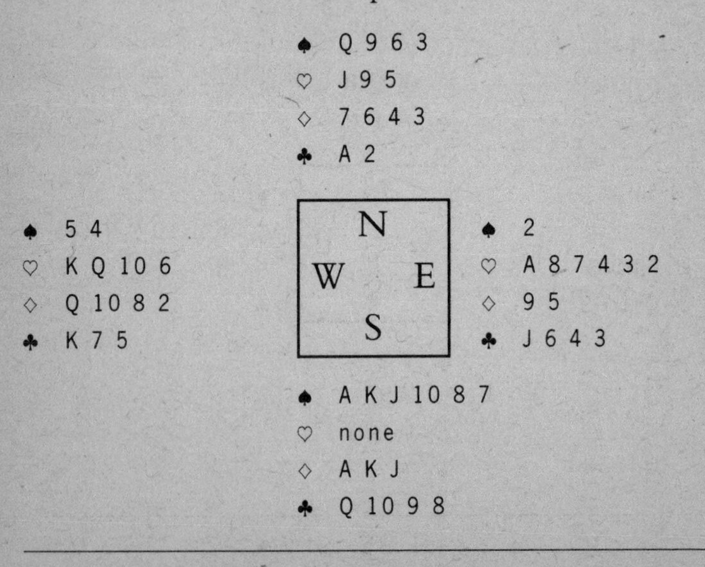

With nothing further to show North signed off with Five Spades, but South felt that he had enough in reserve to bid the small slam.

Against Six Spades West led the King of Hearts and declarer ruffed. Following his natural instincts, he drew trumps and played Ace and another Club, finessing the nine when East played low.

This drew the King from West but when the Jack did not fall on the third round declarer was reduced to trying a losing Diamond finesse.

A better bet would have been to play West for the King of Clubs. Try drawing trumps and leading **C** Q. As the cards lie West covers and, after losing to **C** J, declarer can discard two of dummy's Diamonds.

And should **C** Q lose to the King? There are still two chances – the Jack of Clubs may fall on the next round and there is still the Diamond finesse in reserve.

CHAPTER TWO

Deception

Deception in this game can take many forms. In the bidding it can be an out-and-out psychic bid – 'An attempt to persuade the opponents that you hold the cards that they can see in their hands', as the humorist put it – or altogether more delicate. For example, on the way to a Spade game which may prove difficult on a Diamond lead, a player throws in a diversionary bid in Diamonds after which, with any luck, an opponent may find a less punishing attack.

One of the most brazen deceptions was once successfully employed by John Collings. With **S** K Q 10 9 5 **H** 4 **D** 3 **C** A K Q J 10 4 he opened One Spade (!) and was raised to Three Spades. In reply to a Blackwood enquiry his partner showed one Ace and John bid Six Spades! Yes, the player on lead attempted to cash the Ace and King of Diamonds and now his partner's Ace of Hearts did not feature in the play when all of dummy's Hearts went away on the Clubs. It was an unusual use of Blackwood – not to stop at the Five level because two Aces were missing, but to persuade the opponents that two Aces were not missing.

Most deceptions in the play are false cards, although there is always the possibility of declarer deliberately playing on his weakest suit first in order to deter his opponents from continuing the suit. False cards in defence, however, have to be chosen with some care. There is often the very real danger that they will only fool your partner and leave declarer completely unimpressed. If you can judge, though, that your partner will not be side-tracked and that your play may confuse declarer, then away you go.

The only false cards that are completely accident-proof are those played by declarer. It really does not matter how much he puzzles dummy, even assuming that dummy is paying any attention!

Creating a Losing Option

Sometimes you look at a hand, read that declarer went one off in his contract and simply cannot see why.

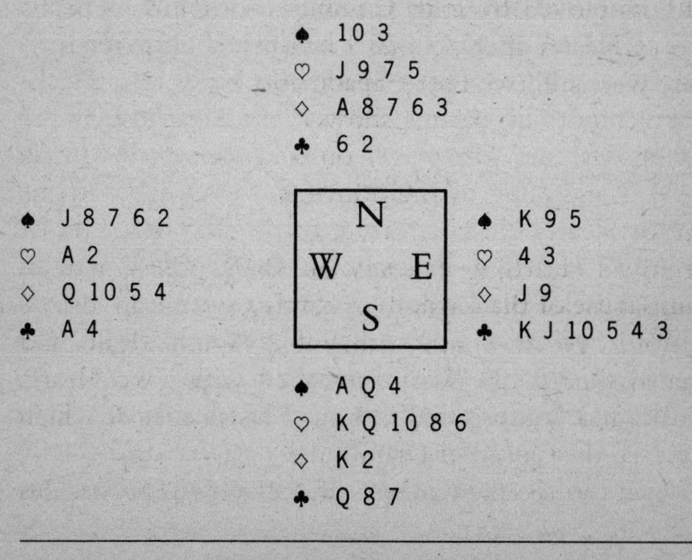

Take this deal which South played in Four Hearts, and see if there can be any logical reason for him to have ended with only nine tricks.

South dealt at love-all and opened One Heart, which North raised to Two Hearts. Optimistically South went directly to game and all passed.

Can you see what I mean about a contract in which it should be impossible to fail? The trumps are 2-2, the Spade finesse is right; the defenders seem powerless.

East, however, created a neat diversion. West led the Ace of Clubs and continued with the four to his partner's King. Now East switched to the nine of Spades and suddenly declarer found himself with an alternative to risking the Spade finesse. He went up with the Ace of Spades and led his established Queen of Clubs.

His plan was to discard a Spade from the table and cross-ruff, losing eventually to the Ace of trumps.

Disaster! West ruffed the Queen of Clubs with his two of Hearts and, although dummy could over-ruff, there were still two more inescapable losers.

An Odd Idea

I enjoyed watching *International Bridge Club* on television. One of the (unshown) hands gave me an idea:

With North-South vulnerable South dealt and opened One Club. West overcalled with Two Hearts (weak) and South ended in Four Spades against which West led the Queen of Diamonds.

You can see the danger – if declarer simply tackles

trumps, it is sure that East will win and return his singleton Heart. After he has taken a ruff, that will be four tricks for the defenders. Is there any way to avert a Heart ruff? Or at least make it difficult for the defenders to find?

There is a curious solution that might work. After winning the opening lead with the King of Diamonds, declarer leads the four of Hearts himself!

If a sleepy West plays low or, after taking his Ace, cannot decide whether his partner's three is a singleton or not, then declarer is home and dry. For the defenders can no longer come to their ruff.

I would like to report that the British player featured in the TV series, Tony Forrester, found this play and made an impossible contract. He found the play all right but the cards did not lie quite as they do in my diagram and the defenders came to their ruff.

West		East
	♠ Q 9 6 2 ♡ Q 6 ◇ A 10 8 2 ♣ A 7 4	
♠ 7 4 ♡ A J 10 9 8 5 ◇ Q J ♣ 10 8 3	N W E S	♠ A K 3 ♡ 3 ◇ 9 7 6 5 4 3 ♣ 9 6 5
	♠ J 10 8 5 ♡ K 7 4 2 ◇ K ♣ K Q J 2	

It is a pleasing thought, though. To avoid a Heart ruff it may pay you to lead the suit yourself.

Better Things were Coming

False-carding is a practice which many players seem to over-do. Nevertheless, there are occasions when a judicious false card will not confuse your partner and may throw declarer out of his stride.

This hand, from rubber bridge, gave me a great deal of pleasure.

With North-South vulnerable, North dealt and opened One Club. East, my partner, overcalled with One Spade and South bid Two Hearts. This suited me very well and I passed, hoping for better things.

They were not long in coming: for North bid Two

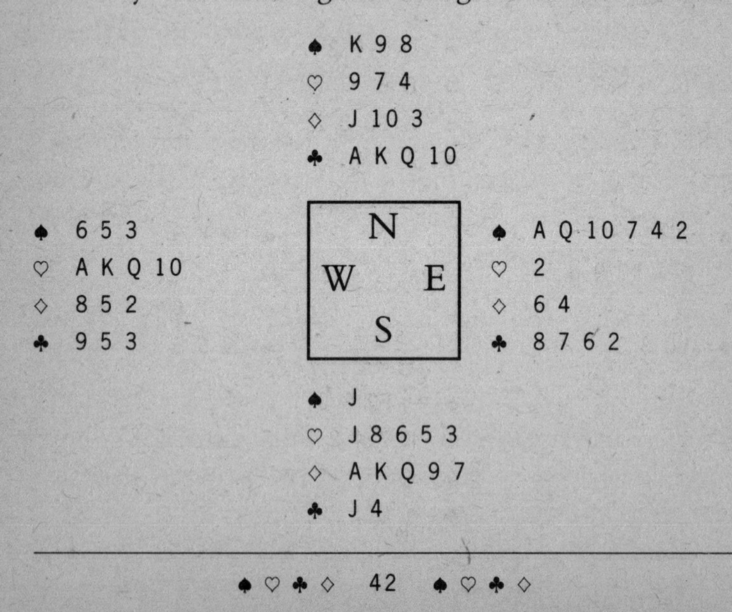

No-trumps, South tried Three Diamonds and North gave preference to Three Hearts.

South unwisely pressed on to Four Hearts and, as West, I felt that I was prepared to take my chances with a double. Against Four Hearts doubled, I led six of Spades and East won with the Queen and shrewdly returned a trump.

South played low – and as there was clearly no rush to win a trick with my ten of trumps, I won with the Queen. This could hardly confuse partner, but you may guess what effect it had on declarer.

He ruffed the next Spade lead and, expecting the trumps to be divided 3-2, tried to escape for one off by leading a second round of trumps. Now the roof fell in – I was able to draw the remaining trumps and still had a Spade left to give my partner the next four tricks.

For the final insult I was able to claim 100 for honours and we collected 1,800 points.

South would have been better advised to take out insurance. He should abandon any hope of one off and cut his losses by playing on Diamonds. That way he could not make less than eight tricks and would lose only 500 points (plus 100 for honours).

Worth Trying!

Every so often you come across a new situation in this game. The idea on the hand below, although simple, was quite a revelation to me.

It really is rather curious that the order in which you follow suit with three losing cards may put your opponents off the scent.

South opened One No-trump and, without a care in the world, North raised to game. The play was very soon over – West led the King of Spades to the two, seven and eight.

He continued with the Queen to the three, four and ten and, when the nine of Spades followed, East had no difficulty in winning with his Ace and taking two more Spade tricks.

It looks a completely uninteresting hand: Five Diamonds has no chance and surely Three No-trumps was the best bet. The missing Spades might be divided 4–4, the suit might be blocked or even not led.

'Very unlucky,' observed South at the end of the hand – and his partner agreed. It looks an innocuous

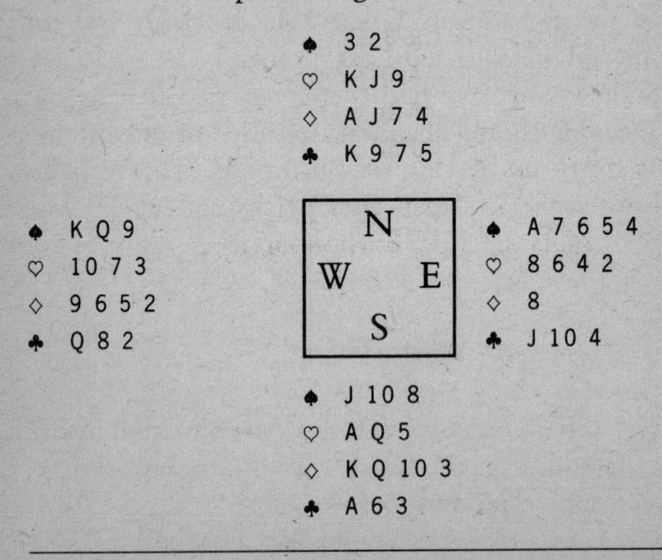

manoeuvre, but try the effect of dropping the ten and Jack of Spades under the King and the Queen.

Now, when the nine is led, East has a genuine problem. As the play has gone, which seems more likely – that West has started with **S** K Q 9 8 (when for East to play his Ace would block the suit) or that West has his actual holding when it is vital to overtake the nine with the Ace?

Especially if South has played smoothly, I think that most Easts could get this one wrong.

Combined Operations

What do you lead from three low cards, such as 7 6 2 in an unbid suit? Fashions change. 'Top of nothing' used to be universal; MUD (middle, up, down) had a vogue;

West	North / South	East
	North ♠ 9 8 3 ♡ A Q 10 8 ◇ A Q J 6 ♣ J 4	
♠ 5 ♡ 7 6 2 ◇ K 10 9 5 ♣ 10 8 7 6 3	N W E S	♠ K Q J 10 2 ♡ K J 3 ◇ 8 4 2 ♣ 9 5
	South ♠ A 7 6 4 ♡ 9 5 4 ◇ 7 3 ♣ A K Q 2	

and now a number of pairs are trying out an earlier American idea of leading low.

All these methods have their advantages (if you are dealt the right hand) but this deal proved a success for the modernists.

South opened One Club and North responded One Diamond. East's failure to overcall was, to my mind, inexplicable and South's rebid of One No-trump was raised to game. This left West with an awkward lead.

With little enthusiasm for the suits bid by his opponents and faithful to his modern ideas, West selected **H** 2 for his opening salvo. Dummy played low and, not to be outdone in trickiness, East won with the King and switched to the King of Spades. After holding off for two rounds declarer won the third Spade and, looking at eight certain tricks, decided to take the 'marked' finesse in Hearts.

Unlucky! East produced a completely unexpected Jack of Hearts and two more Spade tricks.

Of course, if East had won the first Heart with the Jack, declarer might still have gone wrong – by trying a second Heart finesse rather than playing on Diamonds.

Certainly the actual defence left South with real problems; while if West had made the more orthodox 'top of nothing' lead, then declarer would surely have got things right by relying on the Diamond finesse.

An Un-Safety Play

South fell for a very neat trap on this deal. It is true that he could have avoided it, but only with a distinctly far-sighted play. I am glad that I was not set the problem at the table.

South opened Two Clubs at love-all, North responded Three Diamonds and South elected to suppress his Heart suit in favour of a bid of Three No-trumps. Now, with little excuse, North raised to Four No-trumps and, with even less excuse, South went on to Six No-trumps.

West led the Queen of Clubs against the small slam. South won and, at trick two, led a Diamond from hand on which West made the excellent play of the King. With no entry to dummy outside the Diamonds, declarer had to allow for the possibility of the King

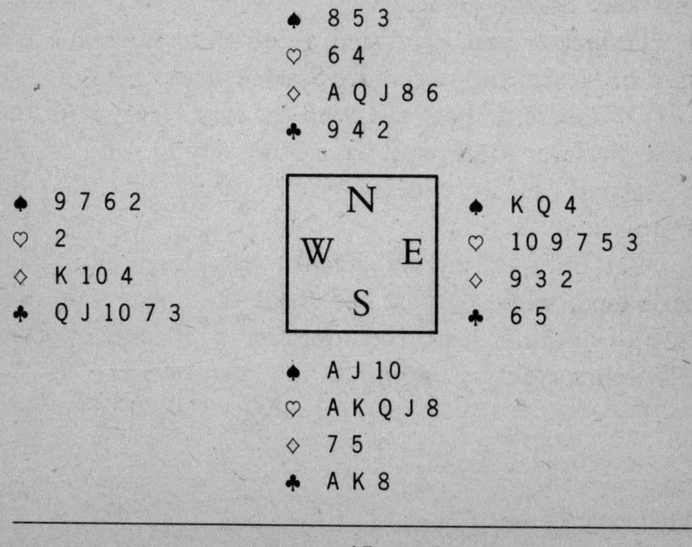

being doubleton. So he ducked in dummy to ensure four Diamond tricks unless the suit was 5-1.

When the Hearts failed to provide five tricks, South was short of his contract and had good reason to regret his safety play.

With hindsight South should have tested the Hearts before the Diamonds. He would then have known that five tricks were required from the Diamonds and, whatever antics West tried, he had to rely on a 3-3 break with the King well placed for him.

It was New to East

In a tricky contract of Four Hearts, South tried an old idea. Fortunately it was a new idea to East; so declarer got home.

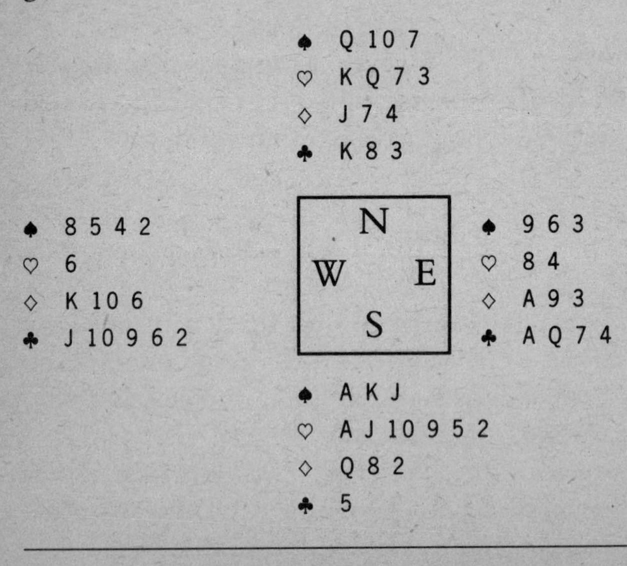

At game-all East dealt and passed, South opened One Heart and went on to game after his partner and raised to Three Hearts. West led the Jack of Clubs against Four Hearts and declarer ruffed the Club continuation.

The problem lay in avoiding the loss of three Diamond tricks. If West had held both the Ace and the King, he would surely have led the suit; if East had held both Diamond honours as well as the Ace and Queen of Clubs, he had already shown he would certainly have opened the bidding.

One possibility was to find either opponent with a doubleton honour in the suit, but South tried a psychological coup. He drew trumps in two rounds and led the Jack of Diamonds from the table.

As you can see, if East had covered this with his Ace, the defenders could have taken three tricks in the suit.

East played low, however, imagining that declarer was about to take a finesse, and a subsequent Diamond lead towards the Queen gave South his 10th trick.

Be Tactful if You Can

'Why did you play the trumps like that?' demanded my partner after we had achieved a lucky result on this deal. 'In case West held the singleton Jack,' I replied tactfully. But that was not the real reason.

East opened One No-trump (12-14 points) and as South, I overcalled with Two Spades. It was not a bid to be proud of but partner and I had not arranged any conventional defence to One No-trump. North raised to Four Spades, all passed, and West led the nine of Hearts.

To make the contract I had to restrict the trump losers to two. If the Spades were 2-2 any play would succeed and there was also the possibility of finding West with the singleton Jack.

After crossing to dummy with a Diamond I led with Queen of Trumps. This proved an undeserved success when East covered with the King, only to see his partner make sure of the trick with his Ace!

Subsequently, a trump lead towards my ten held East to only one more trick in the suit.

It was perfectly true that my play catered for the singleton Jack but it also gave East the chance to cover if he held the A J 9 or K J 9. He did cover (and it was a

West		East
	North ♠ Q 8 3 2 ♡ Q 7 5 4 ◇ K Q 8 3 ♣ 10	
♠ A ♡ 9 8 7 3 2 ◇ 6 5 2 ♣ 9 7 6 3	N W E S	♠ K J 9 ♡ K J 10 ◇ J 9 7 ♣ A 8 5 2
	South ♠ 10 7 6 5 4 ♡ A ◇ A 10 4 ♣ K Q J 4	

bad mistake) but I could hardly explain that to my partner while East was still within earshot.

It Should Have Been More Difficult

'That was a good switch!' declarer congratulated West, who had just found a good defence to defeat Three No-trumps. True, but South could have set West a much more difficult problem.

South opened One No-trump (15-17 points) at game-all and North raised to game. West led the Six of Spades, dummy played low and declarer won East's ten with his Jack.

There were only seven top winners and the Clubs had to be brought in. At trick two a Club went to West's King and he stopped to think. The play to the

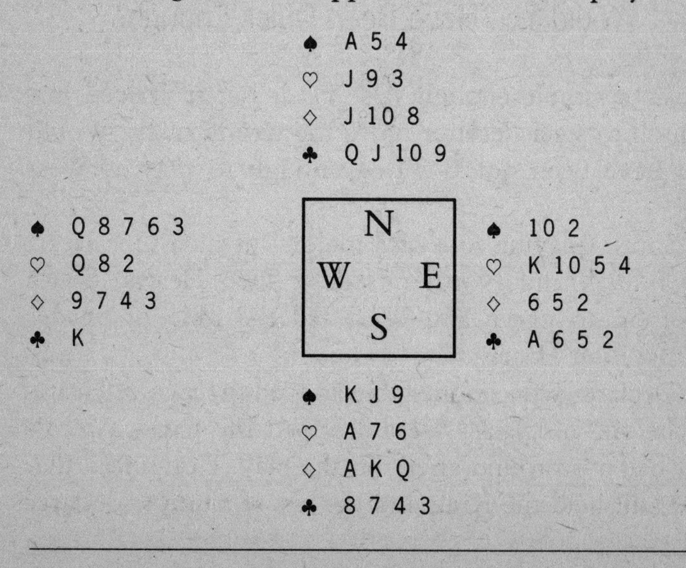

first trick marked declarer with the King of Spades, so there was no future for the defenders in that suit.

Instead of futilely persisting with Spades, West brightly switched to the two of Hearts. East covered dummy's Nine with his Ten and the defence now came to three Heart tricks as well as two Clubs.

What could South have tried? He should have won the first Spade trick with the King, not the Jack. (He still has two more Spade tricks to come with the aid of the marked finesse.)

The difference is that West will be convinced that his partner holds the Jack of Spades and will be extremely likely to continue the suit when in with the King of Clubs. Then South has time to drive out the missing Club honour and come to nine tricks.

Would You Have Been Quick Enough?

It was a simple enough false card, but it proved just enough to steer declarer on to the wrong track. Would you have been quick-witted enough to play as West did?

South (playing five card majors) opened One Heart at game-all and North raised to Two Hearts. South went on to game and West led the nine of Spades against Four Hearts.

Declarer won on the table and led the two of Hearts to the six and Jack. West dropped the ten – a move that had a profound effect on the play. Convinced that East still held the King and the six of trumps, declarer used dummy's second spade entry to lead another trump.

This proved quite unnecessary when both opponents followed suit, but now there was no entry left to the table to take what would have proved to be a winning Diamond finesse. Despairingly South got off lead with a Club, but East–West defended carefully and eventually declarer lost two Diamond tricks as well as two Clubs.

Of course South could have made his contract by playing the Ace of Hearts at trick three and using dummy's Spade entry for a Diamond finesse, but West's play of the ten of Hearts had given him a gentle push in the wrong direction.

West	North	East
	♠ A K J	
	♡ 4 3 2	
	◇ 6 5 3	
	♣ 8 6 4 3	
♠ 9 8 7 5	N	♠ Q 10 4 3
♡ 10 7	W E	♡ K 6
◇ J 9 7	S	◇ K 10 8 2
♣ A J 9 5		♣ K 7 2
	♠ 6 2	
	♡ A Q J 9 8 5	
	◇ A Q 4	
	♣ Q 10	

Two More Tricks Than Anyone Else?

The Charity Challenge Cup is played simultaneously at more than 500 clubs and I have often contributed a hand for the souvenir booklet.

Most clubs run heats – try to make sure you play at yours in order to help the excellent causes.

This was a deal I submitted – no, it won't help you this year, it was used in 1983.

South dealt with East-West game. Sitting North in a big pairs competition, I heard my partner open One No-trump (16-18 points) and I had an automatic raise to game.

Away from the table for a couple of minutes to make a telephone call, I returned to find that partner had made two more tricks than anyone else.

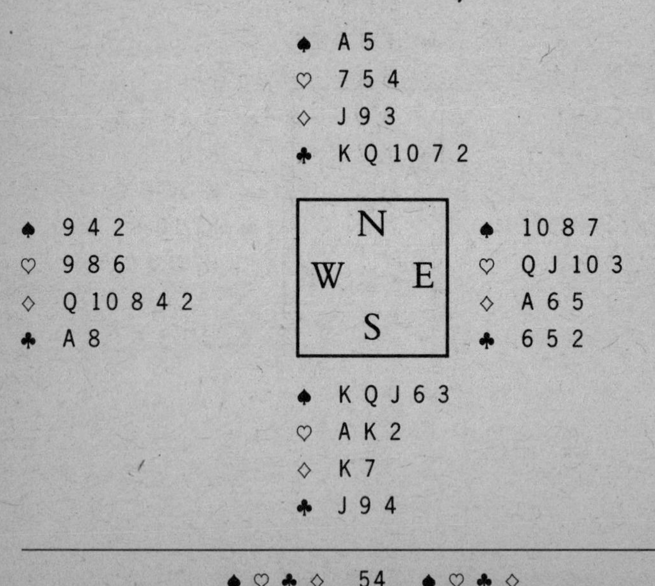

At the end of the session I found out what had happened. At practically every other table West had led a Diamond to his partner's Ace and a Diamond return cleared the suit. When West got in with the Ace of Clubs it was all over – one off.

At my table, under the Ace of Diamonds partner had dropped the King. Convinced that declarer must have both the King and Queen, East now switched to the Queen of Hearts and, as there was still a Diamond guard on the table, South had time to build up ten tricks.

The Game Failed, But The Slam Made

To go down in an easy game is always embarrassing – and on this deal from match play, matters were made

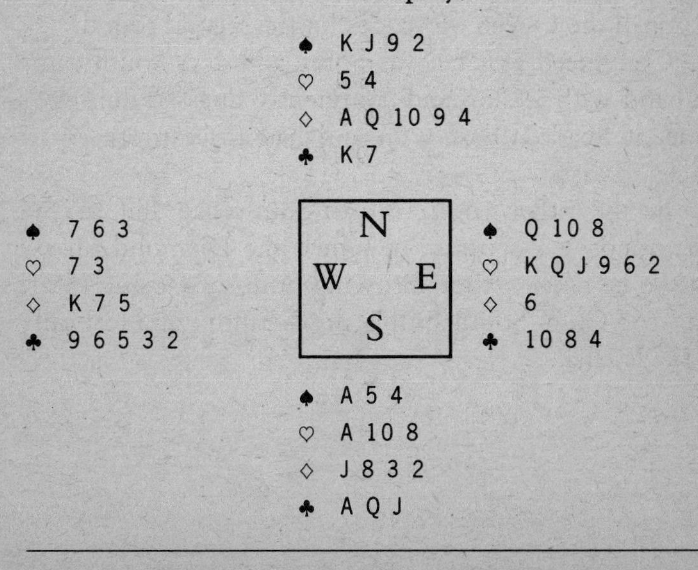

much worse when South discovered that the opposition had bid and made a slam on the same cards at the other table.

South played in Three No-trumps after East had overcalled in Hearts.

West led the seven of Hearts and declarer held off his Ace until the third round. He was extremely reluctant to stake everything on a simple Diamond finesse and, as a straightforward Spade finesse would be just as risky, looked for a way by which he might improve his chances.

The idea was to play off the Ace and King of Spades first before falling back on the Diamonds. Then, if he succeeded in dropping a doubleton Queen in East's hand, a finesse of the nine would yield nine tricks without the aid of the Diamond finesse.

East, however, was wide awake and smoothly dropped the Queen of Spades on the second round.

Convinced that he was home and dry, South came to hand with a Club and confidently finessed dummy's nine of Spades. East won and had three more Heart tricks to cash.

In the other room North-South had bid to Six Diamonds – a contract in which the Diamond finesse had to be taken. After throwing dummy's losing Heart on a top Club, South simply drew trumps and lost only a Spade trick.

CHAPTER THREE

Timing

It is difficult to think of any game where correct timing is not of the essence. This is manifestly true of any physical game and only slightly less obvious for a sedentary game like bridge.

There are the technical aspects of correct timing. In which suit should tricks first be developed in a No-trump contract? Which entries in the opponents' hands should be attacked first? In a suit contract, is it right to draw trumps? Or has something vital to be tackled first? It is extremely difficult to lay down any hard and fast rules – every hand has to be treated on its own merits – but I suppose that the advice given to beginners has considerable value: draw trumps unless there is a good reason not to. It is beautifully safe advice – if someone draws trumps and subsequently goes down you can always suggest that there was a good reason not to.

The psychological aspects of timing are interesting too. Does it pay to play quickly? A ponderously slow player, even if technically accurate, is easy to play against. By contrast, someone who plays quickly and confidently (even if making the occasional inaccuracy) is a much more difficult proposition. The theory is that you should try to slow things down against the Martin

Hoffmans of this world and attempt to speed up matters against more deliberate opponents.

It can hardly be considered sporting but I know of at least one match where slow play during the last set of boards achieved undeserved success. Why? Because the opponents had a last train to catch and had been getting more and more agitated as time ticked by!

A Little Naive . . .

One of the most unsatisfactory contracts in which to end is Five of a major suit.

It is always difficult to judge that you can make exactly 11 tricks; one extra and you have missed a slam; one less and you have gone down instead of stopping in

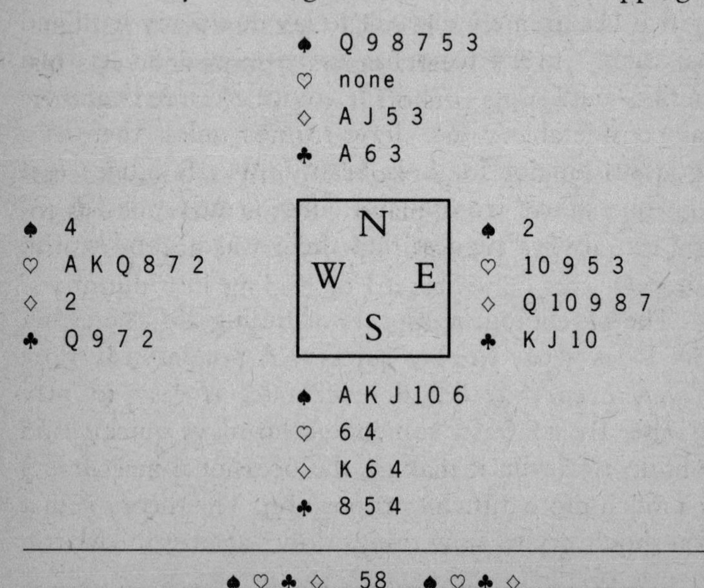

	North	
	♠ Q 9 8 7 5 3	
	♡ none	
	◇ A J 5 3	
	♣ A 6 3	
West		**East**
♠ 4		♠ 2
♡ A K Q 8 7 2		♡ 10 9 5 3
◇ 2		◇ Q 10 9 8 7
♣ Q 9 7 2		♣ K J 10
	South	
	♠ A K J 10 6	
	♡ 6 4	
	◇ K 6 4	
	♣ 8 5 4	

a game. Sometimes, as on this hand, you have little option, for the opponents have bid to the Five level themselves.

South dealt with North-South vulnerable and opened One Spade. Keen competition in the major suits led to South doubling Five Hearts but North judged that this would not yield much (in fact it only goes one off) and decided to go on to Five Spades.

West led the two of Diamonds and declarer saw no harm in trying dummy's Jack. This went to the Queen and King and, after drawing trumps, South tried the Diamonds. The 5-1 break meant that there was no way to avoid the loss of a Diamond and two Clubs and the contract failed.

It was a little naive to hope for a 3-3 break in Diamonds – the lead had all the earmarks of a singleton. Suppose declarer wins in hand (without wasting dummy's Jack), ruffs a Heart, draws trumps and ruffs his last Heart. Then he gets off lead with Ace and another Club.

The defenders take two Club tricks but whoever wins the second is end-played. If it is West, he has to concede a ruff and discard; if it is East he has the choice of giving a ruff and discard or leading into dummy's Ace and Jack of Diamonds.

Weak Or Strong?

I once gave a hand where, although contrary to my normal methods, a weak No-trump would have scored heavily. To redress the balance, here is a hand from match play where it led to a complete catastrophe.

North dealt at love-all and after two passes South opened One No-trump. (Even if playing a weak No-trump, I think I would have preferred One Diamond). West doubled, North decided not to stage any rescue attempt, and all passed. West led the four of Spades and dummy apologised as he spread his hand. ('Sorry, partner – the ten of Hearts spoils it!') Declarer won with the ten but it was to be his first and last trick.

He led the Jack of Diamonds but West rose with the

	North	
	♠ 7 6 3 ♡ 10 7 6 ◇ 8 6 3 ♣ 8 5 4 3	
West ♠ A K 9 4 2 ♡ Q 5 2 ◇ A 10 ♣ A 10 2	N W E S	**East** ♠ 8 5 ♡ A K 9 3 ◇ 7 5 4 2 ♣ K 7 6
	♠ Q J 10 ♡ J 8 4 ◇ K Q J 9 ♣ Q J 9	
	South	

Ace and ran off four Spade winners. Then he switched to the Queen and another Heart.

East, who had carefully kept all his Hearts, took three more tricks in the suit. When the last one was played declarer had to find a discard from **D** K **C** Q J 9. It did not matter what he chose for West, playing after declarer, still had **D** 10 **C** A 10 2 and could wait and see what South threw.

Declarer found himself squeezed and ended up six down, doubled. At the other table? South opened One Diamond, East-West ended in a peaceful Three No-trumps and made nine tricks after a Diamond lead.

Anybody For Stayman?

Players will always argue about whether it is worth while using the Stayman convention in reply to One No-trump when you have only one, very poor, major suit and a very natural raise in No-trumps.

Sometimes a fit allows ten tricks in the major suit; sometimes there are only nine tricks however you play; sometimes exploration gives too much away and makes the defence easier.

On this deal the scientific approach had the edge, but one swallow does not make a summer.

South dealt at game-all and opened One No-trump. Most players would simply raise to Three No-trumps with the North hand – and, in practice, this contract would be likely to fail – but this particular North's veins ran with scientific blood and he was convinced that he was right when he bid Two Clubs (Stayman) and raised South's rebid of Two Spades to game.

West, with no temptation to try for a ruff, led the Queen of Hearts and declarer vindicated his partner's 'judgement'. He won in dummy, ducked a Club to West's seven and won the Heart continuation. He followed with two top trumps, the Ace of Clubs, a Heart ruff on the table and a Club ruff in hand.

Next came the King of Diamonds and, when West showed out on the next Diamond lead, he played dummy's nine. East won but had to return a Diamond into dummy's tenance or concede a ruff and discard. It would not have helped West to ruff the second round of Diamonds.

It was a very elegant demonstration of what is termed a partial elimination.

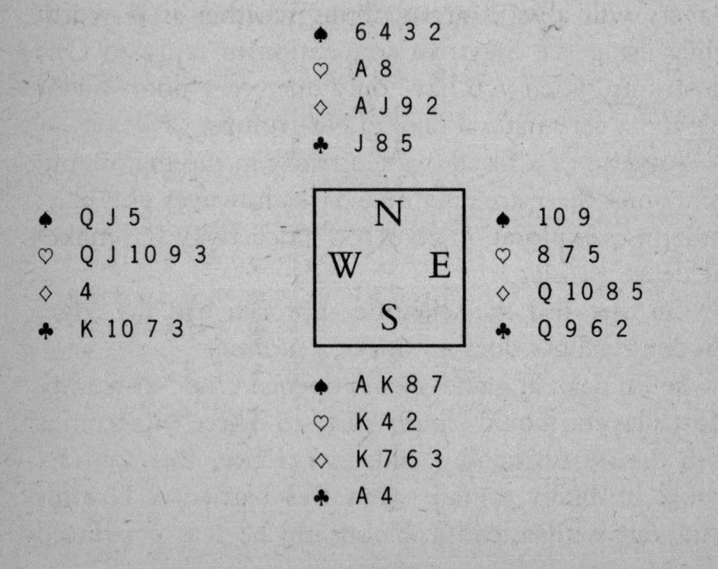

A Good Try

There was an exciting struggle on this hand. The deal had everything – there was keen competitive bidding and the result of the final contract (doubled, of course) was in doubt until the last moment.

It was a pleasing change from the auction going One No-trump–Three No-trumps and declarer claiming an immediate nine tricks.

North dealt with North-South vulnerable and opened One Diamond. East overcalled with Two Hearts, South chanced his arm with Two Spades and the battle was on. After East-West had bid as far as Five Hearts (which would have gone three off), South ended in Five Spades doubled.

Judging that there was little future in a Heart lead,

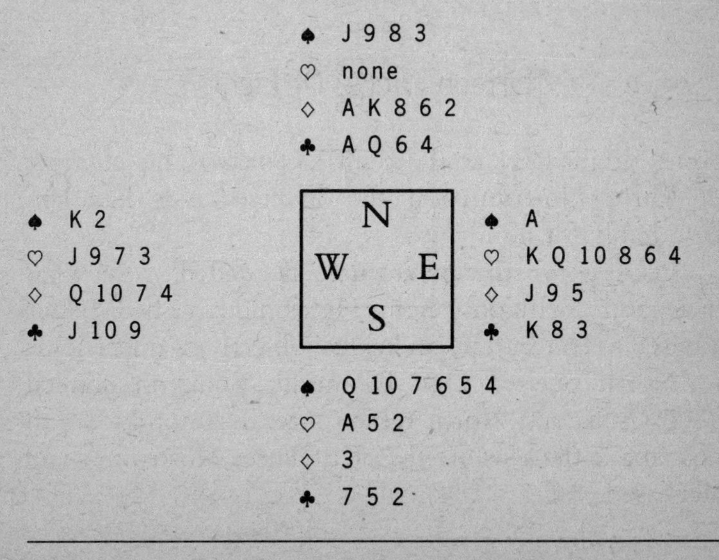

West seemed to have struck oil when he led Jack of Clubs. Declarer won with dummy's Ace, cashed the Ace and King of Diamonds to discard a Club and ruffed a Diamond.

Next came a Heart ruff and another Diamond ruff, while East discarded a Heart. A second Heart ruff afforded an entry to the established Diamond. Again East discarded a Heart and away went South's last Club. West ruffed but when King and Ace of Spades came down together declarer was home.

Would it have been better for East to have discarded two Clubs on the last two rounds of Diamonds – the idea being that, after West ruffs the fifth Diamond, the defenders can make their two top trumps separately?

It does not work, though, if declarer ruffs the last Diamond. Then, with no Club loser, he loses just two trump tricks.

Thirteen Tricks? Or Eight?

South might have come to all 13 tricks in his contract of Three No-trumps if the adverse cards had lain favourably for him.

Playing for the maximum, he ended, somewhat inelegantly, with only eight. He would have been better advised to concentrate on his real objective – nine tricks.

North opened One Diamond, South responded Two Clubs and North rebid Three Diamonds. South now made the sensible choice of Three No-trumps and all passed.

West led the four of Spades and Declarer played low from the table. It looked a natural enough play but East won with the King and, in an inspired moment, switched to a low Heart. (I am sure that I would simply have returned my partner's lead.)

Declarer won in dummy and started on Diamonds, but the King and the Ace revealed the bad news. When the King and another Club worked equally badly, it was all over.

Well, what was Declarer's best chance? He should win the opening Spade lead with dummy's Ace and finesse the nine of Diamonds.

Even if this loses to the Jack, he is still protected in both major suits and will come to at least nine tricks. As the cards lie, an overtrick rolls in.

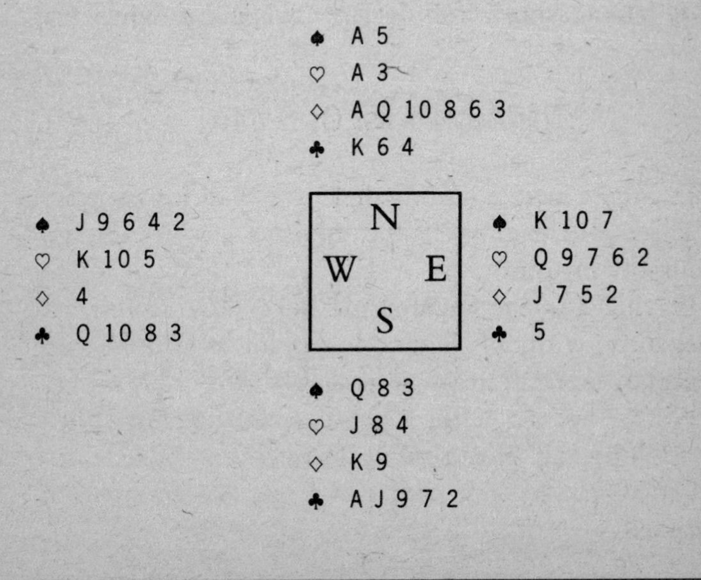

'A Winner On A Loser'

The phrase 'winner on a loser' is usually only used whimsically to describe one of partner's little accidents, but it seemed a good move on this deal and was certainly intentional.

South dealt at game-all and opened Two Clubs. North responded Two Diamonds (the conventional negative). South showed his Hearts and the partnership seemed to lose its way when it bypassed Three No-trumps (which would have been easy) and ended in Four Hearts. Perhaps it was South's 150 for honours that influenced him!

West led the Queen of Clubs, East overtook with his Ace and returned the Jack.

It was a shock for declarer when his King was

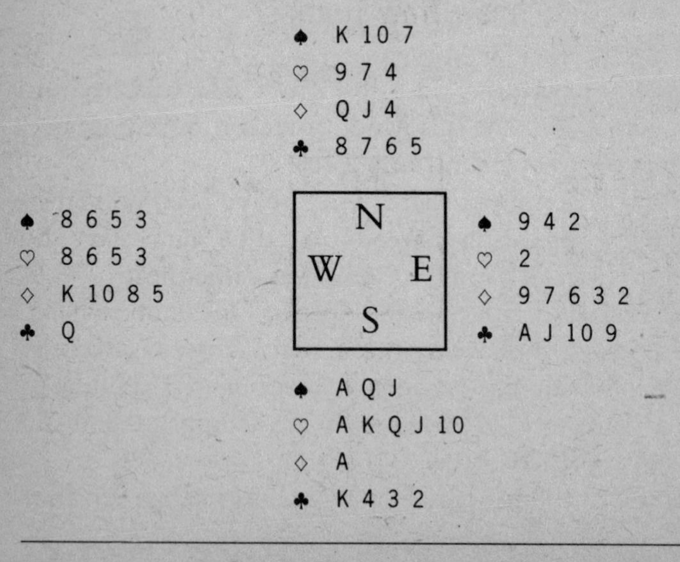

trumped and his apparent 10 winners had dwindled to nine. It looked as though, with only one entry to dummy, there would be two more inescapable losers in Clubs.

Declarer neatly escaped. He won the trump return, drew the remaining trumps and played off the Ace of Diamonds. Then came the Ace and Queen of Spades, overtaking with dummy's King. The Queen of Diamonds followed and South discarded his winning Jack of Spades.

Without a doubt his was a 'winner on a loser'. West took his King but, with only Diamonds and Spades left, his next lead put dummy in to enjoy the ten of Spades and the Jack of Diamonds for declarer to shed his losing Clubs.

Why Draw Trumps?

Throw-in plays to avoid a loser in a side suit are not that uncommon. On this hand, however, South organised matters to avoid a trump loser.

Mind you, I think that I would have been prepared to take my chances in Three No-trumps, but I have to admit that his play in Five Clubs was rather neat.

South dealt at love-all and opened One Club, which West doubled. Following the modern style, North bid One Spade (forcing as normal) instead of redoubling and, although South suggested No-trumps, the final contract was Five Clubs.

West led the King of Hearts and, assuming that the

Spade finesse was right, there were certain losers in both red suits. The success of the contract, therefore, depended on finding the Queen of Trumps. Rather than rely on guesswork, South found a clever way to bypass his problem.

He held off the opening lead and won the continuation with the Ace. Then he finessed the Queen of Spades, cashed the Ace and ruffed a Spade in hand.

Next came a Heart ruff in dummy, followed by the last Spade. East discarded a Diamond and declarer ruffed.

Now the Ace, King and another Diamond left West on lead. Declarer had **C** A J 9 in his own hand and **C** K 10 8 in dummy and was bound to win the last three tricks.

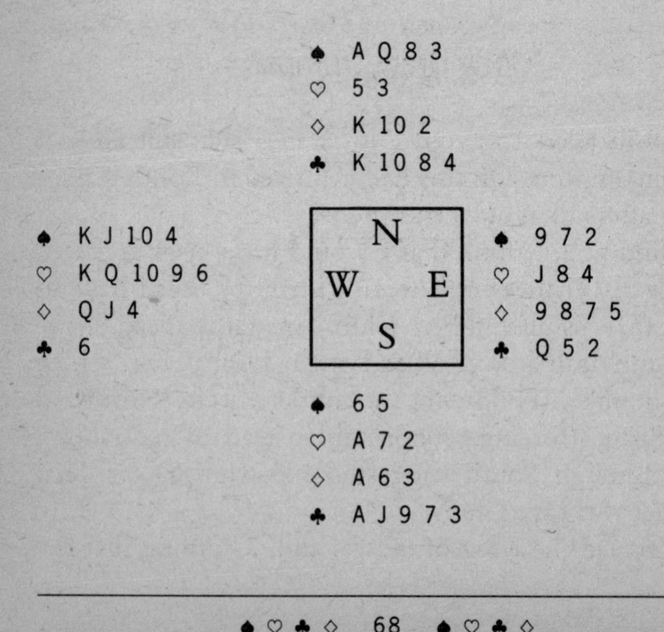

Keeping Control

It may seem a simple point; but if you hold the Ace and two other trumps in defence, it often pays to refuse the first round. In that way you retain control and, if declarer had hoped to draw exactly two rounds of trumps, you can thwart his plans. Here is an example:

At love-all North opened One Diamond and rebid Two Clubs over the response of One Spade. South might have tried No-trumps now but he bid Two Hearts and, after jump preference to his first suit, went on to Four Spades.

West led the eight of Diamonds and declarer won in hand. He followed with a trump to the King, which East allowed to hold.

A finesse of the Queen of Hearts lost to the King

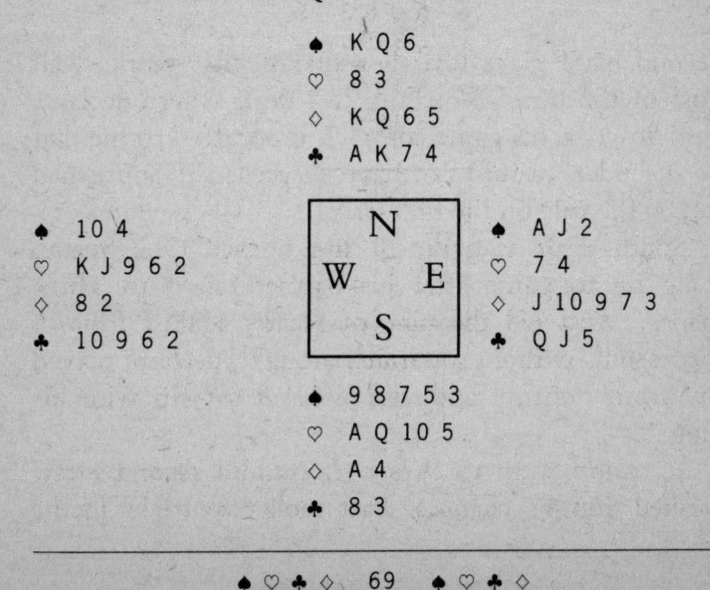

and West played another Diamond. (A trump would have been equally effective, allowing East to clear dummy's holding in the suit and keeping South to nine tricks.)

Now when declarer ruffed the third round of Hearts on the table, East over-ruffed and gave his partner a Diamond ruff. That was three tricks for the defence and the Ace of trumps was still out.

If East plays the Ace of Spades on the first round, the contract is easily made. Say that East exits with a Heart; South finesses, wins the Diamond return and cashes the Queen of trumps. Now he throws one losing Heart on a Diamond and ruffs the other. The defence can make only two Spades and a Heart.

When To Break A Rule . . .

'Second hand plays low' is a maxim that works well most of the time. Watching this deal, where declarer went down in his game contract, it occurred to me that the defenders would not have succeeded if South had broken the rule on the first trick.

South dealt at game-all and opened One Spade, going on to game after his partner raised to Three Spades. West led the nine of Hearts against four of Spades and, without too much thought, declarer played low from dummy and was allowed to win with his King.

A trump went to West's Ace and a second Heart finished South's chances. East took two tricks in the suit and the defenders eventually came to a diamond trick as well.

Suppose that declarer had tried the Queen of Hearts from dummy on the first trick – East has to win and cannot profitably return the suit. Say that he switches to a Diamond – resisting all temptation, declarer wins with the Ace and tackles trumps.

As he still controls the Hearts, there is plenty of time to draw the last trump and discard his losing Heart on the King of Clubs. In all he loses a trump, a Heart and a Diamond.

Second hand plays low? Well, at least think about it.

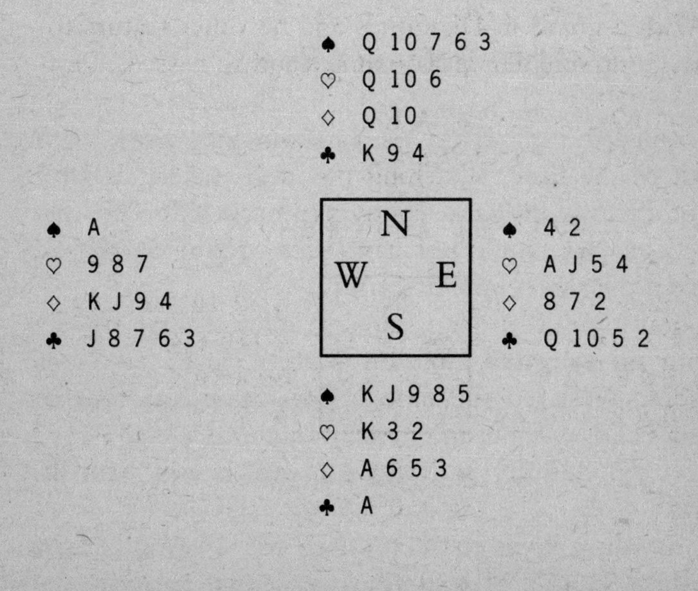

A 6-0 Break Proved Good News

I recently overheard a heated argument among the four players involved in this deal. Called in to give an impartial opinion, I agreed with the way that the auction had gone even though it led to what appeared to be a hopeless contract.

South dealt at game-all and opened One Spade, North responded Two Clubs and South rebid Two Hearts. Now North, with game-going values but no clear idea as to which contract might prove best, bid Three Diamonds. This was the fourth suit – not necessarily showing anything in Diamonds but suggesting progress.

With a guard in Diamonds and no other feature to show, South bid Three No-trumps and all passed. West

West	North	East
	♠ A J	
	♡ A 6 2	
	◇ Q 4	
	♣ A 10 9 8 5 3	
♠ none	N	♠ Q 10 9 8 7 3
♡ J 9 7	W E	♡ 10 8 4
◇ 8 7 6 5 3 2	S	◇ A 10 9
♣ K Q 6 2		♣ 7
	♠ K 6 5 4 2	
	♡ K Q 5 3	
	◇ K J	
	♣ J 4	

led the eight of Diamonds to his partner's Ace and a Diamond came back to clear the suit for the defenders.

With the Diamond suit wide open and at least one trick to be lost in the suit before the Clubs could be established, it seemed all over for declarer.

Then he had his first thought. Suppose that both Spades and Hearts divided 3-3 and West held the Queen of Spades?

So, after winning the second Diamond in hand, he led a Spade but everything seemed lost when West showed out. Giving up and hoping to settle for one down, South won with dummy's Ace and led a low Club.

You can see what happened – West won, the Diamonds were blocked and nine tricks rolled in with the aid of a Club finesse. It was a possibility that declarer had not taken into his calculations.

But wasn't he lucky to find the Spades 6-0? If West had followed to the first round of the suit with a low Spade, he would surely have set off on a losing line of play.

Two Finesses, One Entry

There are some hands that you prefer to watch rather than play.

I am quite sure that I would have made a losing decision in the bidding of this hand but, having seen the critical suit combination before, would have done better in the play than the actual declarer.

South dealt at love-all and opened Two Clubs. West overcalled with Two Hearts and, after two passes I must confess that I would have chanced my arm with Three No-trumps. South preferred Three Diamonds, however, and ended in Five Diamonds after a raise from his partner.

West led the King of Hearts and declarer won. He played off the Ace of trumps and the bad break made it clear that bidding Three No-trumps would have been a disaster.

South cleared the trumps and ruffed the third round of Hearts in hand. Then he crossed to the table with the nine of Diamonds and turned his attention to taking finesses in the black suits.

First he ran the ten of Spades successfully but, when he continued with the Queen of Spades, East covered.

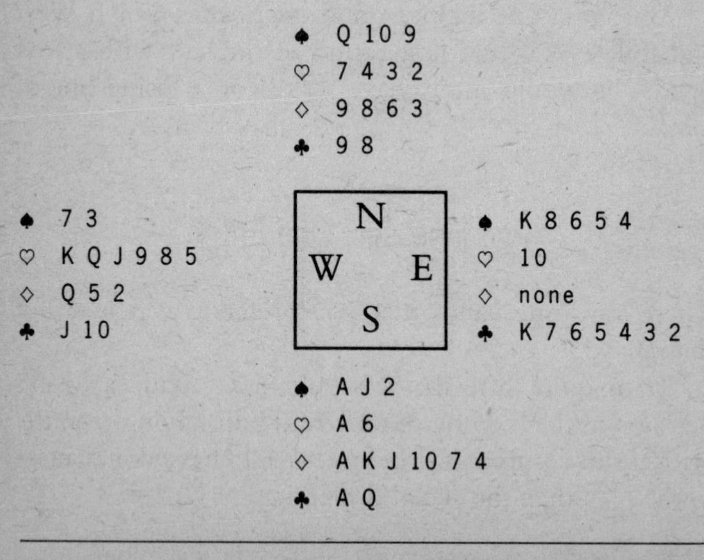

Now there was no way back to table for the Club finesse and the contract failed.

The right way to have tackled the black suits was to lead the Queen of Spades, not the ten and (if not covered) with the Jack from hand. Then, after the next Spade finesse succeeds, the lead is still in dummy for the Club finesse.

Another Broken Rule . . .

All the textbooks suggest that you should have a good five-card suit before you overcall, but the modern game is becoming increasingly aggressive. A lead-directing overcall at the One-level, even on only a four-card suit, may cramp the opponents' style and possibly lead them to the wrong contract.

West		East
	North ♠ A 2 ♡ 8 7 5 ◇ K Q J 10 5 ♣ K J 3	
♠ 8 7 6 5 ♡ K 4 3 ◇ A 8 3 ♣ 9 4 2	N / W E / S	♠ K Q J 9 ♡ Q J ◇ 9 7 6 2 ♣ 8 6 5
	South ♠ 10 4 3 ♡ A 10 9 6 2 ◇ 4 ♣ A Q 10 7	

North dealt with North-South game and opened One Diamond. Intrepidly, East joined in with One Spade, South bid Two Hearts and West raised to Two Spades. This made things uncomfortable for North-South. They could have taken a small plus score by defending Two Spades but they were reluctant to play in Three No-trumps (which would have been easy with Spades dividing 4-4) and they ended in Four Hearts.

Prospects were not good after a Spade lead – it looked to declarer as though he would have to lose a Spade, a Diamond and at least two trumps.

There was just a chance, however, which lay in playing on Clubs. You can see what happened on the fourth Club – dummy's Spade went away and whichever defender ruffed did so at the expense of a trump trick.

The play went smoothly. It was East who ruffed the last Club and he returned the Queen of Hearts to the Ace.

A Diamond lost to West's Ace but now the only remaining trick for the defenders was the King of trumps – declarer was in charge and could throw his losing Spades on the established Diamonds.

Perfect Defence

It needed a perfectly timed defence to beat Three No-trumps on the deal below. The slightest deviation would have allowed South to make his contract.

South opened One No-trump (16-18 points) and

North raised Three No-trumps. West led the two of Spades and declarer played the King from dummy.

The winning defence is for East to duck this trick. It does not help declarer to finesse in Hearts immediately, for West wins and, seeing little future in Spades now that his entry has gone, switches to Clubs. Then East still has the Ace of Spades as an entry to the 13th Club.

Instead, declarer may try returning a Spade at trick two; East wins now and this time he is the defender who switches to Clubs.

Declarer has to hold off for two rounds, but now the defenders can judge that, as they have no entry to the long Club, it is time to switch back to Spades. This leaves West with the 13th Spade and an entry with the King of Hearts.

It seems remarkable that, with no long suits against

	North	
	♠ K 7 6	
	♡ Q J 5	
	◇ K J 10 6	
	♣ 10 6 4	
West		**East**
♠ 10 8 4 2	N	♠ A 9 5
♡ K 8 6	W E	♡ 9 7 3 2
◇ 5 4 2	S	◇ 8 3
♣ Q 8 2		♣ K J 9 3
	South	
	♠ Q J 3	
	♡ A 10 4	
	◇ A Q 9 7	
	♣ A 7 5	

him, declarer cannot come to the two Spades, two Hearts, four Diamonds and one Club that would give him nine tricks. Did it actually happen?

No, East won the King of Spades with his Ace at trick one! Now, whatever he tried, South had a routine run home.

Should East have known? Well, unless declarer's Spades were as good as QJx, he would hardly have played the King from dummy.

Odd Arithmetic

You might think that if declarer has 'x' winners and 'y' losers, then x + y will equal 13. Arithmetic in bridge, however, is not quite as simple as that – consider this deal:

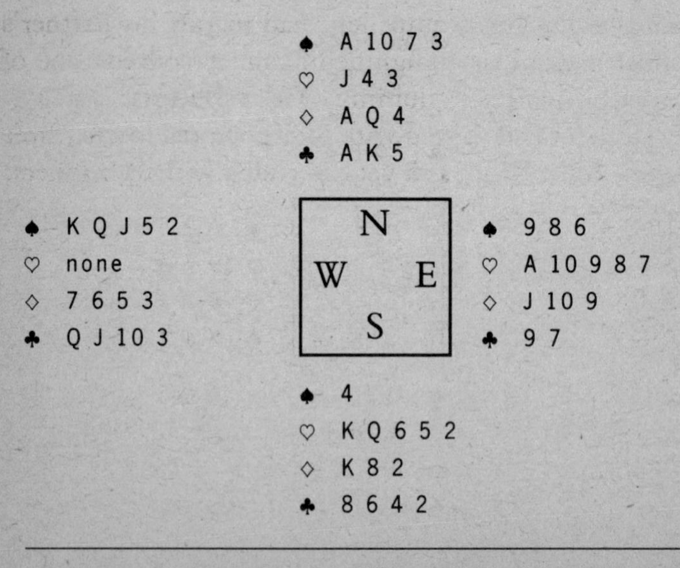

Playing five-card majors and a 15-17 point no-trump, North opened One Club. South responded One Heart and West overcalled with One Spade. North bid Two No-trumps, South showed his Club support and the eventual contract was Four Hearts, unwisely doubled by East who had too many cards in his partner's suit for his double to be a sound proposition.

West led the King of Spades to dummy's Ace and a low Heart to the Queen confirmed the expected bad trump break. Declarer crossed to the Queen of Diamonds and ruffed a Spade in hand. Re-entering dummy with a Diamond, he ruffed another Spade.

Next came the King of Diamonds and two top Clubs; then came the last Spade from the table. East could do no better than ruff low and declarer over-ruffed with his Jack.

All that remained to do was exit with a Club. East, with nothing but trumps left, had to ruff his partner's winner and, in an undignified manner, concede one of the last two tricks to dummy's Jack of Hearts.

Declarer had started with four potential losers (three trumps and a Club) and yet had ended with 11 winners.

CHAPTER FOUR

Humour in Bridge

It proved very difficult to disentangle the material for this chapter from the one entitled 'Remarks at the Table', but a wide variety of amusing things happen in the bridge world – not always at the table. For example, most major tournaments feature a daily bulletin (giving results, hands and news) and there is often a light-hearted competition for the most disastrous bid or play of the event. Believe it or not, some players positively enjoy seeing their horror stories published.

In championship play it is obligatory for both members of a partnership to have a detailed description of their system on the table. Not for themselves, of course, but for the benefit of their opponents. At a recent tournament the new arrivals at the table were puzzled to find only one system card on the table. A polite enquiry as to the whereabouts of the other copy elicited the reply 'Oh, we only need one card – we both play the same system!'

It was in the same tournament that a player in the Mixed Pairs exhibited pronounced male chauvinistic tendencies. (In a Mixed Pairs event, rather like a Mixed Doubles in tennis, there is the strong feeling by the male partner that he should make every *conceivable* effort to be declarer rather than dummy – although in practice this may not be such a good idea.) The gentleman in question was due to be declarer but an opponent led out of turn. The tournament director started to intone the various options open to declarer but he was interrupted: 'Don't bother to tell me about the one where partner plays the hand!'

The absent-mindedness of bridge players is legendary. A well-known player was in the middle of a rubber at the club when he was interrupted by a telephone call. Making his excuses, he left the room. The other three players waited . . . and waited . . . and waited . . . Finally they sent out a search party, only to find (just two tables away) the absentee, who had happily cut into another rubber.

Again, a distinguished player finished a session and, still thinking about the hands, boarded the lift. Next to him was a face that seemed familiar. 'How did it go today?' he enquired politely. 'For goodness sake!' was the reply, 'I was sitting opposite you all afternoon!'

It Is Usually A Disaster

There have been countless examples over the years of players contributing the wrong card to a trick by mistake.

It happens to us all, usually leading to total disaster. But every once in a while the error proves to be a spectacular winning play.

South opened Two No-trumps at game-all and North raised to game. West led the four of Hearts against Three No-trumps and dummy won with the Ace.

On any other lead there would have been an easy run to at least nine tricks, but the lead took away the entry to dummy before the Diamonds could be unblocked.

In the hope of creating a new entry (the ten of Spades) declarer led a low Spade from the table at trick two and finessed the Jack. West started thinking – what should he lead after winning with the Queen of Spades?

On the bidding his partner was marked with practically nothing in the way of high cards and West made his decision. He would exit peacefully with the nine of Spades.

Something went wrong – planning a trick ahead, West suddenly realised that he had allowed South's Jack of Spades to win, having followed with the nine!

West		North		East
		♠ 10 7 2		
		♡ A		
		◇ Q J 9 7 3		
		♣ 6 5 4 3		
♠ Q 9 8		N		♠ 6 4 3
♡ K J 6 4 3	W		E	♡ 9 7 5 2
◇ 5 2				◇ 10 8 6 4
♣ A Q 7		S		♣ 10 8
		♠ A K J 5		
		♡ Q 10 8		
		◇ A K		
		♣ K J 9 2		

I expect you can see what happened: cut off from dummy's winning Diamonds, declarer had only seven top tricks. One more came in but the contract failed.

Everybody congratulated West on his shrewd defence – losing one trick but gaining at least two – and his prestige in the club rose considerably.

Only West – and now my readers – know the truth.

West's Discard Was Critical

No matter how bad a hand you are dealt, you should never give up. West, with one of the worst hands that he was ever likely to hold, carelessly parted with a card that would have helped his cause.

South dealt at game-all and opened One Spade.

West	North	East
	♠ 10 6 5 ♡ J 10 6 2 ◇ A J 8 7 ♣ 5 4	
♠ 4 3 2 ♡ 5 3 ◇ 6 3 2 ♣ 8 7 6 3 2	N W E S	♠ 9 7 ♡ A K Q 8 7 ◇ Q 10 9 ♣ K Q J
	♠ A K Q J 8 ♡ 9 4 ◇ K 5 4 ♣ K 10 9	

West passed, North raised to Two Spades and East doubled. South bid Four Spades, West passed thankfully and, although East gave the matter some thought, this became the final contract.

West led the eight of Clubs and declarer allowed the Jack to hold. East cashed two top Hearts and followed with a low one which South ruffed high.

Any interest that West might have held in proceedings had long since gone and he discarded a low Diamond. South cashed his Ace of Clubs and ruffed his last Club in dummy.

Judging that the Diamond finesse was sure to be wrong, he played off the rest of his trumps; discarding Diamonds from dummy.

At the end South held **D** K 5 4; North **H** J **D** A J and East had to discard from **H** Q **D** Q 10 9. Clearly he had to keep the Queen of Hearts, so he let a Diamond go.

Now the Ace and Jack of Diamonds to his Queen gave South the last trick with his five.

If only West had discarded a completely useless Club instead of an apparently useless Diamond, he would have had the satisfaction of taking the setting trick with his six of Diamonds.

Accidents Can Happen

We all experience accidents at the bridge table. Sometimes partner makes the wrong bid, sometimes partner plays the wrong card – much more rarely you are to blame.

Most of the time accidents are costly, but this deal from the early 1960s was a curious example of the accidentees (is that the right word?) falling on their feet.

East dealt at game-all and opened One Spade. Most Souths warmed up with a direct overcall in the opponent's suit and ended in a variety of unsuccessful contracts. Five Diamonds failed miserably and Three No-trumps stood no chance after a Spade lead, in spite of North-South; 27 points.

One South decided to double One Spade and, after partner's response of Two Hearts bid Two Spades in order to extract further information. The quest failed when North, misunderstanding the call, passed.

Declarer won the opening Spade lead, cashed two

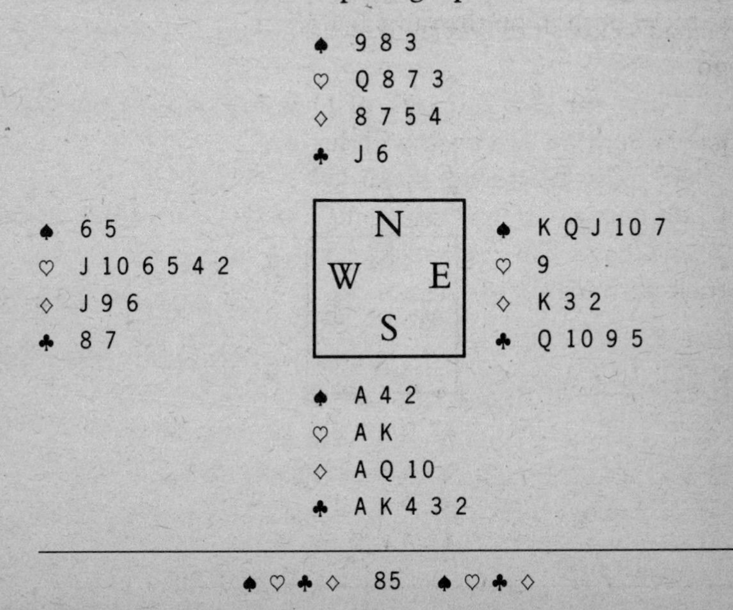

Clubs and ruffed a Club on the table. A successful Diamond finesse was followed by the Ace of Diamonds and, when another Club was ruffed with dummy's nine of Spades, a top Heart yielded eight tricks. Yes, they were the only North-South pair to end with a plus score.

Two In One

'Well, that was all right,' commented East after what seemed to be a multiple disaster for his side.

'What?' expostulated his partner. 'Yes,' continued East (who was not a great striker of the ball, but was fully prepared to admit it), 'I usually do about two bad things in every rubber and I find it economical if I can fit them both in on the same hand.'

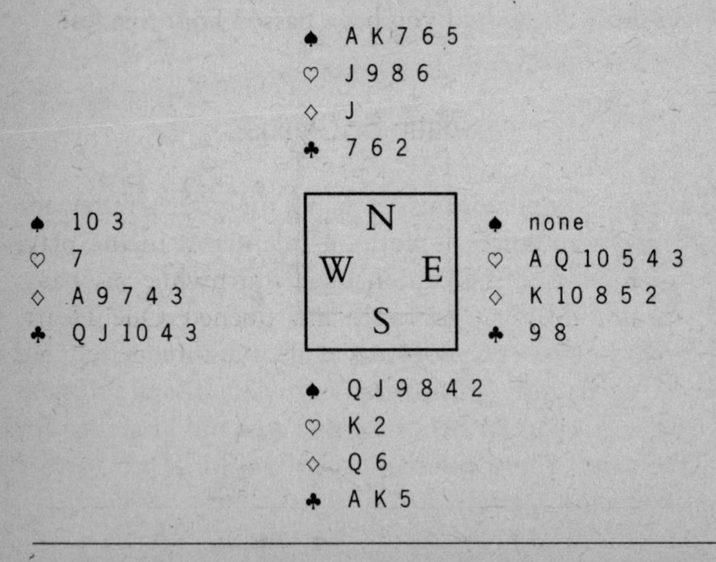

To be perfectly fair I would say that neither of his 'bad things' was criminal – they just worked out badly as the cards lay. South dealt at love-all and opened One Spade. North raised to Three Spades, East overcalled with Four Hearts and South bid Four Spades. It would have gone well for him if East had fought on with Five Diamonds but he decided to pass.

West led the seven of Hearts to East's Ace and, thinking quickly, South dropped the King. It was clear to him that West's seven was a singleton but by no means clear to East who now placed his partner with **H** 7 2 and switched to the nine of Clubs. South won, drew trumps and conceded a Heart. He won the next Club lead but could now enter dummy with a trump and take a ruffling finesse against East's Queen of Hearts to land ten tricks.

You cannot really blame East for falling for South's false-card, but would you have passed Four Spades?

Lunatic Or Genius?

Though I rarely discuss a hand on which, after the opening lead, there is nothing of interest in the play, several points in this deal make it worthwhile anyway.

South dealt at game-all and opened One Heart. North could see no problems at all and immediately bid Four No-trumps (Blackwood). It was a disappointment to hear that partner held only one Ace and he settled for Six Hearts, confident that there would be no further problems for his side.

North was in for a shock, though, for East doubled. With West on lead, North reasoned, this had all the earmarks of a Lightner double.

East was suggesting that he could trump something and (looking at North's hand) surely it was Diamonds. After the expected ruff, the defenders would have an Ace to cash.

Too late North regretted not bidding Six Diamonds instead of Six Hearts, but he made what he regarded as an intelligent attempt to retrieve the situation by converting to Six No-trumps. East doubled again (on firmer ground now, for he was on lead) and all passed.

North's 'rescue' did not work well and the slam failed by four tricks, but what do you think of East? Lunatic or genius?

He could not have defeated Six Hearts but his first double caused his opponents to panic.

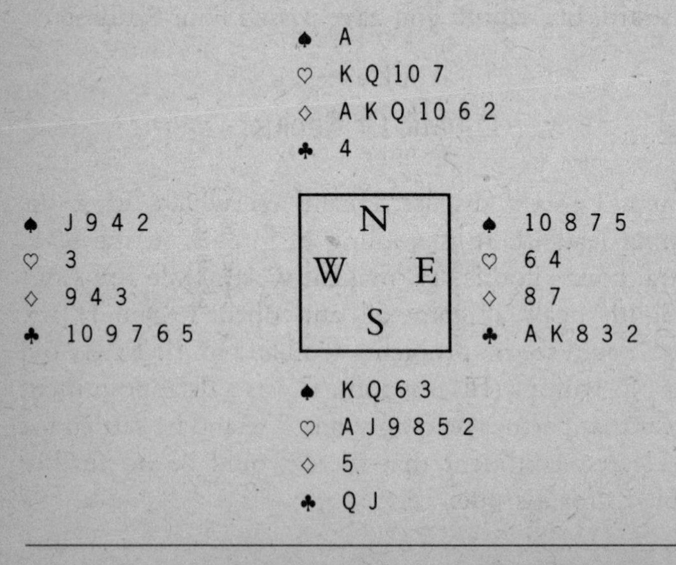

Horror Story

Some years ago I resumed an old partnership with Pietro Forquet (of the famous Italian Blue Team) in the Philip Morris European Pairs Championship at Salsomaggiore. Although we did not feature in the main prize list, I have to confess that Pietro won the Bulletin prize for the best entertaining horror story of the tournament. This was the hand.

As West at game-all I dealt and passed, North opened One Spade and Pietro overcalled with Three Clubs. South bid Three No-trumps, North asked for Aces and raised to Six No-trumps (a doubtful decision).

Now, can you see East's problem? If he doubles – a Lightner slam double suggesting, on the bidding, a Spade lead after which the contract will almost surely

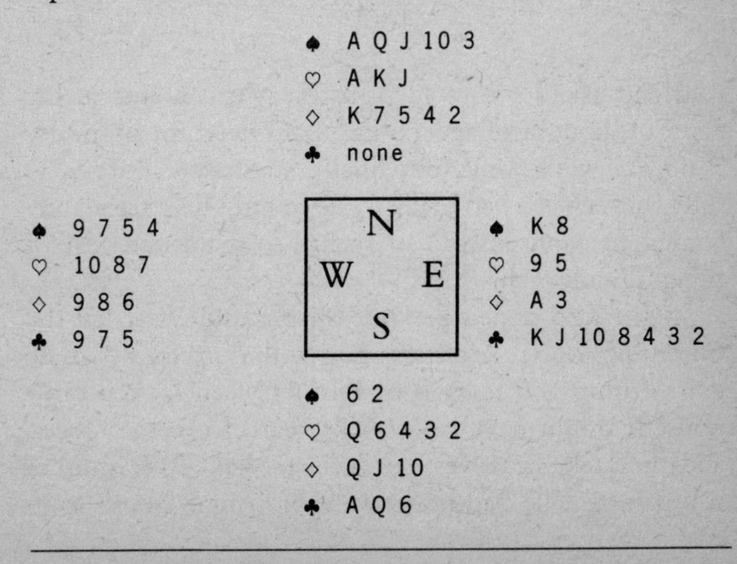

be defeated, I would certainly have led a Spade as requested and, indeed, the slam would have failed by one trick.

But, reasoned partner, without a double I would be sure to lead his suit (Clubs) and with two almost certain entries in the shape of the King of Spades and the Ace of Diamonds, the contract seemed likely to go several off. So he passed, I dutifully led a Club, and it proved easy for declarer to establish 12 tricks without taking a Spade finesse.

Yes, a Spade lead would have defeated the contract and – the ultimate horror – it was only the Club lead that gave declarer his twelfth trick for, with the void in dummy, he could not have taken the marked Club finesse himself.

Tact?

A friend asked me to identify the weak points in his game. I thought of several good answers; for example, 'You *deal* very well', but finally suggested more tactfully that when a bad break came to light he, as declarer, tended to panic instead of trying to make the best of things. Look at this hand.

My friend ended in Four Spades and West led the Queen of Hearts. After winning with dummy's Ace, he led a trump and the fall of East's Queen looked ominous. It might have been a false card from the Queen and the Jack, however; so declarer played off another top trump. The bad news was confirmed. South led a

Diamond, West took his Ace and drew two more rounds of trumps before forcing out declarer's last trump with the Jack of Hearts.

Now South crossed to the King of Diamonds and, despairingly, took a finesse off the Jack of Clubs. West won and the defenders took three more Heart tricks. Four down was inglorious to say the least.

How should South have played? After one round of trumps, he should force out the Ace of Diamonds.

Say West continues Hearts. Declarer ruffs and only now plays his second top trump. Then he crosses to the King of Diamonds and ruffs a Heart, cashes his third Diamond, goes over to the King of Clubs and trumps dummy's last Heart.

West can over-ruff and draw dummy's last trump, but he has nothing but Clubs to lead and South is home and dry.

West		North / South		East
		♠ 7 4 3 ♡ A 10 6 2 ◇ K 10 4 ♣ K 6 3		
♠ J 10 9 6 ♡ Q J 4 ◇ A 7 3 ♣ Q 7 4		N W E S		♠ Q ♡ K 9 8 7 5 ◇ 9 8 6 5 ♣ 10 9 5
		♠ A K 8 5 2 ♡ 3 ◇ Q J 2 ♣ A J 8 2		

Where Was The Two Of Clubs?

Everyone knows that Blackwood can be used to track down Aces in your partner's hand but rather more of a rarity must be this old deal that I found in my files.

Everything depended on placing the two of Clubs. And you can never find that out, no matter how sophisticated your bidding methods may be.

South dealt at game-all and opened One Spade. West doubled, North raised to Two Spades and South went on to game. West led the King of Hearts to declarer's Ace. It was clear to South from West's double that the Ace of Clubs was likely to be wrong. The best chance, he decided, was to hope that it would fall in three rounds.

At trick two, therefore, he led a low Club from

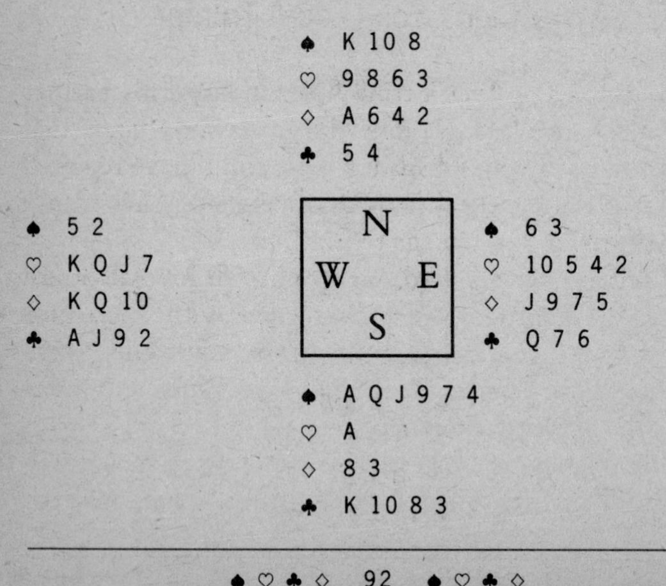

hand. East won and returned a trump. West won the next Club lead and was able to lead a second trump. Now, although South could ruff one Club on the table, there was still a third trick to be lost in the suit as well as a Diamond.

Just suppose that declarer had crossed to the Ace of Diamonds before touching Clubs. The five is covered by the six, eight and nine. The trump return is won in dummy and the next round of Clubs goes four, seven, ten and Jack.

The second Trump lead is won in hand and the King of Clubs led, covered with the Ace and ruffed in dummy, pinning East's Queen.

And at the end? Wait for it! South's three of Clubs beats West's two and wins the trick by force.

Why Didn't You Lead A Trump?

'Why didn't you lead a trump?' East asked his partner after this hand. It was a joke, for everybody knew that West had been void in Spades. East could have repaired the omission, but the idea of sacrificing a possible trump trick simply did not occur to him.

The bidding was wild and woolly. At love-all South opened One Spade, West overcalled with Two No-trumps to suggest length in the minor suits, and North raised to Four Spades. East tried Five Clubs and, after two passes, North doubled.

Not fancying his defensive prospects, South removed to Five Spades and – from somewhere or another – North found a raise to Six Spades. West led the King of Clubs and South ruffed the second round.

He then set about a cross-ruff – he trumped a Heart, cashed two Diamonds and ruffed another Heart.

Two more Clubs and two more Hearts were ruffed and there were three more trump tricks to follow. East's Queen of Spades fell soundlessly on the last trick.

Suppose that East had tried the effect of overtaking the Club lead with the Ace and returning a trump. South would no longer have been able to come to the 12th trick.

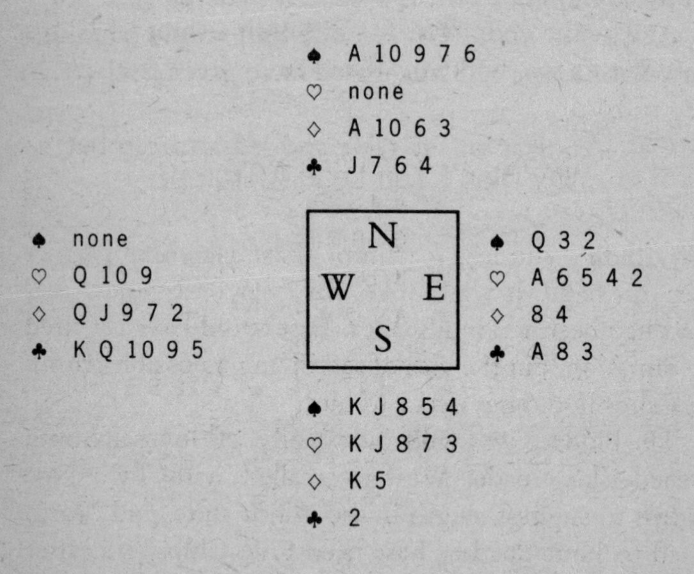

A Partner's Pleasing Mistake

Here is a bridge riddle: can you think of any reason for a player to be pleased when his partner makes a mistake? The answer, of course, is that he writes a weekly column and his partner has just provided him with the material for a good article.

South dealt and opened One Heart. Feeling that he was a little too good for a direct raise to game, North temporised with Two Clubs and, when his suit was supported, jumped to Four Hearts.

West made an excellent start for the defence when he led the Jack of Clubs. A spade lead would have cost a trick and either red suit would have given declarer an easy run.

Declarer won on the table and led a trump but, as

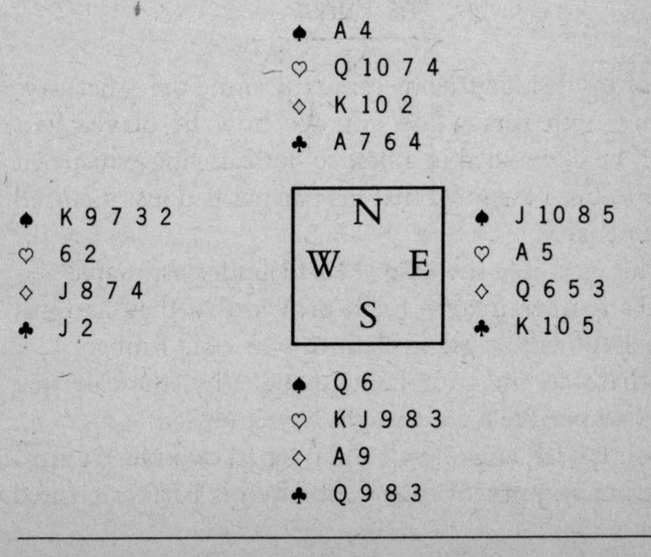

East, I went in with my Ace, cashed the King of Clubs and gave partner a Club ruff. It was clear to West that a Spade lead would not work well and he was reduced to leading Diamonds.

But the four went to the two, Queen and Ace and now declarer finessed the ten of Diamonds successfully. Now he was able to discard his losing Spade on the King of Diamonds and take the rest of the tricks.

The defence had started splendidly, but what should West have led after taking his ruff? The *Jack* of Diamonds! Now declarer cannot make a third Diamond trick, and eventually he loses a Spade.

Very neat, and you can see why I was almost happy to lose the rubber.

The Purist

One of my bridge friends came up to me the other day, shaking with fury. 'Did you see how he played that hand?' he demanded in a hoarse but carrying whisper. I had not, but I assumed that his partner had just incurred a vast penalty.

This was not the case – I had under-estimated my friend's temperament – for it proved that they had just made a vulnerable grand slam to win a big rubber.

What was the complaint, then? Why, the *way* that hand had been played. I might have guessed . . .

South dealt at game-all and opened two No-trumps. A Gerber enquiry of four Clubs by his partner elicited the reply of four Diamonds (none or four Aces) and North bid a firm seven no-trumps.

West led the ten of Diamonds and the play was soon over. Declarer won on the table and, with only 11 top winners, knew that he had to bring in the Clubs without loss. He played off dummy's King, studied West's Queen for some while, and successfully finessed the nine of Clubs to claim the rest of the tricks.

The Principle of Restricted Choice certainly suggested a finesse in Clubs on the second round rather than playing for the drop of the Jack. For if West had started with both the Queen and the Jack, he would have been equally likely to play either card on the first round; with the Queen alone, he would have had no choice.

It worked, but can you see why dummy was so agitated? It was only when shown the full hand that I

West		North		East
		♠ K J		
		♡ K Q 3		
		◇ K J 4		
		♣ K 10 7 6 3		
♠ 9 5		N		♠ 10 8 7 6 4 3
♡ 10 8 7 6 4		W E		♡ 9 2
◇ 10 9 8 6 2		S		◇ 5 3
♣ Q				♣ J 5 2
		♠ A Q 2		
		♡ A J 5		
		◇ A Q 7		
		♣ A 9 8 4		

saw the point. Certainly the Clubs had to be brought in, but suppose that declarer puts off his decision as long as possible?

Three rounds of Spades, Hearts and Diamonds make it crystal clear that West has started with two Spades, five Hearts and five Diamonds. Therefore he has only one Club and, when the Queen falls under the King, the winning finesse is now guaranteed to succeed.

Of course, if both defenders had followed suit all the time there would still have been a genuine guess at the end.

An Odd Problem

I was posed an odd bridge problem the other day: What was unusual about the following deal from a Danish team tournament?

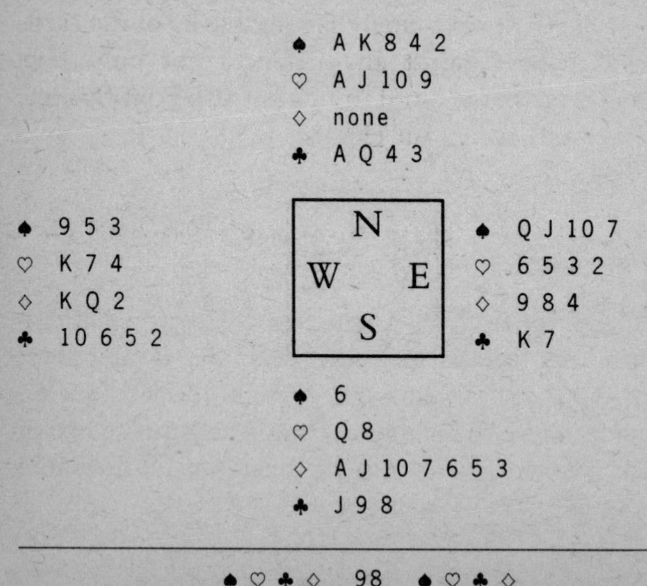

I was told that South had ended in Five Diamonds rather than the more normal Three No-trumps and had made his contract elegantly.

A misunderstanding in the bidding had led to Five Diamonds, but South recovered well after the worrying lead of the six of Clubs. He won with dummy's Ace, cashed two top Spades discarding a Club, and ruffed a Spade in hand. Then came the Queen of Hearts (West did not cover), and a further Heart finesse was followed by the Ace of Hearts on which declarer threw his last losing Club.

Next came a Club ruff and the Ace and another Diamond. Now South was home, losing only two trump tricks. I still could not see what was particularly unsuitable about the hand and finally gave up.

Perhaps you spotted it? The amusing thing is that North-South can make game in whichever suit they choose. Due to the extremely favourable lie of the cards they can make (against any defence) not only Five Diamonds and Three No-Trumps but also Four Spades, Five Clubs and even Four Hearts.

Six Tricks Or Eleven?

How many tricks would you expect North-South to make in No-trumps on this deal? Assuming best defence, you will probably guess at six (declarer losing two Spades and five Diamonds) but in a Camrose match between England and Northern Ireland it did not quite work out like that . . .

North dealt at game-all, and at one table, the Northern Irish South opened One No-trump. All passed and West led the seven of Spades. As you can see, declarer would have been well advised to try dummy's Queen – ending with no fewer than 11 tricks – but instead he played low from the table.

In some circumstances this could have been the right play, but not here – East won with his Jack, returned to Spade and the defenders now took the first ten tricks to score 400 points.

At the other table the English South opened One Club and West overcalled with One Spade. North tried One No-trump (this was before the days of negative doubles), but the subsequent auction to Three No-trumps did not sound convincing to East and he doubled.

East led the Jack of Spades and West had to make

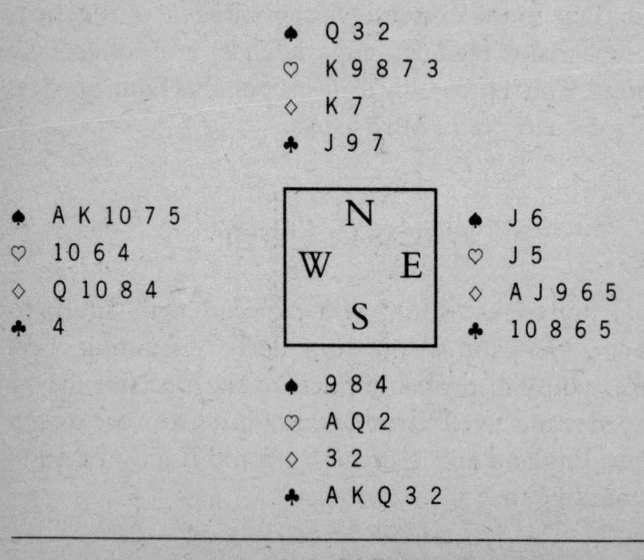

the critical decision. In the fervent hope that his partner had the Clubs held, he judged that it was safe to duck. Now 11 tricks were made for a score of 1,150 points.

He Had A Point, But Something Was Odd

This hand produced some interesting possibilities. Declarer had the right idea but slipped slightly. West definitely went wrong. It was the post-mortem that left us all wondering . . .

South opened One Heart and North responded Two Clubs. South reversed with Two Spades and North jumped to Four Hearts to end matters. Both players had done a little more than was justified, but the final contract was not unreasonable.

West led the Jack of Diamonds and South was

	North	
	♠ 8 2 ♡ A 10 7 ◇ Q 8 3 ♣ Q J 10 9 5	
West ♠ A Q 9 ♡ J 5 2 ◇ J 10 9 2 ♣ 8 6 3	N W E S	**East** ♠ J 10 6 3 ♡ 6 4 ◇ A 7 6 5 ♣ K 7 4
	♠ K 7 5 4 ♡ K Q 9 8 3 ◇ K 4 ♣ A 2	
	South	

allowed to win with the King. He returned a Diamond and let West's nine hold. With little else to do, West continued the suit and declarer ruffed with the eight of Hearts.

Next came the three of Hearts, and dummy's seven was finessed successfully – to get the Clubs working it was necessary to have three entries to dummy. A Club finesse followed, then the Ace of Clubs and the nine of Hearts to dummy's ten. A Club ruff in hand and South's last trump to dummy's Ace clinched matters.

Declarer made one Diamond, four Clubs and five Trumps.

'I could have defeated that!' observed West. 'If I play the Jack on the second round of trumps, you are one entry short.'

True enough, but he replied: 'If you were going to play the Jack on the second round of trumps, I would have ruffed the Diamond with my Queen.'

His analysis was spot on. Try it out – now there are three entries to dummy whatever West tries.

Way Back . . .

The Lederer Memorial Trophy always provides an excellent opportunity to watch top-class bridge in London. One of my favourite stories comes from this event back in 1960.

South dealt at game-all, and at table one ended in a routine Four Spades. The defence was beautifully accurate – West led the three of Clubs and East was allowed to win with the ten. A Diamond came back and West won to return a second Club.

There was no escape for declarer and he lost two tricks in both minor suits to go one off.

At comparison time West asked what had been the opening lead at the other table. On hearing that it was the King of Diamonds, West was delighted – surely that should represent a good gain for his side! But there was a nagging suggestion all was not well . . .

It appeared that South had opened Two Spades, North had bid Three Diamonds, and a flurry of cue bids had led to a wild Seven Spades. And the opening lead was the King of Diamonds.

Now, after drawing trumps and driving out the Queen of Diamonds, declarer escaped for one off and a miraculously flat board. Has the standard of play improved in the last 30 years?

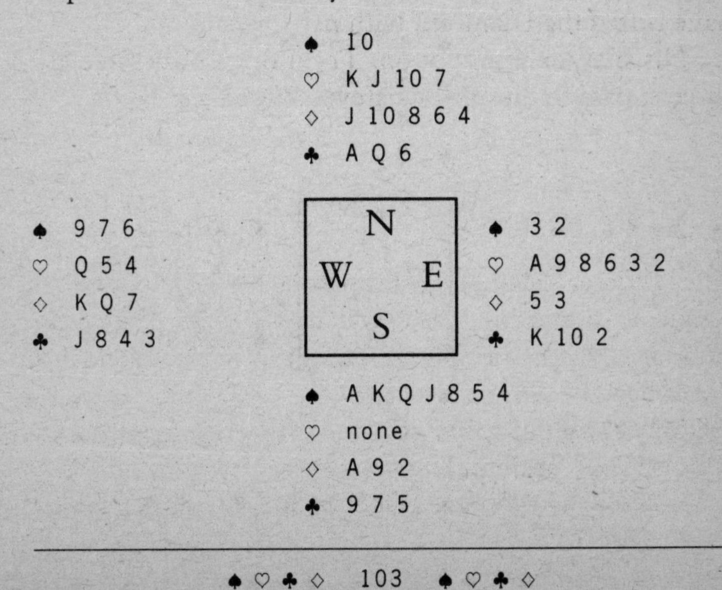

There Is Always One Pair . . .

Most bridge clubs have a pair who – how can I put it kindly? – seem to antagonise other pairs.

So I could fully understand a friend's enjoyment of this deal during which one of the unpleasant pair misdefended and, as a result, his partner was squeezed.

North dealt at game-all and, after two passes, South opened Five Clubs. All passed, although East gave the matter some thought.

West led the King of Hearts and declarer ruffed the third round. Clearly there were no problems if the missing diamonds broke 3-3, but to improve chances South played off the Ace of trumps, crossed to the Queen of Clubs and led a low Spade from the table.

It was a cost-nothing play: for players in the East

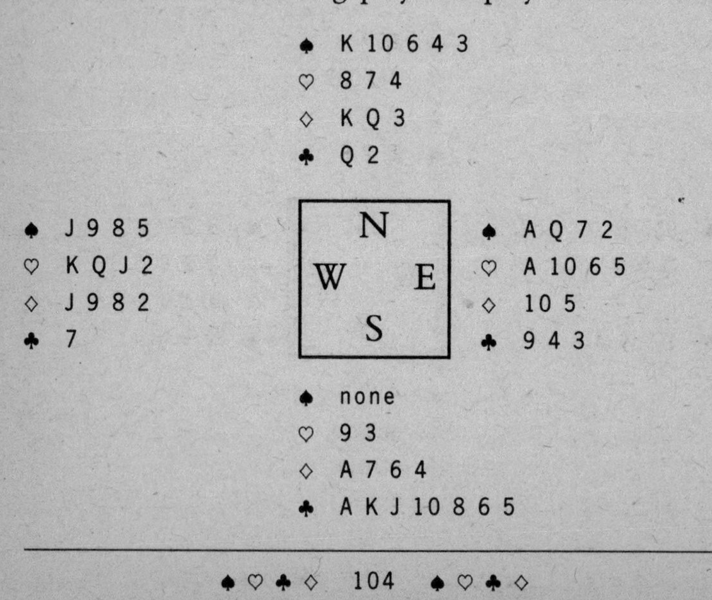

seat with the Ace of Spades but not the Queen have been known to fall for this sort of trap.

There was no reason for East to play his Ace here, but his actual choice of the Queen proved just as costly.

South ruffed, drew the last trump and entered the dummy with a top Diamond.

The King of Spades was covered with the Ace and ruffed and declarer followed with the rest of his trumps.

At the end West had to keep his Jack of Spades in front of dummy's ten and was forced to unguard the Diamonds.

Tactful as Ever

'What do you think is the weakest part of my game?' asked a friend. It was a difficult question to answer

	North	
	♠ K 7 4 ♡ J 10 9 5 ◇ A J 6 4 ♣ 8 2	
West ♠ Q 9 6 2 ♡ A 8 4 ◇ 3 ♣ A 10 6 4 3	N W E S	**East** ♠ J 10 3 ♡ 7 2 ◇ Q 10 8 7 2 ♣ J 9 5
	♠ A 8 5 ♡ K Q 6 3 ◇ K 9 5 ♣ K Q 7	
	South	

tactfully but, remembering a recent rubber, I was able to suggest he had a tendency to lead singletons rather too often.

That was the downfall of West in this game. South opened One No-trump at game-all; North explored with a Stayman Two Clubs and raised South's response of Two Hearts to game. All passed to leave West on lead against Four Hearts. He immediately led his singleton three of Diamonds. This did not prove to be a success when East's ten lost to the King and South was able to start on trumps.

It was too late now for the defender to establish a fourth trick. After his nine of Diamonds had lost the Queen, declarer was able to discard his potential Spade loser on the established Jack of Diamonds.

The singleton lead was poor tactics, for West himself held the quick entries and there was little likelihood of him being able to put his partner in quickly before trumps were drawn.

The lead also gave declarer three tricks in a suit where he might easily have made only two. To have led a low Spade would have been more purposeful and, as the cards lie, successful.

He Knew What He Was Doing

'There is only one chance,' observed declarer after inspecting the dummy opposite. Then he took a finesse that the bidding had made absolutely clear was wrong. Even his partner joined in the laughter when, unsurprisingly, the finesse lost. But declarer knew exactly what he was doing . . .

West dealt at love-all and opened Three Hearts. After two passes, South selected Three No-trumps as the most practical bid (Four Clubs would have taken the partnership past the No-trump game). North closed his eyes and raised to Six No-trumps to end the auction.

Against the slam, West led the nine of Spades and declarer assessed his prospects. With West marked with the King of Hearts, there were only 11 winners in sight. The 12th trick had to come from a squeeze – if East held the Spades, then both defenders might have to unguard Diamonds. But first, a trick had to be lost to correct the timing.

South won the Spade lead in dummy and took the Heart finesse, occasioning all the merriment. West won and played another Spade, but now South was in

West	North / South	East
	♠ A K 5 ♡ 4 3 2 ◇ A 9 6 ♣ Q 9 6 3	
♠ 9 8 ♡ K J 10 9 7 6 5 ◇ Q 8 3 ♣ 4	N W E S	♠ Q J 6 4 3 ♡ 8 ◇ J 10 7 5 2 ♣ 5 2
	♠ 10 7 2 ♡ A Q ◇ K 4 ♣ A K J 10 8 7	

control. He won the Spade in dummy, cashed the Ace of Hearts and ran his Club winners.

West had to keep a Heart in front of dummy and so could save only two Diamonds. After dummy's four of Hearts had gone away at trick ten (its work done), East had to keep the Queen of Spades and also came down to two Diamonds. Now three Diamond tricks gave declarer his contract.

Can Spot Cards Be That Important?

It would have been easy to go off in Four Hearts on this deal but the declarer was a keen student of the spot cards. As he said afterwards: 'It would not have been as easy if I had not been dealt the seven of Clubs!' He was right, too.

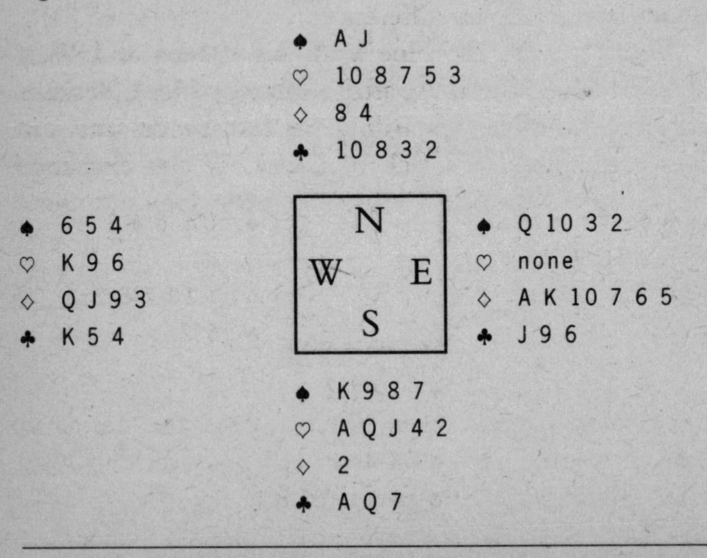

South dealt with East-West vulnerable and opened One Heart. North raised to Two Hearts, East over-called with Three Diamonds and South (not famed for the delicacy of his methods) bid Four Hearts.

The level was too high for West to compete and all passed. West led the Queen of Diamonds and switched to the six of Spades, covered by the Jack, Queen and King. After a Spade to the Ace declarer tried a trump and, when East showed out, played the Queen.

West won and led a second Diamond but South ruffed, trumped a Spade on the table and drew trumps ending in dummy. Next came the two of Clubs. East played low and declarer put in the seven. As the cards lay, this forced the King and South was home and dry.

West suggested that his partner might have done better to play the nine on the first round of Clubs but it would have made no difference.

South covers the nine with his Queen and West takes his King. But now, after a Diamond lead, declarer ruffs on the table (discarding his last Spade) and can finesse against East's Jack of Clubs. If you exchange the six and seven of Clubs, the play does not quite work.

Bidding Only

It is not often that I write about a hand that seems to depend entirely on the bidding, but this deal illustrates an interesting and little-known point.

I was asked by a friend how North-South should bid to their slam if they were playing a natural system. Oddly enough, there was a scientific way to reach the optimum contract.

South dealt at love-all and found himself looking at 11 certain tricks. A slam depended upon finding his partner with the King of Hearts *or* either the Queen or a doubleton in Clubs.

The bidding I suggested was for South to open Two Clubs and, after his partner's negative response of Two Diamonds, rebidding Three Spades. As Two Spades would have been forcing to game, Three Spades conventionally carries a special message. It says, 'Do not worry about trumps – my Spades are self-sufficient', and asks if partner has any Aces.

The bidding proceeds with Three No-trumps by North ('No, I have no Aces') and Four Clubs by South.

West	North	East
	♠ 10 7 4 ♡ J 8 3 ◇ Q 7 6 4 3 ♣ 8 5	
♠ 3 ♡ 10 7 5 2 ◇ A 8 2 ♣ Q 9 6 4 2	N W E S	♠ 8 ♡ K Q 9 6 ◇ K J 10 9 5 ♣ J 10 7
	♠ A K Q J 9 6 5 2 ♡ A 4 ◇ none ♣ A K 3	

Remember that Spades have been set as trumps. Four Clubs is merely a 'mark time' bid.

Four Spades by North (a return to the agreed suit) shows no Kings and now Four No-trumps by South goes even further by asking for third round controls.

North shows his doubleton Club with Five Clubs (Five Spades would have been his bid with, perhaps, **S** 10 7 4 **H** J 8 3 **D** 7 6 4 3 **C** 8 5 2) and now South can bid Six Spades with confidence. Very elegant, and the play is easy.

'How did you bid it?' I asked my friend.

'Oh, I just opened Six Spades,' he replied. Well, he saved time but he might have missed an easy grand slam.

It Can Go Either Way

'When you are playing a strong No-trump,' asks a reader, 'is it better to play a 15–17 point range or 16–18?' On the brink of replying that it really does not matter a scrap as long as the partnership is on the same wavelength, I watched this hand played in a friendly teams match.

South dealt at game-all and at one table (where the North-South methods included a 16–18 point No-trump and five-card majors) opened One Club. North scientifically responded One Spade, East passed (well pleased) and South raised to Two Spades.

Now North tried Three No-trumps and, on lead, East doubled. He would not have been averse to a retreat to Four Spades either. All passed and East whimsically led the Jack of Spades ('Fourth highest of my longest suit, partner!') and took the first five tricks.

At the other table South was able to open One Notrump (15-17) and, without exploration, North raised to game. Again East doubled – conventionally a lead-directing double for, if the opponents have bid as they have, with no suit mentioned and apparently plenty of values, it suggested a solid or near-solid suit and usually requests partner to lead his shortest suit. Unfortunately West, although eager to lead a Spade, was unable to oblige and nine tricks rolled in.

Does this mean that 15-17 is better than 16-18? Of course not – just try exchanging the East-West hands!

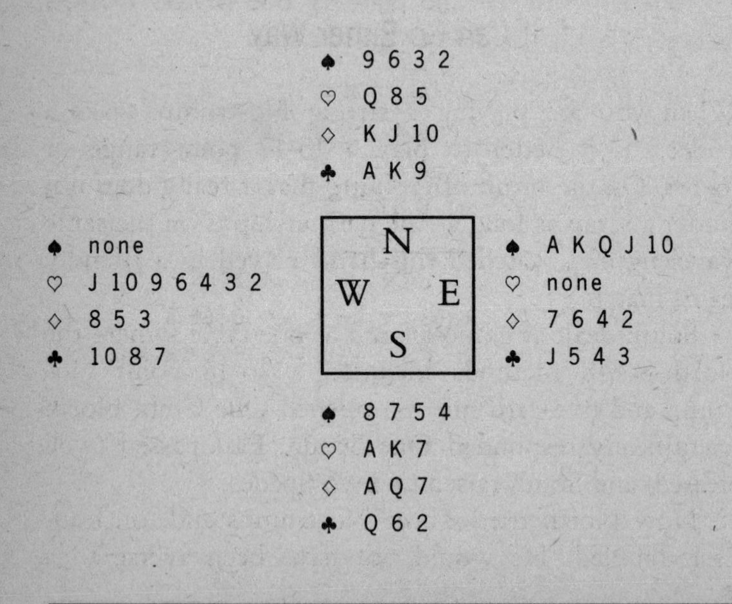

An Unappreciated Joke

There was an amusing side to this old deal from the 1978 Olympiad but I doubt whether the joke was appreciated by either defender.

Try to be honest, cover up the East-West hands, and decide which black suit you would tackle if as South you played in the distinctly poor contract of Three No-trumps and had been allowed to win the opening Heart lead with your King.

West led the three of Hearts against Three No-trumps and declarer won East's Queen with the King. Now, consider my question. Obviously a Club finesse looks a much better bet than trying to do anything with the Spades. And yet the play by one of the world's shrewdest declarers did not go like that.

West	North	East
	♠ A J 7 4 2	
	♡ 6 4	
	◇ A	
	♣ Q 10 7 6 5	
♠ K 5 3	N	♠ 10 6
♡ A J 7 3 2	W E	♡ Q 10 5
◇ J 10 9 3	S	◇ 8 7 6 5 4 2
♣ K		♣ 9 2
	♠ Q 9 8	
	♡ K 9 8	
	◇ K Q	
	♣ A J 8 4 3	

Gabriel Chagas, playing for Brazil, saw an extra chance and (after winning the Heart) led the Queen of Spades. He knew perfectly well that the Clubs were more promising and he had not the slightest intention of finessing in Spades – he planned, if the Queen was not covered, to go up with dummy's Ace and take the percentage Club finesse.

However, West, quite reasonably, covered with his King. The Ace won and when the Jack dropped East's ten there were suddenly five Spade tricks and no need to risk a Club finesse. So, after cashing the nine of Spades and crossing to dummy's Ace of Diamonds to take the next two Spade tricks, Chagas came to hand with the Ace of Clubs. As a result, nine tricks turned into 13 . . .

CHAPTER FIVE

Defence

What can you say about defence in bridge? Primarily, it is much more difficult than declarer play. For every sound defender in this game there must be at least 20 thoroughly competent declarers. It is easy to appreciate why this should be so. Although it is true that, after the opening lead, all of the active participants can see 26 cards, it is only the declarer who can see exactly what are his side's total assets in every suit. The advantage of having the opening lead is dubious – if a player strikes the right one, he may well gain his side a vital tempo; but he can see only his own 13 cards at the time that he makes his possibly critical choice. And this critical choice is notoriously difficult – whole books have been written on the subject.

I am sure that two factors, more than any others, contribute to the making of a good defender. First, he must be able to count as the play proceeds and he mentally constructs the unseen two hands – both points and suit lengths. Second, his partnership should be on the same wavelength as far as signalling is concerned. Distribution; encouragement, discouragement; reverse signals . . . everyone has their own pet theories and the actual choice of method is not all that critical – as long as the partners are in accord!

Do you remember the story of the player who had to discard from the Jack, ten and nine of Hearts and wanted to discourage his partner from leading the suit? Even the nine would be likely to have fatal results. His solution to the problem was to drop the nine on the floor and spend so long in retrieving it that an impatient declarer finally asked what he proposed playing. 'A small Heart!' was the reply – but I do not seriously recommend this way of improving your defensive skills.

Curate's Egg

Like the curate's egg, West's defence on this hand was good in parts. He was right on target with his opening lead, but found the next hurdle too difficult . . .

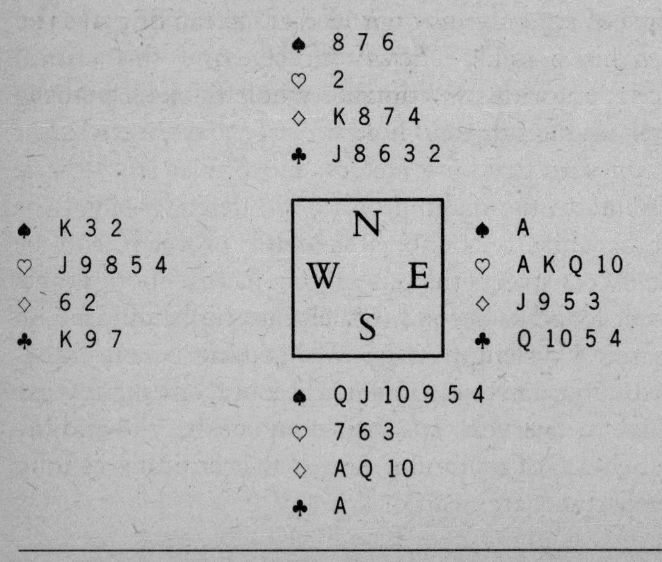

East dealt at love-all and opened One Heart. South overcalled with Two Spades, West raised to Three Hearts, North (with little excuse) competed with Three Spades and East went on to game in Hearts. Judging that his partner was short in Hearts, South persevered with Four Spades. East's double ended the auction.

Rather than lead Hearts, which would have given Declarer an easy run, West shrewdly led a low trump. East won and, unable to continue what looked to be a promising attack, switched to a low Club. Declarer won and led a low Heart from hand.

West went up with the nine but his partner was forced to overtake and still could not lead a second round of trumps. As a result, South had time to ruff both of his remaining losing Hearts on the table and so landed a distinctly thin game.

West was dozing. He should have appreciated that his nine of Hearts might not win. If instead he plays the Jack, his partner can follow with the ten.

On lead, West can continue with two more punishing rounds of trumps to hold declarer to eight tricks.

Strong And Silent

Some players never say anything after a hand – unless provoked by their partner. This usually means that, when they do make a comment, it is worth listening to.

East on this deal was the strong silent type and his analysis was far more revealing than that of his volatile partner.

South dealt at love-all and opened One Club. North responded One Spade, South rebid Two Clubs (I would have preferred One No-trump) and North showed his Hearts. South's next bid of Two No-trumps was optimistically raised to game by his partner.

West led the Jack of Diamonds and, seeing little future in the suit, East turned his attention to driving out dummy's side entry before the Spade suit could be established. After winning with the Ace of Diamonds, he thoughtfully returned the Jack of Hearts.

Declarer followed with the eight, won on the table, and forced out the Ace of Spades. He won the Diamond return in hand and led the two of Hearts to the four and dummy's seven. It was all over and, whether East won or not, ten tricks rolled in.

'Why the *Jack* of Hearts?' West was quick to attack – 'a low Heart gives him a guess!'

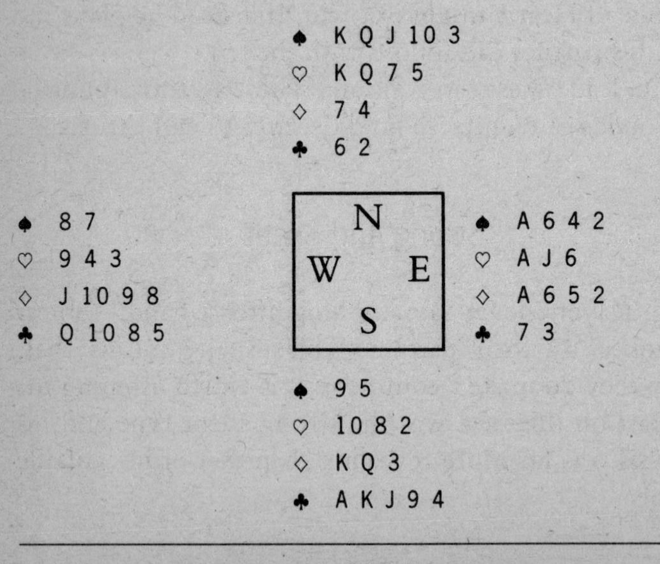

East patiently explained that leading the six of Hearts would only have given a 50 per cent chance of defeating the contract, but the Jack of Hearts should have made it a certainty.

Can you see his point? On the second round of the suit West should have played his nine. Then, whatever declarer tries, there is no entry for dummy.

Not Many Would Have Got It Right

Would you have got the defence right against Four Hearts as West on this deal? In practice a very experienced player missed his chance and I have to agree that it was not obvious – just possible, I suppose, for someone gifted with considerable imagination.

East opened One Diamond at game-all, South over-

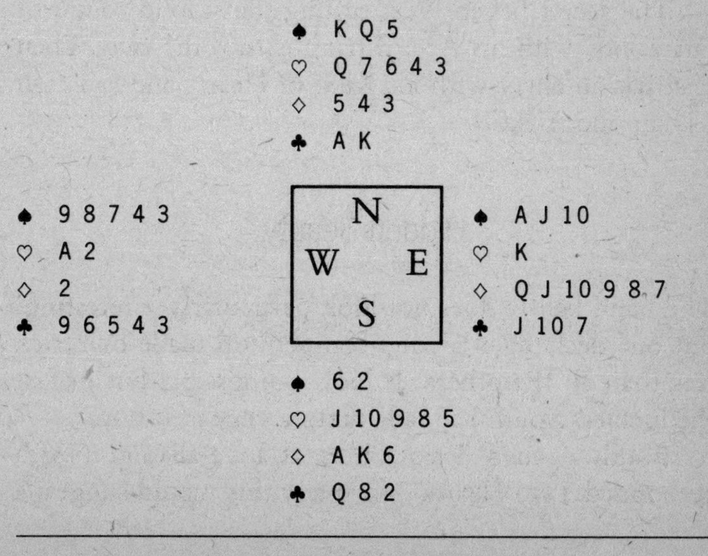

called with One Heart and North raised to Four Hearts. West led the two of Diamonds and East's contribution of the seven made it easy to read the lead as a singleton.

With three top losers, the danger lay in losing a Diamond trick as well. Any attempt to discard a Diamond from dummy on the Queen of Clubs was sure to fail; another thought was to lead trumps immediately.

This fails if West plays low for, although he ruffs South's second top Diamond with his Ace of trumps, he can put his partner in with a Spade to cash a Diamond. Instead, South tried a Spade at trick two. East won and returned a Diamond for West to ruff South's Ace. Although declarer still had a Diamond loser, the Ace and King of trumps fell together and the Diamond loser went away on the Queen of Clubs: for East could not longer get in in.

The secret lies in West ruffing the second round of Diamonds with his Ace of trumps, not the two. Then East has an entry with his King of Hearts and can cash a Diamond trick.

Hidden Beauty

The hand below does not look particularly interesting, but one declarer in a pairs competition made one trick less than all the others. It looks impossible but in fact the luckless South had fallen into a very neat trap.

South opened Two Clubs at love-all and North responded Two Hearts. Normally this would suggest a five-card suit; but North judged that Ace, King, Queen and another was better than most five-card suits. South rebid Two No-trumps and, having already given a positive response, North contented himself with raising to game.

West led the Jack of Spades against Three No-Trumps. Declarer won, crossed to dummy with a top Heart and played back a Diamond, finessing the nine.

You can see what would have happened – and did happen at the other tables – if West had won with the Queen. With nothing else to play for, South would win the return, force out the Ace of Diamonds, and claim 11 tricks. Instead, West won with the Ace of Diamonds and led a second round of Hearts.

Convinced the finesse against the Queen of Diamonds was right, declarer took dummy's top Hearts (discarding a Diamond, for it was not certain the Queen

<table>
<tr><td></td><td>♠ 7 5 4
♡ A K Q 2
◇ 6 4 3
♣ 8 7 2</td><td></td></tr>
<tr><td>♠ J 10 9 2
♡ 10 8 5 3
◇ A Q 2
♣ 9 6</td><td>N
W E
S</td><td>♠ 8 6 3
♡ J 9 6
◇ 8 7 5
♣ 10 5 4 3</td></tr>
<tr><td></td><td>♠ A K Q
♡ 7 4
◇ K J 10 9
♣ A K Q J</td><td></td></tr>
</table>

would fall in three rounds), and finessed the Jack of Diamonds. West won and cashed the ten of Hearts for the defenders' third trick.

An Unusual Complaint

'I wish that I had not been dealt so many high cards,' was West's complaint. It was an unusual thing to worry about, but I could see what he meant. He need not have been so distressed, however, if he had thought of discarding one of his treasures.

With East-West vulnerable, South opened One Spade and West doubled. North raised pre-emptively to Three Spades and, with very little excuse, South went on to Four Spades.

West led the Ace of Diamonds and switched to his

West	North	East
	♠ 10 9 7 6	
	♡ K 9 6 5	
	◇ 7 5	
	♣ A 10 4	
♠ 4	N	♠ 5 3
♡ A J 10 7 3	W E	♡ Q 4
◇ A K 4	S	◇ J 10 9 6 2
♣ K J 8 3		♣ 9 6 5 2
	♠ A K Q J 8 2	
	♡ 8 2	
	◇ Q 8 3	
	♣ Q 7	

singleton trump. Even assuming that West held most of the outstanding high cards, there looked to be only nine tricks. The extra winner had to come from some sort of end-play against West.

At trick three declarer led the Queen of Diamonds from hand – good technique preparing for a Diamond ruff without letting East in for a damaging Club return. West took his Ace and exited safely with a Diamond.

South ruffed on the table and played off all his trumps. West came down to **H** A J **C** K J and dummy to **H** K 9 5 **C** A. Now a Heart towards the King established two tricks in the suit and gave South his contract.

Well, how could West have done better? Suppose that he had thrown away his Ace of Hearts on the last trump – then East gets in with the Queen of Hearts and has a long Diamond to defeat the contract.

There Was No Hurry

Every so often you come across a hand on which it seems impossible to make a sensible bid. South's problem on this deal is a good example, but at least he ended in a sensible contract and went on to collect a plus score.

West dealt at game-all and opened One Diamond, North doubled and East passed.

What should South bid? He cannot try No-trumps with so little in Diamonds; Two Clubs seems very feeble with 10 points (he would have been forced to respond with nothing), and to cue-bid the opponents' suit with Two Diamonds would be too pushy. His actual choice of Three Clubs, which was passed out, worked quite well but would not have been everyone's choice.

West started with three top Diamonds, dummy ruffed low and East over-ruffed with the Jack. With the Spade finesse right for declarer, East later came to the King of Clubs but that was the defenders' last trick. It is worth noting that East does better to discard a Heart instead of over-ruffing.

Declarer *can* still get home (a Heart to hand, three Spade tricks, then two more Hearts – East ruffs this but can later be end-played), but after East's failure to over-ruff, he is far more likely to take an early finesse in trumps. After that there would be no recovery.

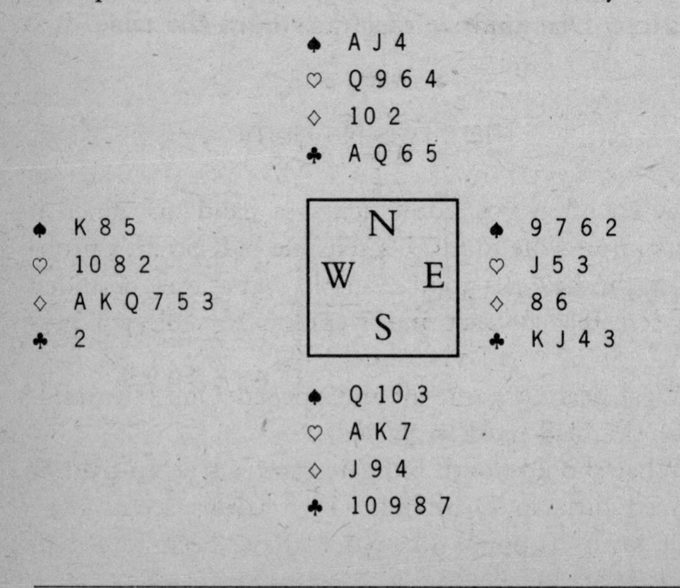

One Of Partner's (Rare) Mistakes

Nobody said anything at the end of the deal below, and it was only much later that my partner, who had been the declarer, admitted to me that he had made (as he put it, modestly), 'one of my rare mistakes'. Fortunately the defenders had not spotted it either and we had made our contract.

As North, at game-all, I opened One Diamond and raised my partner's response of One Spade to game. Against Four Spades, West led the Queen of Diamonds.

Declarer won with dummy's Ace and followed with the two from hand. East's nine had the appearance of a singleton so, to avoid immediate defeat, South drew three rounds of trumps ending in dummy.

Next came the five of Hearts from the table. It is

West	North	East
	♠ A K J 3	
	♡ 5	
	◇ A K 7 6 5 4	
	♣ 7 5	
♠ 6 4	N	♠ 9 5 2
♡ J 9 6 4	W E	♡ A 10 8 3 2
◇ Q J 10 3	S	◇ 9
♣ A J 8		♣ K 10 9 4
	♠ Q 10 8 7	
	♡ K Q 7	
	◇ 8 2	
	♣ Q 6 3 2	

usually right to duck in these situations, and East played low allowing South to win with the King. In practice East would have done better to take his Ace.

South followed with the eight of Diamonds to the ten and King, then came the seven of Diamonds on which declarer threw a Club. West could take his Jack of Diamonds and Two Clubs, but dummy's Diamonds were established and the game rolled in.

Well, what was South's tiny error? He should have followed to the first trick with the eight of Diamonds.

As the play went, West could have defeated the contract by not covering when the eight was led. The eight wins but the lead is in South's hand and the rest of the suit (except for the King) is shut out and declarer is left with only nine tricks.

Would *You* Have Done Better?

Both West and South made intelligent plays on this deal. Oddly enough it was East, who apparently had nothing whatsoever to worry about, who missed his chance.

West dealt with East-West vulnerable and opened Two Spades. East gave the negative response of Two No-trumps and an intrepid South joined in with Three Hearts.

Having already shown a good hand, West passed to see what action his partner might take. North raised to Four Hearts and then West took his chances in defence.

His lead of the Ace of Spades, dropping his partner's Queen, clarified the position in the suit.

West might have switched to the King of Diamonds at this point, but instead tried the King of Clubs. His plan was to win the first round of trumps, put his partner in with a Spade ruff and trump the Club return.

Declarer won the Club switch in dummy and, instead of playing trumps immediately, tried the Ace and another Diamond. When East followed with the six, South threw his losing Spade; for he knew that West would have to overtake his partner's six.

On lead West could no longer put his partner in and declarer lost only one Spade, a trump and a Diamond.

It looks unnatural, but try the effect of the ten of Diamonds by East on the second round of the suit. Now he cannot be kept from gaining the lead (either in

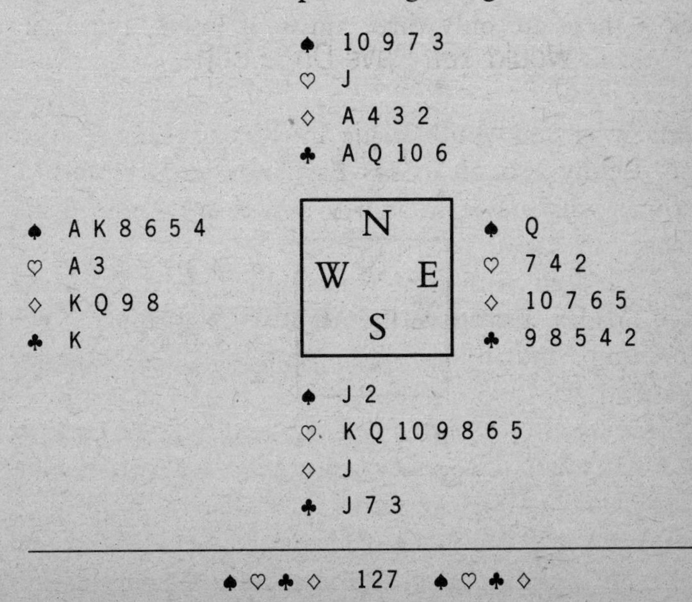

Diamonds or with a Spade ruff) and West gets his Club ruff to defeat the contract.

Much Later . . .

I always enjoy hands where only the most unnatural-looking play leads to success, especially when the play has to be made by a defender.

Even after this hand had been completed, it still did not dawn on East that he might have done better. It was only much later, after looking at all four hands, that the declarer spotted what might have happened.

South dealt with East-West vulnerable and ended in Four Hearts after East had completed in Spades. In fact Four Spades by East would have failed by only one trick – there are only three apparent losers, but East

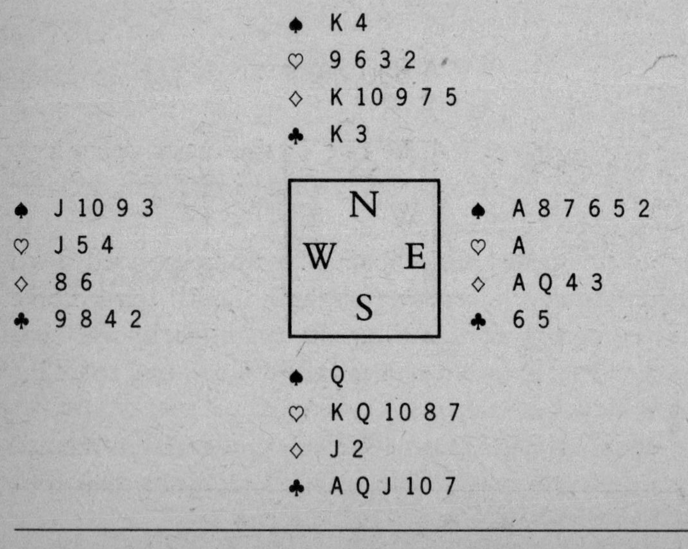

cannot conveniently get his dummy in to take the winning Diamond finesse.

Against Four Hearts, however, West led the Jack of Spades to the four, Ace and Queen. East returned a Club to dummy's King and the play was soon over when one of South's losing Diamonds went away on the King of Spades, and a trump lead from dummy ensured that declarer lost only one trick in the suit.

Well, what did they all miss?

Suppose that East, after taking his Ace of Spades at trick one, had played the Ace and another Diamond. It looks a terrible play with the Ace-Queen sitting over the King, but observe the effect.

Now when East wins the first round of trumps with his Ace, he leads a third round of Diamonds. This promotes a trick for his partner's Jack of Hearts and defeats the contract.

A Sad Sight

Unless you happen to be one of the lucky defenders, there are few sadder sights in bridge than the declarer who squeezes himself.

South opened One Spade, North responded Two Diamonds and, stretching slightly, South tried Three Clubs (forcing to game on the methods in use) and went on to Three No-trumps after North had rebid his Diamonds.

West led the nine of Hearts and declarer relaxed visibly – how could he possibly lose more than four tricks? He won in hand and started work on the Diamonds.

East won the third round of the suit and returned a Heart. Suddenly declarer saw problems – if he won in hand, he would cut himself off from any potential black-suit winner.

Accordingly he took the Heart in dummy and cashed the established Diamonds, coming down to **S** K Q **H** A **D** none **C** K J.

It did not help, for when he led a Spade from the table East went in with his Ace and switched to a Club for West to take three more tricks. Nor would refraining from cashing the last Diamond or two have assisted matters.

Declarer went wrong at the second trick. After winning the Heart lead in hand, he should lead a top Spade. East wins and plays a second Heart – but South

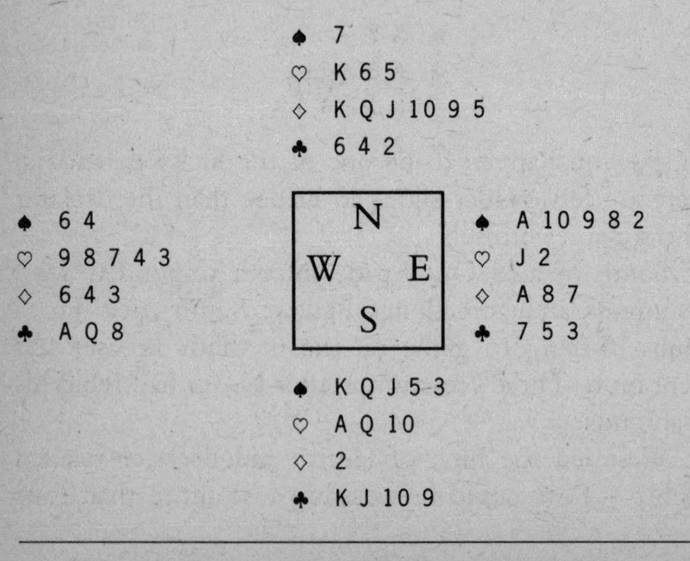

takes this in hand, cashes just one Spade winner and only then establishes the Diamonds. Now the defenders can come to only four tricks.

Play The Card You Are Known To Hold

Play the card that you are known to hold is an excellent maxim. For example, consider this hand.

North-South bid to an adventurous Six Spades and West led his singleton trump.

This scotched any idea of relying on a Club finesse and ruffing two Clubs on the table, and declarer realised that he would have to bring in dummy's long suit.

In order to retain an entry to the table South won in hand and led the nine of Diamonds to the ten, Jack and Ace.

West		East
	North ♠ K 5 ♡ A 8 7 2 ◇ K J 7 6 5 4 ♣ 2	
♠ 8 ♡ Q 10 6 4 3 ◇ Q 10 8 ♣ K J 9 3	N W E S	♠ 7 4 3 2 ♡ J 9 ◇ A 3 2 ♣ 8 7 5 4
	South ♠ A Q J 10 9 6 ♡ K 5 ◇ 9 ♣ A Q 10 6	

East played a second trump to dummy's King and declarer continued by cashing the King of Diamonds. West followed mechanically with the eight, and after that South could not go wrong.

He ruffed a Diamond (bringing down the Queen), drew trumps, and crossed to the Ace of Hearts to cash the established Diamonds.

Suppose West drops the Queen of Diamonds (the card he is known to hold) under the King?

Declarer may still get it right by ruffing a Diamond, but he will have been left with the genuine alternative of taking a ruffing finesse against the supposed eight in East's hand.

Do You Remember?

Sometimes people say that hands in bridge columns look familiar. I cannot vouch for other journalists, of course, but inevitably I may sometimes repeat a theme or occasionally adjust an old deal to make a new point.

If you remember this hand, well done; for it appeared in 1938!

South ended in Four Spades, having bid Hearts on the way. West led the two of Diamonds to his partner's Ace, and East decided to return a Heart. (A trump or another Diamond might have been more purposeful, but I am only describing what happened all those years ago.)

Declarer played low, West took his King and led another Heart to dummy's Queen. A finesse of the

Queen of trumps followed and West, rather shrewdly, played the nine.

If he had taken his King then declarer, faced with a loser in all four suits, could have released the two top Clubs, drawn just one more round of trumps and continued with two winning Hearts to discard dummy's losing Clubs. Then a Club ruff on the table would have seen him home.

With the nine of Spades falling under the Queen, however, it might have looked to declarer as though the trump finesse was right and he could continue with a Club to the King and another trump finesse.

This would have been a disaster for South for, when the second trump finesses loses, another trump is returned and his chances have been killed.

What went wrong? Why, when South finessed the Queen of Spades, East reached across the table to pick

	North	
	♠ 8 7 2 ♡ Q 9 ◇ 6 5 4 3 ♣ A K 7 5	
West ♠ K 9 4 ♡ K 6 4 2 ◇ Q 10 2 ♣ Q 9 6	N W E S	**East** ♠ 6 5 ♡ 8 5 3 ◇ A J 9 8 7 ♣ J 10 3
	♠ A Q J 10 3 ♡ A J 10 7 ◇ K ♣ 8 4 2	

up the expected trick! Now there was no temptation to repeat the finesse.

Old Theme In New Guise

One of the textbook situations in defence arises when declarer (call him South) is playing a trump suit of, say, K 10 8 7 6 facing Q 3 2 and has no outside entries to dummy. He leads the six to the Queen and East, holding A 9 4, ducks smoothly.

Dummy returns trumps; East follows with the nine and South (convinced that West has the Ace), finesses the ten and loses to the doubleton Jack. If East had taken the first trick, declarer would have had no option but to drop the Jack.

The theme came up in a new guise on this deal.

West	North	East
	♠ Q 3 ♡ J 10 6 ◇ J 4 3 ♣ J 9 7 6 3	
♠ 10 4 ♡ 9 8 7 3 ◇ K 9 6 2 ♣ Q 5 4	N W E S	♠ K 7 5 2 ♡ 5 4 2 ◇ Q 10 7 ♣ K 10 8
	♠ A J 9 8 6 ♡ A K Q ◇ A 8 5 ♣ A 2	

South rated his hand as worth a conventional Two Clubs and, after giving the negative response of Two Diamonds, North raised his partner's rebid of Two No-trumps to game.

West led the nine of Hearts and declarer won in hand. It was clear that four Spade tricks were needed for the contract, so South started by leading low to the Queen. Without any tell-tale hesitation, East let this win.

I expect that you can see the sequel. Declarer continued spades from the table and East played low. 'Knowing' that West held the missing King, South tried the nine.

West won and continued hearts and, with a trick still to lose to the King of Spades, South was held to eight tricks.

And if East had won the first Spade trick? It would have been all over. With no entry to the table there would have been no choice for declarer other than to play Spades from the top, dropping the ten.

A Helpful Discard

It is not enough for your opponents to go wrong at this game – you have to spot their mistake! My partner found a thoughtful defence on this deal.

I was East and heard South open One No-trump (12-14 points) which was raised to game by North. All passed and West made his natural lead of the Queen of Spades.

Concerned about a switch to Hearts, if he ducked the first trick, declarer won and started on the Clubs. All followed to the first round but West discarded a low Diamond on the second.

Clearly South needed to bring in the Club suit, so he played a third round to my Queen. But before I won the trick, my partner made his good play – he discarded a Spade, making it easy for me to switch to a Heart.

Declarer could make his Clubs now, but there was no way back to his hand to enjoy the second top Spade and he ended with only eight tricks.

Suggestions for improving declarer's play? Try the Ace of Clubs, then a low Club (not the King). He gives up the chance of an overtrick but is sure of nine winners.

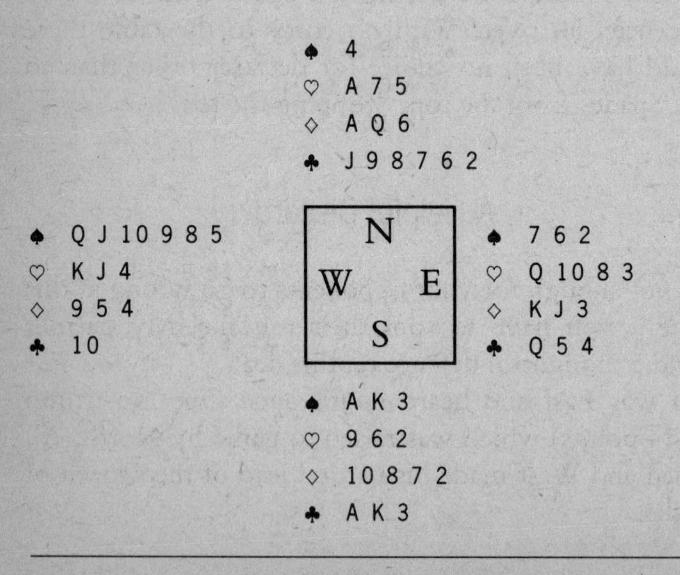

A Good Try

Among bridge columnists it is considered bad form to point out mistakes by colleagues.

On this hand, however, I have a clear conscience. The deal was first presented as a defensive problem for East, and the original idea was good. It might well have worked in slightly different circumstances – but it occurred to me that declarer had a neat counter.

South opened One Club, North responded One Diamond, South rebid One Spade. After a fourth-suit bid of Two Hearts by North, South ended in Three No-trumps.

With all suits bid, West led the five of Clubs to his partner's Ace. East saw little future in Clubs and

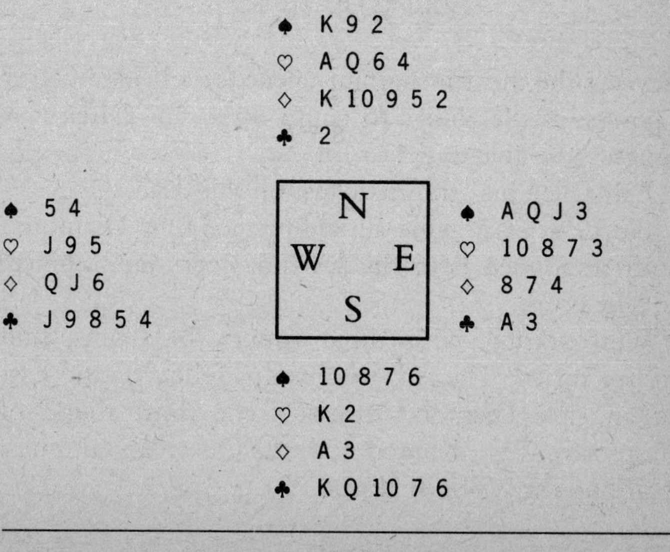

considerable danger in dummy's long Diamond suit if he defended passively.

He switched to the three of Spades. Declarer won cheaply with his six but with only eight tricks in sight, it looked impossible to develop a ninth without letting West in. Then a Spade return would give the defenders five tricks.

Very neat, but suppose that (after winning the Spade switch in hand) South plays off his two winning Clubs. What does East throw on the second? He cannot part with either a Spade or a Heart and must discard a Diamond.

Now declarer cashes his two top Diamonds and follows with four rounds of Hearts. On lead, East has to concede declarer's ninth trick to the King of Spades.

Adding Up To 13

They say the most important talent for a bridge player to possess is the ability to count up to 13. Often it is enough to be able to get to 10!

East failed his arithmetic test on this deal.

North dealt at game-all and opened One Diamond. South responded Four Spades (not everyone's choice) and all passed.

West started with three rounds of Clubs, and declarer ruffed. The two top trumps followed and East had an easy Diamond discard. The third round of trumps saw West winning with the Queen and dummy discarding the seven of Hearts.

East found himself with a problem – he had to retain the Queen of Clubs, but which red suit should he discard? He chose to keep the same length as dummy in both and parted with the five of Hearts.

As you can see, this proved fatal, for now declarer had the rest of the tricks.

Counting up to ten would have been sufficient to guide East to the logical defence. He knows that South has six Spade tricks and he can see three winners on the table.

If declarer is missing the King of Diamonds, the finesse lands the contract.

The one slim chance is to hope that declarer is void in Diamonds and unable to take the winning finesse. So East should stick, leechlike, to his Hearts. If nothing else can help, why not try it?

West	North	East	South
	♠ 10 3		
	♡ A K 7		
	◇ A Q 9 4		
	♣ J 6 4 3		
♠ Q J 8		♠ 4	
♡ 10 8 3		♡ Q 9 5	
◇ K J 5 2		◇ J 10 8 6 3	
♣ A K 8		♣ Q 10 9 7	
			♠ A K 9 7 6 5 2
			♡ J 6 4 2
			◇ none
			♣ 5 2

Creating A Losing Option

This hand ended in an odd fashion. With the four players reduced to three cards each, all in the same suit, there was still considerable scope for subtlety.

At game-all, South dealt and opened One No-trump. North raised to game and, against Three No-trumps, it was natural for West to lead the Jack of Hearts.

East took his three Heart tricks and switched to a Club; declarer played off four Club winners and three top Diamonds to end in hand. This left everyone with just three Spades apiece. As the cards lie, a winning play is to run the ten of Spades round to East and end-play him but instead South led the five of Spades.

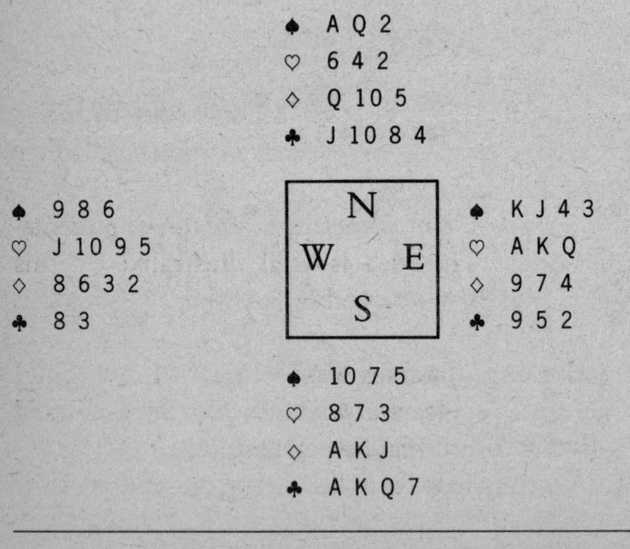

West, who could well have been excused for losing interest after parting with his solitary picture card on the first trick, stayed awake and followed with the nine. The Queen was finessed, losing to the King, and the four of Spades came back.

Can you see South's problem in the two-card ending? If East holds the Jack of Spades, the ten is the winning play. If West holds **S** J, the seven may force it and establish the ten.

There would have been no story if declarer had got it right, but he tried the seven and so went one off.

The key point, of course, is that if West had followed automatically to the first spade lead with the six, South would have been left with no option but the winning play of the ten on the second round of the suit.

Easy to Miss

One type of defence that seems a blind spot to many players is deliberately leading dummy's long suit before declarer has drawn trumps.

In this way you can sometimes cut the opponents' communications. The idea is well illustrated by this deal from a match where, oddly, neither West got it right.

The action at both tables was identical – a rare thing! South opened One Heart at love-all; North responded Two Clubs and South bid Two Diamonds.

Now North tried Two Spades – the fourth suit,

asking for further information – and South bid Three Diamonds to show his distribution. North jumped to Four Hearts and all passed.

West started with the King and Queen of Spades, then made the natural-looking switch to the King of Diamonds. Now it was all over: South won and played off five rounds of trumps.

Suppose that West had appreciated that his partner might well hold four trumps? Remember that declarer held one Club at most.

A Club return at trick three finishes South's chances. He cannot draw trumps and get back to the winning Clubs and, if he draws only one or two rounds of trumps before continuing Clubs, East will ruff the third round and South will come to only nine tricks.

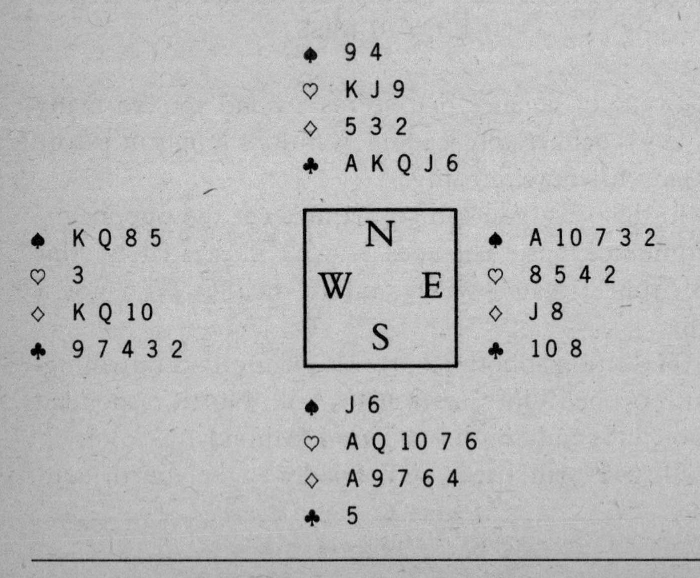

Laziness Is Easy

It is very easy to be lazy when you are defending. One of the most natural things to do is leading a high card and making declarer ruff in his own hand. On this hand, however, it proved fatal.

South opened One Heart, North raised to Three Hearts and South went on to game.

With little to go on, West led a Heart and declarer drew trumps in two rounds. Next came three rounds of Diamonds. If the suit had divided 3-3, South would have been home and dry, for his losing Spade would have gone on the long Diamond.

East showed out on the third round, however, and discarded the four of Clubs in a well-intentioned effort to tell his partner that a Club switch would be welcome.

	♠ A 10 7 ♡ K Q 6 4 ◇ 9 8 5 2 ♣ Q 5	
♠ Q 6 5 ♡ 8 2 ◇ Q 10 6 3 ♣ A 10 9 7	N W E S	♠ J 8 4 2 ♡ 7 5 ◇ J 7 ♣ K J 4 3 2
	♠ K 9 3 ♡ A J 10 9 3 ◇ A K 4 ♣ 8 6	

The message was not clear to West, who followed the line of least resistance when he exited with the Queen of Diamonds. South ruffed and got off lead with a Club.

The defenders could take two tricks in the suit but, no matter who won the second, they were left with the choice of conceding a ruff and discard or opening up the Spades.

After the (eventual) Spade lead, declarer played for divided honours in the suit and landed his contract.

The defence, to succeed, has to be timed exactly. When West wins with the ten of Diamonds, he must lead a low Club.

On winning the next Club with his Ace, he exits with his carefully preserved Queen of Diamonds. South can ruff this but now has to play Spades himself.

A Depressing Game

It is important in defence to help your partner as much as you can. Even if it is impossible to suggest what you would like him to do, you can sometimes make it difficult for him to do the wrong thing.

South opened Two No-trumps, North raised to game and all passed. As West I led the two of Spades to the five, nine and Queen. Correctly, with only one entry to the table, declarer gave up any hope of finessing in Clubs and continued with the Ace, King and ten of the suit.

On lead with the Queen I took stock. From the play to the first trick I could be sure that declarer still held the King and Jack of Spades. So I knew that there was no future in the suit.

It looked as though the only hope was to find partner with the Ace of Hearts when we would be able to take three quick tricks in the suit.

Suddenly I saw a snag. To take three Heart tricks I would have to lead the nine and, even if East held the Ace, he might get it into his head that I was simply trying to give him the lead in order to return my first suit.

I saw the solution – I cashed the Ace of Spades first to make it clear that I had no further interest in the suit, then led the nine of Hearts and waited for a Heart return.

I am still waiting, for back came a Spade and

	North	
	♠ 8 5	
	♡ 8 6 4	
	◇ K J 10	
	♣ J 9 6 4 2	
West		**East**
♠ A 10 7 2		♠ 9 6 4
♡ K J 9		♡ A 5 2
◇ 8 6 3		◇ 9 7 5 4 2
♣ Q 7 5		♣ 8 3
	South	
	♠ K Q J 3	
	♡ Q 10 7 3	
	◇ A Q	
	♣ A K 10	

declarer had ten tricks. Bridge can be a very depressing game . . .

Aces Are Not Always For Kings

When you are defending it is usually a good thing if your Aces can win tricks containing a King or Queen belonging to the other side – it seems a waste if they just gather twos and threes!

The trouble is that you will not always be doing the right thing. The hand below is an instructive example of what I mean.

Playing five-card majors, South dealt at game-all and opened One Heart. North raised Two Hearts, East overcalled with Three Clubs and South ended the bidding with a jump to Four Hearts.

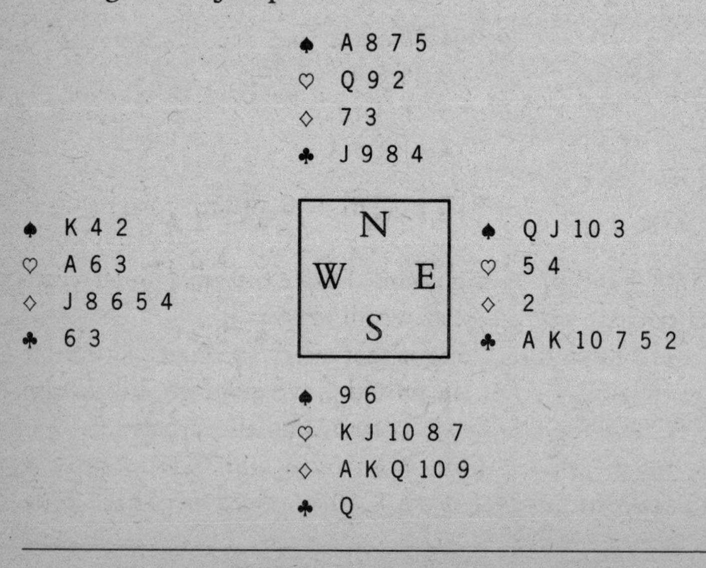

West led the six of Clubs to the four; King and Queen and East, after some thought, switched to the Queen of Spades rather than his singleton Diamond. Declarer won on the table and led a trump to the King.

That was too tempting a bait for West to resist. He took his Ace, cashed the King of Spades and led another Spade which South ruffed. Next came just one more round of trumps before declarer started on the Diamonds.

When East showed out on the second round and was unable to trump, South was home and dry. He took a ruffing finesse in Diamonds to pick up West's Jack, came to hand with a Spade ruff and drew the last trump to make ten tricks.

It is worth noting that South lost nothing by playing on Diamonds before drawing the last trump – if East had held it and was also short in Diamonds, the contract could never be made.

Of course, if the Jack of Diamonds had fallen on an early round, South would have gone back to trumps.

When To Forget The Rules

'Third hand plays high' and 'Don't finesse against your partner' are sayings that we all hear.

The intriguing thing is that every so often a situation comes along when it would have paid to break the rules. The trouble lies in recognising the situation.

South opened One No-trump and North, after a Stayman inquiry of Two Clubs, raised to Three No-trumps. West led the three of Clubs to the five, Queen and Ace and the play was soon over.

Declarer had plenty of time to establish his nine tricks – losing a Spade, two Hearts and a Club – and nobody thought anything much about the hand. But could the defenders have organised themselves a fifth trick?

Suppose that, after the Club lead, East plays the seven rather than the Queen. Effectively he is finessing against dummy's nine rather than against his partner.

Now the defence is in charge. South wins cheaply but, whether he plays on Spades or Hearts next, West wins and leads another Club to the nine and Queen.

When East gets in with his Ace of Hearts he can lead a third Club and his partner has the King and eight sitting over declarer's Jack and six.

I must warn you that it does not always work! East's

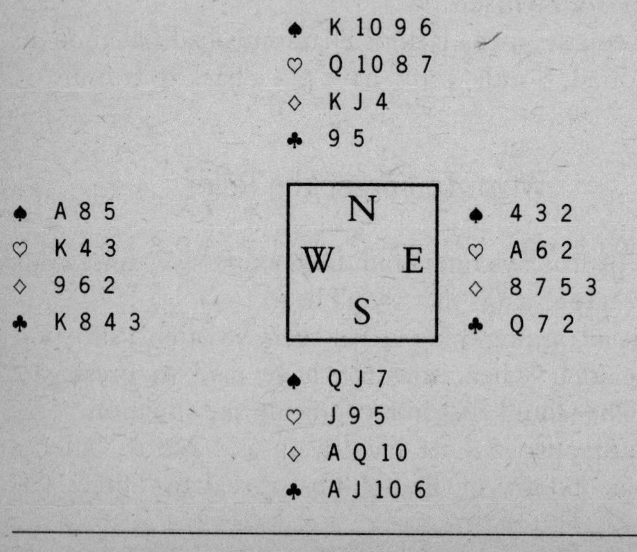

play of the seven of Clubs on the first trick might have proved disastrous if his partner had started with, say, K J 8 3 in the suit.

Even More Rule-Breaking . . .

I always enjoy coming across hands on which the only defence is to break one of the 'rules' that seem to be part and parcel of the game.

How much more important it is to think clearly and be able to recognise the exceptions! Although the following type of play has been written about before, it still seems difficult to find at the table.

East dealt at love-all and opened One Heart. South passed and West raised to Two Hearts. Perhaps a preemptive raise might have proved more effective for

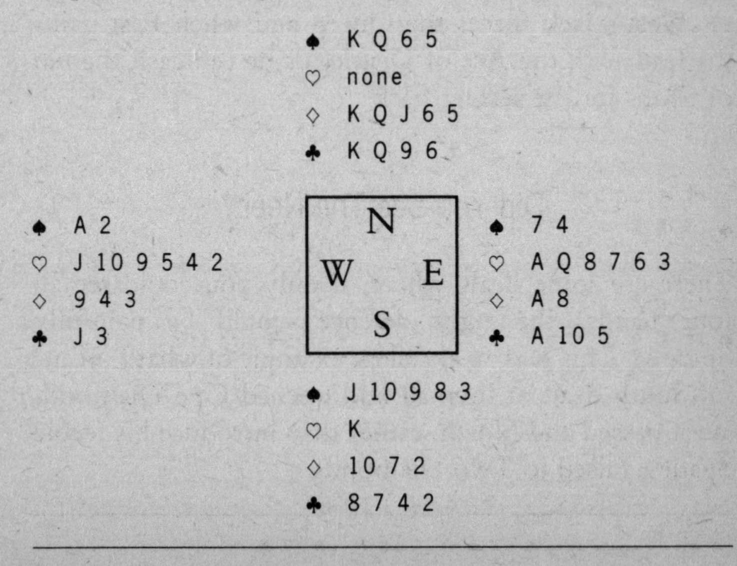

now North came in with a double and North-South bid their way to Four Spades.

West led the Jack of Hearts and declarer ruffed on the table. The King of Spades lost to the Ace and it was clear to West that the only hope of defeating the contract lay in establishing two Club tricks before declarer could get dummy's Diamonds going.

So he switched to the Jack of Clubs (the higher card of a doubleton, as we all are taught) but it was not good enough. The King lost to the Ace – it does not help East to duck – but now there was no safe way for the defenders to continue Clubs. In the fullness of time South's two losing Clubs went away on dummy's Diamonds.

Try the effect of switching to the three of Clubs rather than the Jack. As before East takes his Ace but the difference is that he can now safely return a Club.

West's Jack forces the Queen and when East gains the lead with the Ace of Diamonds he can cash the ten of Clubs for the setting trick.

Did You See The Need?

There are some deals where, if only you could see all four hands, the right defence would be painfully obvious. This was an excellent example of what I mean.

South dealt at love-all and opened One Diamond. West passed and North, rather than introduce his feeble Spades, raised to Two Diamonds.

Rather aggressively East overcalled with Three Hearts and South contested with Three Spades, which North raised to game. East brooded but passed – West had fewer temptations.

West led the six of Hearts and East took his two tricks in the suit before switching to a low Club – a natural enough move. Declarer won but, with no entry to the table, there were problems.

One possibility was to hope for the King of trumps to be singleton but a better bet seemed to be finding East with the singleton Ace of Diamonds. After cashing his second top Club, declarer got off lead with a Diamond.

You can see how East found himself fixed; a Club or a Heart return would give declarer access to dummy for a winning trump finesse. It was all over.

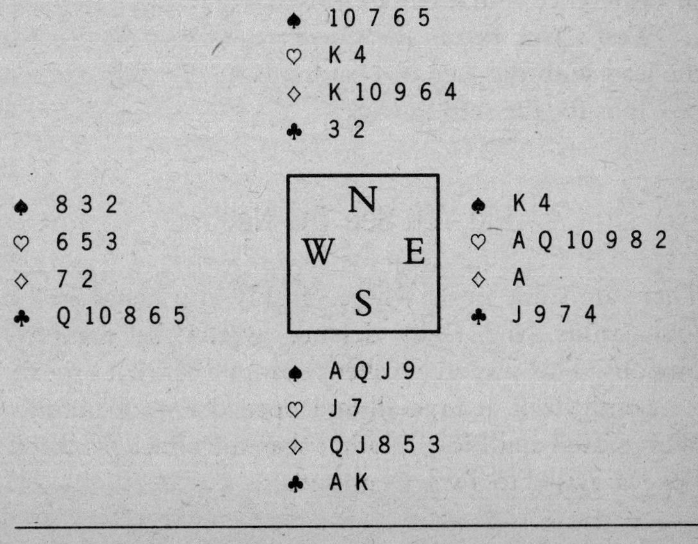

Now, be honest, did you see the need to play off the Ace of Diamonds at trick three before exiting with a Club? And for the right reasons? It all seems so easy now and it defeats the contract.

CHAPTER SIX

Partscores

Partscores have different degrees of importance in the various forms of this game. In match-point pairs, of course, the success or failure of a contract of One Club is just as important as that of a redoubled grand slam, and the extra 20 or 30 points achieved by means of an overtrick can be sheer gold dust. In ordinary rubber bridge, too, they can have a profound effect on the final score. Just think of the times when you had a game and 60 and your opponents (unwisely) sacrificed time and again in a vain effort to 'save the rubber'. It is only in teams play or Chicago bridge (in which the rubber consists of exactly four hands and partscores are not carried forward to the next deal) that matters change. Of course it still helps to make your contract rather than fail but the gain or loss involved is much less than on the big hands, and the odd overtrick makes little or no difference.

Looking back through my files it became painfully clear to me that partscores were poorly represented compared with games and slams. There are two reasons for this. First, they are often not very memorable hands. Everyone remembers (and can reconstruct!) a slam made on two finesses, a misdefence and a squeeze, but who makes a note of a deal on which your partner went one down in a contract of Two Diamonds?

Second – and this is significant for a bridge columnist – there is the question of space. A typical game contract might offer two lines of play, one superior (or more successful) than the other and both alternatives can be discussed reasonably concisely. By contrast, a contract of perhaps One No-trump may have many possible divergences in the play – at several stages more than one player may have varying options – and often a full analysis might have required a loose-leaf insert to the *Sunday Express*.

Never mind, here is a selection of deals that caught my eye.

French Magic

It was a pleasure to come across this rather neat deal from a French tournament.

At game-all, East dealt and passed and all the South players came to rest in a Spade partscore. Without exception the West players led their singleton Diamond.

At one table East won with the King, cashed the Ace and led **D** 3 for West to ruff. This was a clear McKenney signal for a return in the lowest ranking side-suit, so West dutifully played back the ten of Clubs.

The message of **D** 3 was not lost on declarer and his first bonus came when he went up with dummy's Ace and was delighted to see the King fall.

Many of us would have been well satisfied with progress so far, but South was a logical player. East, who had dealt and passed, had shown up with **D** A K and **C** K. Who held the King of Spades?

It could not be East so, with little to lose and much to gain, declarer played a Spade to the Ace and dropped his second black King offside. Now there were nine tricks.

It was not all easy to foresee, but East does much better to return a Heart at trick two. With no clues to the distribution, an innocent declarer might well end up with only four or five tricks.

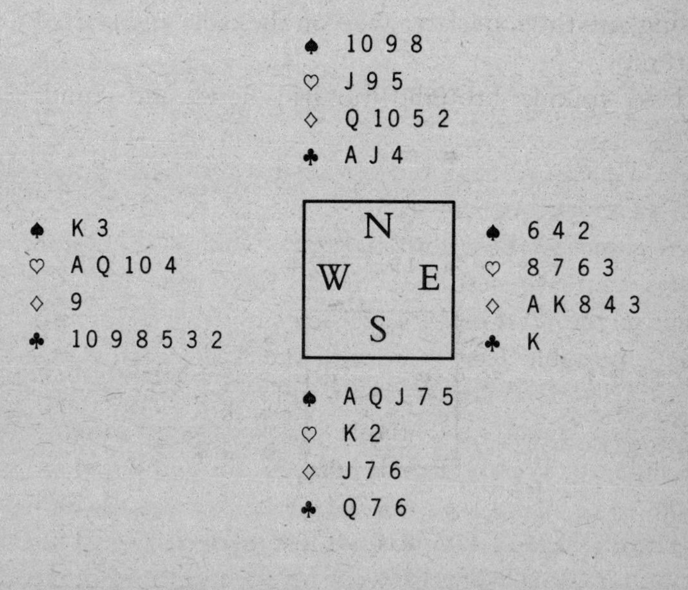

My Opinion Was Asked . . .

'How do you play a suit of A K Q 10 9 2 facing 4 3?' demanded a friend. 'Play for the drop of the Jack rather than finesse, of course!' he continued, answering his own question and jotting down the following hand at the same time.

South dealt with a 30 partscore and opened One Spade. North responded One No-trump and, in view of the score, South stretched a little to rebid Three Spades. (A raise to Two No-trumps instead has considerable merit.)

West led the Queen of Diamonds and, without wasting any time, declarer won on the table and started on trumps.

Two rounds brought the bad news and South

West		East
	North ♠ 4 3 ♡ A 7 6 ◇ A 8 4 ♣ 10 9 7 5 4	
♠ 5 ♡ Q 10 8 3 ◇ Q J 10 6 2 ♣ K Q 8	N W E S	♠ J 8 7 6 ♡ J 9 5 2 ◇ K 9 3 ♣ A 2
	South ♠ A K Q 10 9 2 ♡ K 4 ◇ 7 5 ♣ J 6 3	

changed tack. He played off the King and Ace of Hearts and ruffed a Heart in hand. Then he got off lead with a Diamond.

The defence got things just right when they cashed their three Club tricks and followed with a third Diamond. Declarer ruffed but had to concede the last trick to East's Jack of trumps.

'I can see now what I should have done. The key play is to duck the first Diamond. Then, if they continue the suit, I take the Ace and ruff a Diamond in hand.

'Two rounds of trumps expose the position and now I play three rounds of Hearts, ruffing in hand, before exiting with a Club. Just as before I have the Queen and ten of Spades for my last two cards but it is an *opponent* who has the lead, not me.'

'Very neat,' I agreed, making my solitary contribution to the conversation.

'Ridiculous!'

'Ridiculous!' was my partner's comment after going down in his apparently straightforward contract on this deal. 'What are the chances of finding the cards distributed just like that?'

Small, perhaps, but it would have cost very little to take out insurance.

It was game-all and North-South had a 60 partscore. As dealer, South opened One No-trump and all passed.

West led the two of Hearts and declarer inspected

dummy's two Aces complacently. He was starting to add up the rubber as he won with the Ace on the table and led a low Diamond to the King.

Even though this lost to the Ace, South remained unconcerned. But when the 4-1 Diamond break came to light, there was absolutely nowhere for him to go for honey and he ended with only six tricks.

As always seems to happen, East-West went on to win the rubber.

With no need of *three* Diamond tricks for his contract, South had time to guard against the possibility of West holding the singleton Ace. He should win the Heart lead in hand and play a low Diamond.

If the Ace does not appear, there are still two entries to dummy for subsequent Diamond leads. Then there will be the required two Diamond tricks whenever East holds the Ace or the suit divides 3-2.

	♠ A 9 4 ♡ A 5 ◇ 9 6 5 2 ♣ 9 8 6 4	
♠ Q 8 7 2 ♡ Q 10 4 2 ◇ A ♣ J 10 5 2	N W E S	♠ J 10 5 ♡ J 9 7 6 ◇ J 10 8 7 ♣ K Q
	♠ K 6 3 ♡ K 8 3 ◇ K Q 4 3 ♣ A 7 3	

Elegant Co-operation

This may be rather old but it is still one of the most elegantly organised defences that I have seen.

East dealt at love-all and opened One Spade. South over-called with Two Diamonds (hardly unreasonable) and after two passes East re-opened with a double.

West, with what looked like two trump tricks, passed and this became the final contract. Against Two Diamonds doubled West led with the eight of Spades and discarded a low Heart on the third round of the suit. East switched to a trump.

South won and, placing West with length in the suit, decided to shorten his trumps by crossing to the Ace of Hearts and ruffing a Heart before exiting with a low Club. With any luck, he reckoned, the penalty

	North	
	♠ Q 10 9 ♡ A 7 6 3 2 ◇ 4 ♣ 6 5 3 2	
♠ 8 5 ♡ 10 5 4 ◇ J 9 7 6 5 ♣ Q J 9	N W E S	♠ A K J 7 4 ♡ K J 9 8 ◇ 3 2 ♣ A K
	♠ 6 3 2 ♡ Q ◇ A K Q 10 8 ♣ 10 8 7 4	

would only be 300 points with 100 for honours to mitigate.

The defence timed matters beautifully. East took his two top Clubs and pushed through a Spade. South discarded a losing Club and West ruffed his partner's winner to reduce his trump length to the same as South's. He got off lead with the Queen of Clubs and now it was East's turn to trump his partner's winner.

With the lead in East's hand South could come to only two more tricks and the penalty was 500 points. ('Less 100 for honours!' as South was careful to point out).

Partner To A Prime Minister

In February 1991 I played in a tournament in Reykjavik. Amusingly enough, while I enjoyed mild and sunny weather, my usual partner was snow-bound in Paris.

This led to me playing with a substitute in the pairs event and for the first board I partnered Steingrimur Hermannsson, the prime minister of Iceland. The hand was not without interest.

At love-all North opened One Club and, as East, I doubled. South tried One No-trump and, perhaps not trusting my take-out doubles, West passed.

There was no more bidding and the defence got off to a good start by leading the five of diamonds and cashing five tricks in the suit. West switched to a heart and I won dummy's Queen with the King. The Ace of

Clubs ensured the defeat of the contract and I got off lead with another club.

Everyone had discards to make but, discarding after dummy, I was able to keep **S** K **H** J 7 after dummy had come down to **S** Q **H** A 10 and declarer to **S** A 3 **H** 9.

What had West kept? Ah! With the feeling that he no longer had any interest in the play, he had failed to realise the importance of his eight of Spades and had thrown the six on the fourth club. Now declarer took the last trick with his three of Spades.

Never mind, achieving a plus score proved quite good for East-West.

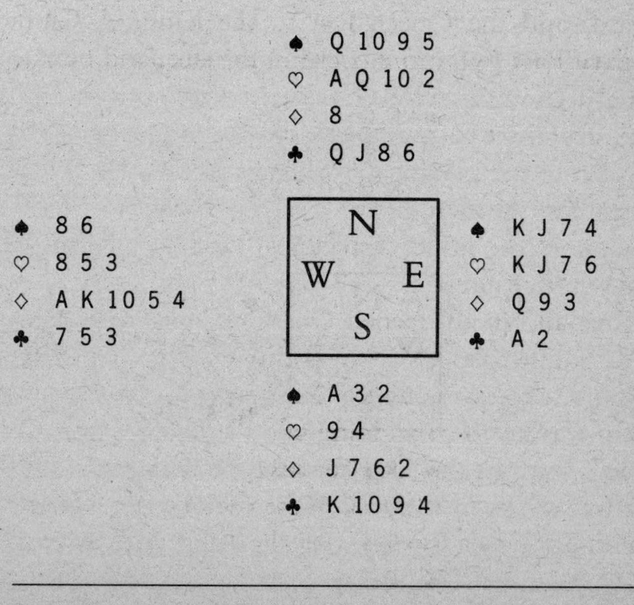

Many Years Ago . . .

Some of the best defensive plays are seen against partscores but, alas, they seldom get any publicity – often because they are not as exciting as slam hands. This deal, from an old championship, struck me as having more than one logical point that could so easily have been overlooked in practical play.

North opened One Diamond, East sportingly overcalled with One Heart, and South ended by playing in Two Spades.

In response to the overcall West led a low heart and declarer allowed East's King to win. Now the defence took over. East returned the Jack of Clubs (just the right card) and the Queen lost to the King. A Club return gave East two more tricks in the suit, and next a

	North	
	♠ K Q ♡ A 9 ◇ K Q 10 7 3 2 ♣ 10 4 2	
West ♠ 8 7 3 ♡ J 7 5 ◇ A J 5 ♣ K 7 5 3	N / W E / S	**East** ♠ J 5 4 ♡ K 8 6 4 2 ◇ 8 6 ♣ A J 9
	♠ A 10 9 6 2 ♡ Q 10 3 ◇ 9 4 ♣ Q 8 6	
	South	

Diamond lead put West in (the fifth trick for the defence) in order to play the 13th Club.

It was unpromising to trump this in dummy, so declarer resolved to ruff in hand.

There might have been a temptation for East to ruff in with the Jack (partner might hold three Spades, headed by the ten, when there would be a trump promotion) but he had the much better idea of discarding his last Diamond.

There was no way now for South to draw trumps – the lead was Jacked in dummy – and East was able to ruff the second round of Diamonds to defeat the contract.

It All Adds Up!

The effect of partscores at rubber bridge is often overlooked. It may not look dramatic on the score sheet, but there is a big difference between collecting 100 points above the line and conceding 60 below to the opponents.

At game-all, East dealt and passed. South opened One Spade and after two passes East reopened with Two Clubs. South fought on with Two Spades and all passed – West's pass was well-judged.

West led the King of Clubs and switched to a Heart at trick two. Declarer won East's King with the Ace and, in view of a possible trump promotion via a third round of Hearts, played off three rounds of trumps to put West in.

West cashed his established Queen of Hearts and got off lead with a Club to his partner's Ace. East switched to a low Diamond and declarer tried the Jack.

It looks completely natural for West to win with his Ace, but if he does so he is end-played and forced to concede an entry to dummy or a lead a Diamond.

As South could be counted as having started with three Diamonds, West let the Jack hold. Now South had to lead away from his King and Jack of Diamonds and so lost two more tricks to go one off.

Even if his partner had held the King of Diamonds, West's clear-thinking duck could not cost.

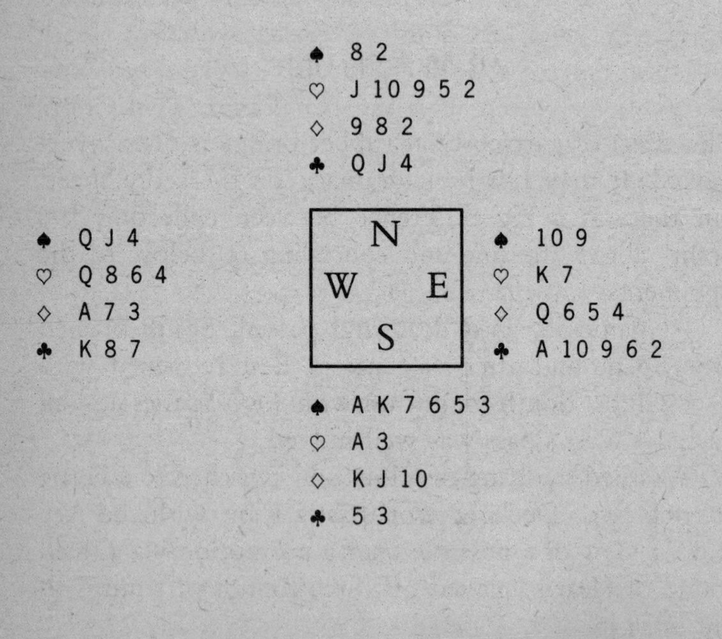

One Trump Trick Should Have Been Two

It seems curious, but players with a natural trump trick always seem reluctant to ruff (or over-ruff) with it.

They tend to overlook the possibility of partner scoring a trump trick independently.

For example, in an extreme case, it may turn out that partner has the singleton King of trumps and failure to trump with the singleton Ace means that the two winners fall, in an undignified manner, on the same trick. The same sort of thing happened here.

East dealt at love-all and the bidding was simple. He opened One Club, South overcalled with One Heart and East passed. North might have tried One No-trump but he passed. East re-opened with Two Clubs

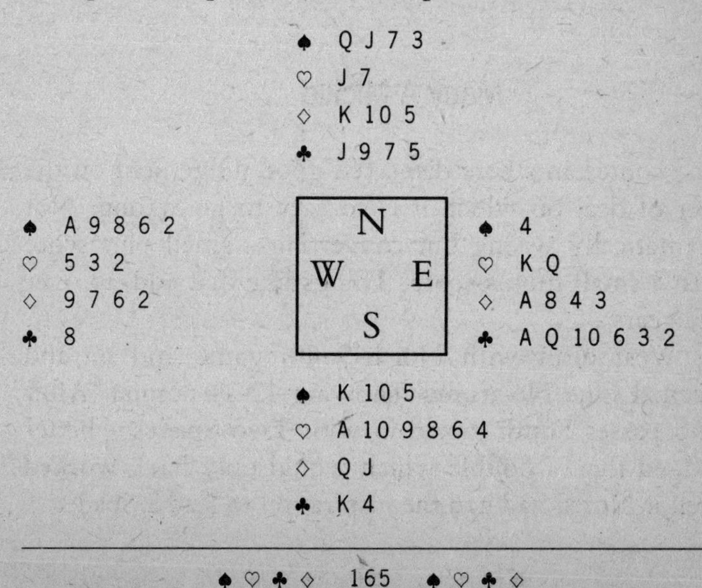

and South fought on with Two Hearts to end the auction.

West led his singleton Club to the Ace and a Club was returned for a ruff. West tried a Diamond to the Ace but declarer ruffed the next Club lead with the eight and followed with Ace and another trump. That was the end of the defence who had only the Ace of Spades to come.

East's argument was that, with a natural trump trick in the shape of the King and Queen of Hearts, he did not want to ruff. He can, however, score tricks with both of them. Although he is sure of giving his partner a Club ruff, suppose he returns a Spade at trick two?

West wins with the Ace, gives his partner a Spade ruff, then regains the lead with a Club ruff for another Spade lead. Then the defenders score three trump tricks as well as their three Aces.

Many A Mickle . . .

The contestants here displayed good judgement on the sort of deal on which it is so easy to go wrong. Not dramatically wrong but converting a small plus score into a small minus score. Things like that add up over the years . . .

West dealt with North-South game and 60 and opened One No-trump (showing 12-14 points). After two passes South joined in with Two Spades – better judged than a double which would only have worked well if North had had the inspiration to lead a Spade.

All passed but how many times have you seen a player with a hand like East's contesting with Two No-trumps or Three Clubs? I couldn't let them play in Two Spades, partner. Look at the score!'

West did well when he led the two of Hearts. East's King lost to the Ace and declarer played off three rounds of trumps to put West on lead again.

He cashed his Queen of Hearts and followed with the Ace and another Club to his partner's King. A low Diamond came back and declarer put in the Jack.

It would have been all too easy for West to win with his Ace but, if he had done so, declarer would have the rest of the tricks and his contract. Instead West let the Jack of Diamonds win. Eventually South had to lead away from his remaining Diamond honours and so concede two more tricks.

A small plus instead of a small minus . . .

West		North		East
		♠ 7 4		
		♡ J 10 9 5 4		
		◇ 7 5 4		
		♣ Q J 8		
♠ Q J 3		N		♠ 10 5
♡ Q 8 7 2	W		E	♡ K 6
◇ A 9 3				◇ Q 8 6 2
♣ A 7 3		S		♣ K 10 9 5 4
		♠ A K 9 8 6 2		
		♡ A 3		
		◇ K J 10		
		♣ 6 2		

Bird's Eye View

They always say that the spectator has a better idea of what is happening at the bridge table than any of the players. I watched the hand below and it was a very see-saw affair.

North dealt at love-all and opened One Club. East overcalled with One Spade and after some close competitive bidding South ended in Three Hearts. (North-South would have done better to double the Two Spade contract that their opponents had reached.)

West led a Spade and, sitting 'South-West' I could see that if declarer had simply finessed twice in trumps he would make his nine tricks. However, South started by winning and returning a Spade.

He ruffed the third round, finessed the Queen of

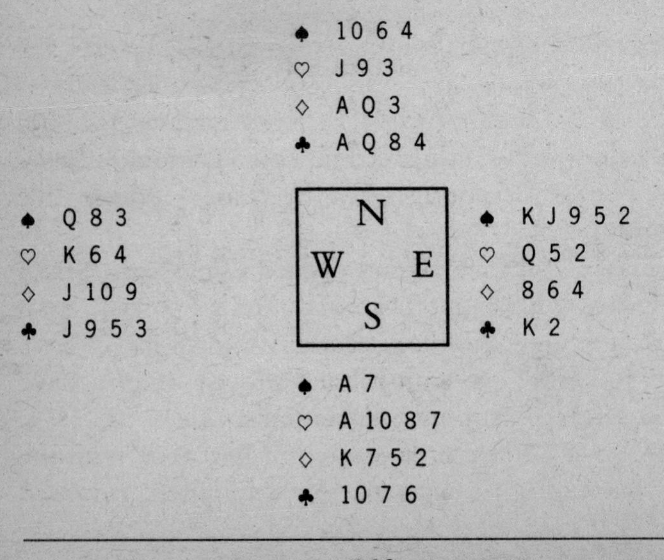

Clubs unsuccessfully and won the Club return with dummy's Ace. There was still time to draw trumps but instead declarer played off three rounds of Diamonds and exited with a Club to West's Jack.

This left West with **H** K 6 4 **C** 3; dummy with **H** J 9 3 **C** 8; East with **S** 9 **H** Q 5 2 and declarer with **H** A 10 8 **D** 7. Mistakenly West now led a low trump (a Club for East to ruff low leaves South on lead and sure to lose two trump tricks).

East did his best by playing low – for it is all over if he plays the Queen – and South won cheaply and led the Ace of Hearts. West played low and was thrown in with his King to concede the last trick to dummy's eight of Clubs.

Bad Bidding Leads To Bad Play

Have you ever noticed how when someone reaches the wrong contract they always seems to play it badly?

Three No-trumps looks all right for North-South on this deal, but South ended in Three Diamonds and – after a neat deceptive play by East – made the minimum.

East dealt at love-all and opened One Heart. South over-called with Three Diamonds and all passed. Both North and South had been cautious. North might have essayed Three No-trumps and South might have doubled before jumping in Diamonds.

West led his singleton Heart and East won with the Ace. Without apparent pause for thought he returned the two of Spades. It had all the earmarks of a singleton, so declarer went up with his Ace and led the King of trumps.

Now the roof fell in: East took his Ace, cashed the King of Spades and gave West a Heart ruff. East carefully chose the ten of Hearts, a clear McKenny signal for the higher ranking side-suit – so West played back a Spade for East to ruff.

Now another Heart lead promoted a further defensive trick for West's Jack of trumps.

When the smoke had cleared the defenders had taken six tricks on a hand where their opponents should have made a game.

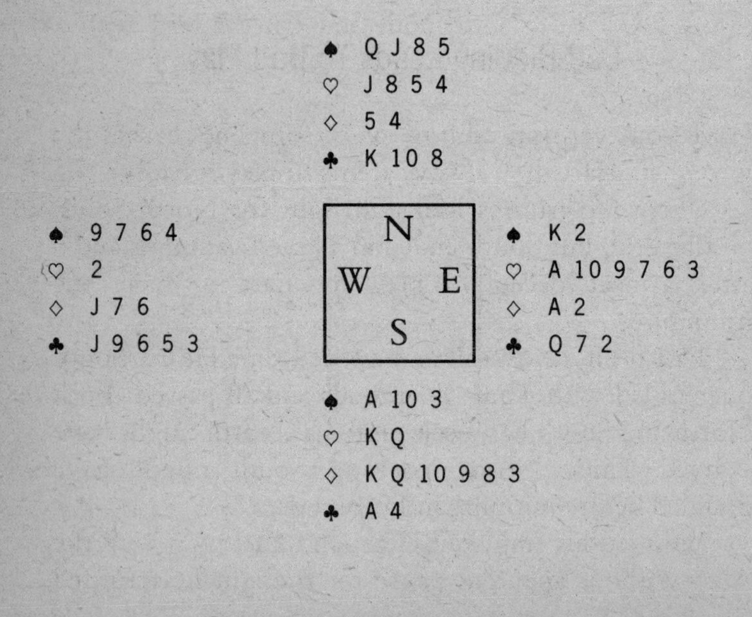

Careless!

There is always a tendency for declarer to be careless when playing in an insignificant partscore. But making these little plus scores rather than losing points makes a difference.

North opened One Club at game-all and rebid One Heart over his partner's response of One Diamond. South now bid One No-trump and all passed.

West led the Queen of Hearts (in spite of North's bid) and declarer won. With no certain entry to his Diamonds, he finessed the Queen of Clubs. East won and the defenders cashed three Heart tricks on which South discarded a Spade and a Diamond. Next West cashed the Ace of Diamonds and got off lead with a Club to dummy's Ace.

West	North	East
	♠ A 5 4	
	♡ 8 7 4 2	
	◇ K	
	♣ A Q J 9 3	
♠ K 7 3	N	♠ J 10 6
♡ Q J 10 6	W E	♡ K 9 3
◇ A 5 4 2	S	◇ 9 8 7
♣ 6 2		♣ K 10 8 5
	♠ Q 9 8 2	
	♡ A 5	
	◇ Q J 10 6 3	
	♣ 7 4	

As there seemed time to test the Clubs later, declarer tried a low Spade from the table and East inserted the Ten.

Who held the King of Spades? South tried the Queen and this proved a disaster. West won, returned a Spade, and East came to the Jack of Spades and another Club to defeat the contract by two tricks. Declarer should have left East on lead with the ten of Spades.

East then has the choice of returning a Spade (giving South two tricks in the suit if he guesses right and inserts the nine), a Club to give declarer four tricks in the suit, or playing a Diamond, which solves all declarer's problems.

Too Late!

There was a simple yet deceptive defence to Two Spades on this innocent looking partscore deal and it competely eluded West at the table. Indeed, everybody missed it. It was only much later that East called his partner to complain!

At game all South dealt and passed and West opened One Club. With nothing sensible to say North passed and East responded One Diamond. Now South overcalled with One Spade and West, with his minimum opening bid and no convenient rebid, passed.

There was no chance of a game facing a passed partner so North contented himself with a raise to Two Spades which ended the auction.

West led the Ace of Hearts to inspect dummy, then

switched to the King and another Diamond. East won and cashed another Diamond trick but, apart from the King of Hearts, that was the end of the defence.

Can you see what West missed? If he cashes his second top heart before switching to Diamonds, he can discard his last Heart on the third round of Diamonds.

Then East leads a Heart, West ruffs, and that is the sixth trick for the defence.

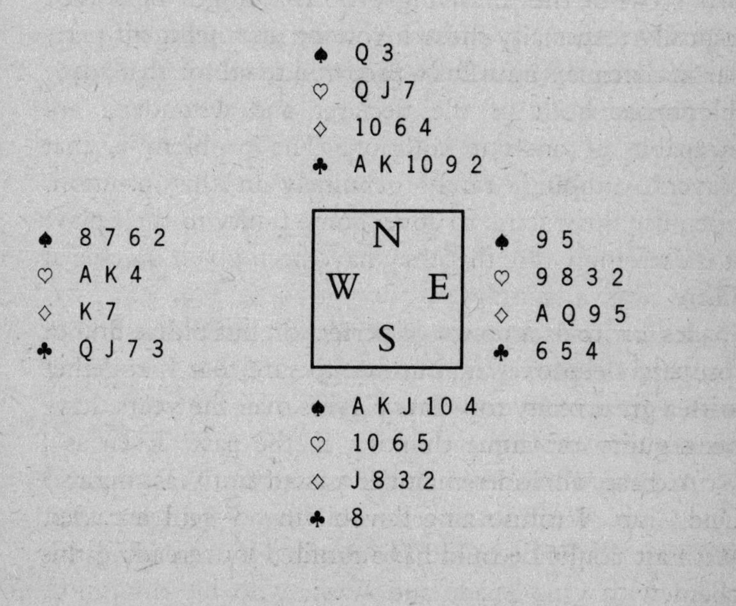

CHAPTER SEVEN

How Could I Tell?

This chapter heading could be the most frequent *cris de coeur* heard at the bridge table. Now, when I suggest that most of the following problems might be solved logically (especially those involving an intelligent partner in defence), I am fully prepared to admit that some dilemmas, both of the declarer and defenders, are incapable of analytic solution. The problem is that players, although rarely genuinely in this position, often use this excuse to cover some frailty in their play. It is extremely rare that they have been given no clue at all!

It all sounds a policy of perfection but please do not lose any sleep over it. I am quite sure that I, together with a great many top-class players over the years, have been guilty of vague thinking in the past. Even as I write these words I remember a hand from last night. I held – no. I refuse to tell you what I held and did. Without doubt I would have profited by rereading this chapter.

Tact!

What do you say at the end of a hand when an opponent asks you if he could have done better and you know that he could?

The formula that I have adopted is to answer: 'You may have made it more difficult for me if you had done so-and-so . . .' In that way no one is offended.

North dealt at love-all and opened One Club. South responded One Heart and soon ended in Four Hearts.

West led his two of Clubs to his partner's Ace, and East returned the nine of Clubs. South played low; West ruffed and switched to a Diamond. Declarer won in hand with the Ace, drew trumps, cashed the three

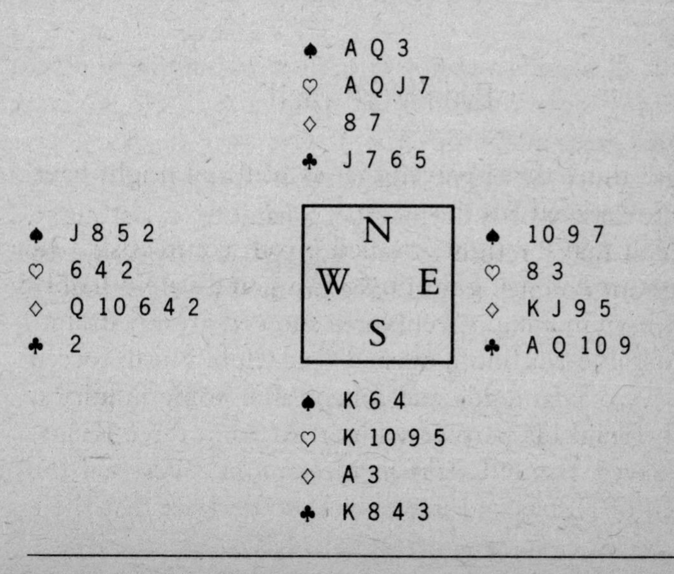

winning spades and got off lead with his remaining Diamond.

It did not matter who won – if it was West, he would have to concede a ruff and discard; if it was East, he would have to give away the same ruff and discard or lead away from his Queen of Clubs. It was all over.

Now East asked South the fatal question: 'Could I have done better?'

Adopting my formula, declarer suggested that his task would have been made more difficult if East had played back the Queen of Clubs at the second trick.

More difficult? That was something of a euphemism, for it would have defeated the contract. West ruffs South's King but East still has **C** 10 9 and can lead the suit safely after making sure that he wins the Diamond trick. Then declarer loses one Diamond, two Clubs and a ruff.

Even More Tact!

'I don't think that I played that as well as I might have done,' observed South.

'You may be right,' agreed North courteously. As his partner had just gone down in a grand slam possibly of his own making, I feel North showed great restraint.

At game-all, South opened One Club, North forced with Two Diamonds and when, after some inquiries, South found his partner with an Ace and three Kings, he essayed a grand slam in No-trumps. West led the Queen of Hearts and it was clear to declarer that there were 12 top winners and that the 13th had to come from one of the black suits.

After winning in hand, he played off the Ace of Clubs (to cater for a possible singleton Queen), tested the Spades to find that they produced only three tricks, ran the Diamond winners and finally fell back on a losing Club finesse.

My opinion? I think South would have done better to cash both top Clubs (gaining if West held the doubleton Queen), then play off all the red suit winners, throwing three Clubs from hand.

Then he is still home if the Spades divide evenly (or the Jack falls), and has given himself the extra chance that either defender (West in this case) will be faced with the impossible task of keeping the Queen of Clubs and guarding the Spades.

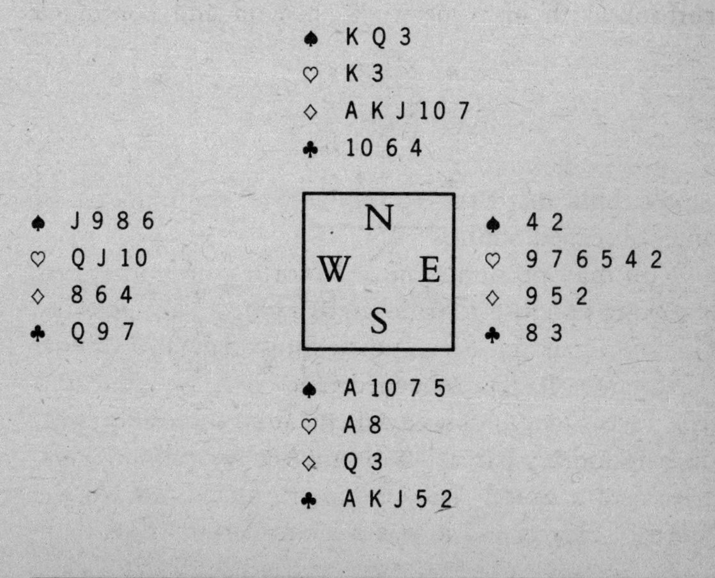

An Old Trick

East fell for an old trick on this deal. I won't say that declarer gave a helpless shrug at the critical moment – he was far too ethical a player for that – but the sequence of play that he adopted led East to believe that defeating the contract was a foregone conclusion.

North dealt at love-all and opened One Diamond. South responded One Heart, North rebid One Spade and South bid his Hearts again. North made a further move with Three-Clubs (Three Hearts would have been better judged if he decided to go on) and South's call of Three No-trumps ended the auction.

West led the three of Clubs and declarer won on the table. He followed with the Jack of Hearts, which he overtook with his Queen. West won and continued

West		East
	♠ K Q 6 3 ♡ J ◇ K Q J 10 9 ♣ A 7 2	
♠ A J 8 4 ♡ K 8 ◇ 8 6 2 ♣ J 9 6 3	N W E S	♠ 10 9 7 ♡ A 6 5 4 ◇ 7 5 4 ♣ Q 10 5
	♠ 5 2 ♡ Q 10 9 7 3 2 ◇ A 3 ♣ K 8 4	

Clubs; South held off this trick and won the Club continuation.

The ten of Hearts (dropping West's eight) went to East's Ace and it looked as though everything was over, for now the defence could cash two more tricks.

However, declarer had cunningly discarded a Diamond from dummy on the third Heart. This convinced East that his partner must hold the Ace of Diamonds but, as you can see, his actual Diamond return was not a success.

It was a neat enough ruse – discarding a winner from dummy – but East only had himself to blame. If he had held up his Ace of Hearts for another round he would have given his partner a chance to signal clearly with the Jack of Spades.

In Spite Of The Poor Dummy . . .

Having reached (or been pushed to) an adventurous contract, declarer did not make the most of his chances.

Playing five-card majors, South opened One Diamond, West overcalled with One Spade, and North doubled. This was the so-called negative double, suggesting that he would have responded One Heart had there been no interference. Clearly he was not quite worth his bid. East raised to Three Spades and South, under pressure, tried Four Hearts and all passed.

West started with two top Spades and declarer ruffed. Inwardly seething over his partner's poor hand, he started with Ace and ten of Hearts. East won and could either return a trump to leave South a trick short or – more elegantly – switch to the King of Diamonds.

After winning, declarer cannot get back to the table to draw the last trump and ruff another Spade, and East comes to a Diamond ruff.

The alternative line of leading the ten of Hearts from hand at trick two does not work either, for East wins and leads his Diamond. Needing another Spade ruff in hand for his tenth trick, declarer is still a trick short.

Try the effect of a low Club at trick three, cutting the defender's communications. A Diamond does not help them now for, after entering dummy with a Club ruff, declarer can draw trumps without loss.

If instead they force with another Spade, South ruffs and plays Ace and ten of Hearts. Then, after entering dummy with a Club ruff, he can draw the last trump.

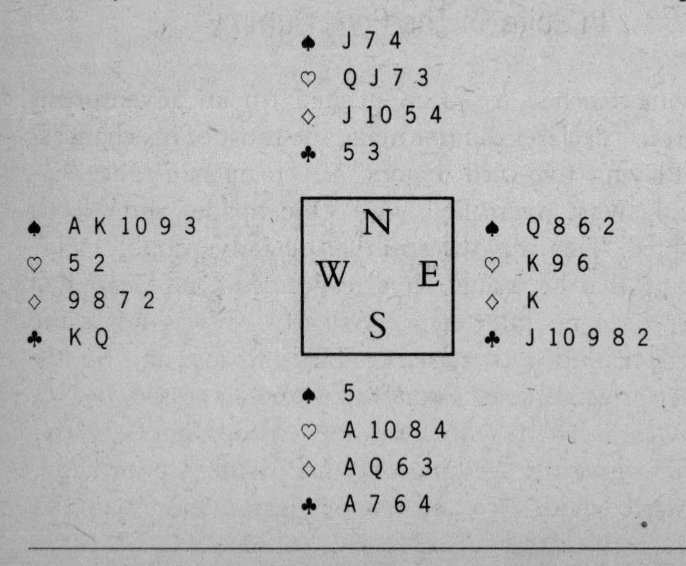

A Trifling Oversight

Playing in a pairs' competition sets a new range of problems unfamiliar to the rubber bridge player. The search for a possible overtrick is critical and sometimes even the success of a contract has to be risked. South failed to combine his chances to the best advantage on this deal:

At game-all South opened with a conventional Two Clubs and ended in Four Spades. West led the King of Hearts to declarer's Ace.

At trick two South crossed to dummy with the nine of Spades and led a Club towards his King. This was not a success, for West won with the Ace and smartly played a second round of trumps. Now, when South

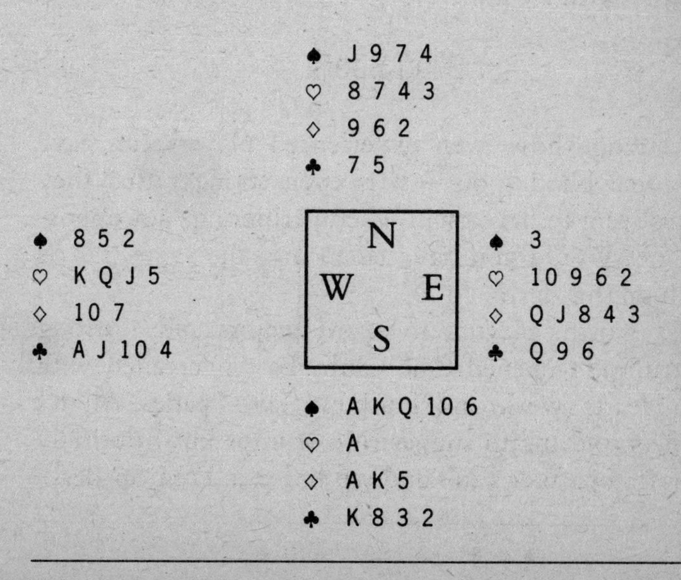

gave up another Club, West was able to win and lead a third trump.

Declarer could ruff only one Club on the table and, rather embarrassingly, ended by losing four tricks.

'I know I could have made that by leading a low Club from hand immediately,' remarked South. 'But wasn't I right to try for the overtrick?'

The point that he had overlooked was that leading a Club from hand at trick two not only guarantees the contract but still gives chances of an overtrick. Presumably the defenders win and lead a trump.

After winning on the table, declarer leads the second Club. If the Ace is well placed for him, his King becomes a trick and later a Diamond can be discarded from dummy. Then a Diamond ruff on the table yields the 11th trick.

Blind Spots

It is strange how even experienced players can have occasional blind spots – it is even stranger that they always seem to have them when partnering, not opposing, me! Would you have fallen into the same trap as South on this deal?

As North, playing five-card majors and a strong No-trump, I opened One Club. East overcalled with Two Hearts (weak) and South bid Two Spades. All my instincts told me to suggest No-trumps but I dutifully supported partner's suit and we ended in Four Spades.

West led the nine of Hearts and the defenders played two more rounds of the suit.

After mature reflection declarer trumped the third round with the Jack of Spades and, having secured his trump promotion, West over-ruffed. He got off lead with a club and, although the Diamond finesse was right, there was no way for South to escape an eventual Diamond loser and so go one down.

With a likely trump loser after the start that the defence had made, declarer would have been better advised to discard his three of Diamonds on the third Heart.

West scores his Spade trick but there are no further problems with trumps, and a simple Diamond finesse brings home the contract.

The Diamond position proved deceptive – if South

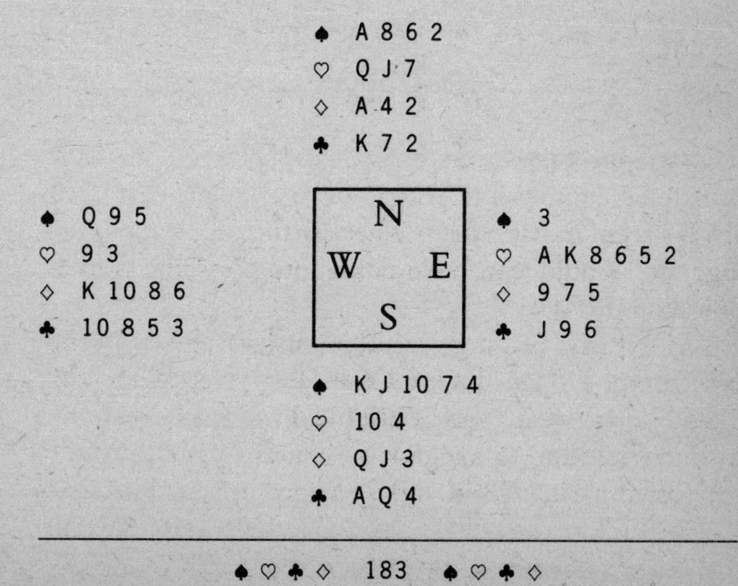

had held **D** K x x instead of **D** Q J 3, he would have had no difficulty in discarding his loser on the third Heart.

A Complete Guess?

'It was a complete guess!' claimed declarer after this hand from rubber bridge. How often have you heard those exact words? And how often does further thought show that it was not, after all, a 'guess'?

South dealt at love-all and, as his partnership was playing a 15-17 No-trump, opened One Club. North responded One Heart and South rebid Two No-trumps to show 18-19 points.

With only six points, but packed with tens and nines, North raised to Three No-trumps. West led the

	♠ 10 8 5 ♡ K 9 8 7 ◇ Q 10 9 ♣ J 10 9	
♠ Q J 3 ♡ A 6 5 ◇ 7 4 2 ♣ 8 6 4 2	N W E S	♠ A K 2 ♡ Q 10 4 3 ◇ 8 6 5 3 ♣ 7 3
	♠ 9 7 6 4 ♡ J 2 ◇ A K J ♣ A K Q 5	

Queen of Spades and East overtook with his King, on which South dropped the six. East continued with the Ace of Spades, collecting the seven, three and eight. On the third round of the suit South played the four and was left with the last Spade.

South was pleased that his innocuous false-carding had persuaded the defenders to establish his eighth trick, but now he was faced with a problem when West switched to a low Heart. Had he led away from the Ace? Or the Queen?

At last declarer played low from dummy – and so lost two Heart tricks.

South should have played dummy's King for two reasons. First, if West held the Queen he was not to know that South did not hold the Ace and the Jack. Second – and this is a theme that occurs more often than you think – if declarer had been left to play the suit himself, he could not have gone wrong as the cards lay.

Only if West leads the suit is South left with a losing option.

How Do They Look When They Lead?

It was Terence Reese who wrote about the demeanour of opponents when they select their opening lead, and how declarer can take advantage.

If, against No-trumps, they lead a low card without much thought, then the lead was an obvious one. Singletons against suit contracts come quite briskly too

– but it is when a player broods for some time before leading with 'an air of foolish expectancy' that you suspect that it was not a clear-cut decision.

The idea might have helped declarer on this deal:

South ended in Four Hearts – a reasonable enough spot – and, after considerable thought, West led the six of Clubs. Declarer played low from dummy and won East's ten with his King. There was no hope of making the contract unless the Clubs could be brought in and, as drawing too many rounds of trumps would lead to immediate loss of control, declarer led a second round of Clubs to the Ace and conceded a trick to East's Queen.

It was not difficult for East to switch to Spades, driving out dummy's Ace – but when declarer attempted to draw trumps (ending with the lead in dummy) he discovered the 4-1 break in the suit. Now

West		East
	♠ A 8 4 ♡ Q J 5 ◇ 7 5 ♣ A J 7 4 3	
♠ K 9 5 ♡ 9 7 6 4 ◇ A J 9 3 ♣ 6 2	N W E S	♠ Q J 10 7 2 ♡ 2 ◇ K 10 8 4 ♣ Q 10 8
	♠ 6 3 ♡ A K 10 8 3 ◇ Q 6 2 ♣ K 9 5	

there was no chance of recovery – and the contract had to fail.

If South had been prepared to follow his intuition and judged that the lead was from a doubleton, he succeeds quite simply by letting East's ten of Clubs win the first trick.

Then, even if trumps break 5–0, everything is under complete control – and there are ten top winners.

Discards Need Not Be Too Difficult

'I never know what to throw away when declarer runs off a long suit,' complained an opponent. He had just demonstrated this quite well, but, as dummy, I was the recipient of his largesse. There were logical reasons for him to have solved his problem successfully.

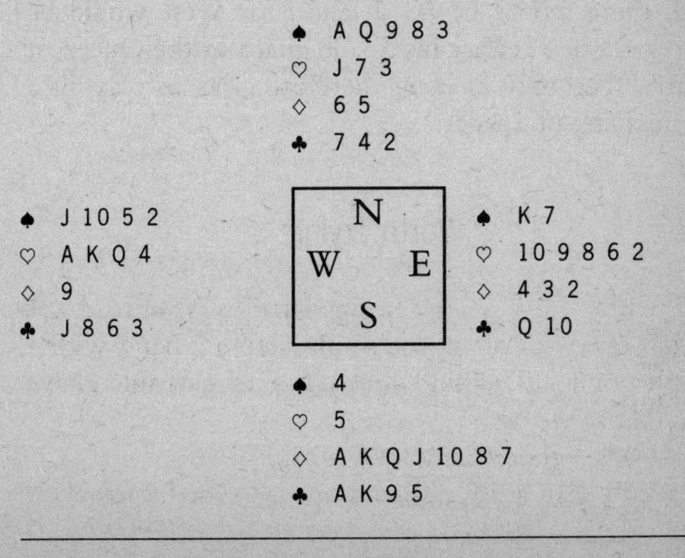

South opened Two Diamonds at love-all and I was just worth a positive response of Two Spades. Partner's immediate enquiry for Aces alarmed me, but I dutifully admitted to one Ace and passed his next bid of Six Diamonds.

West started with the Ace and King of Hearts. Declarer ruffed and took stock. Prospects were not good – even if the Spade finesse was right, there would only be 11 tricks. Hoping for the best, he reeled off all his trumps.

West parted with a low Heart on the second round then and, in order to keep his guard in Spades, he parted with his Clubs. Now declarer found himself with four Club tricks and no need to try the Spade finesse.

West should have reasoned that declarer must hold the Ace of Clubs. If South held the King of Spades as well, there would be no defence: for West would be squeezed out of either his Spade guard or the Queen of Hearts. The only chance, therefore, was to play East for the King of Spades.

Worth Trying

No matter how many bridge articles you read (or write!) every so often you come across a hand with a simple point and yet find yourself asking: 'Would I have seen that at the table?'

This is a good example of what I mean:

South dealt at love-all and opened One Heart. West

overcalled with Two Clubs, North raised to Three Hearts and South went on to game.

Against Four Hearts, West led the Queen of Spades. Declarer won on the table and led trumps – it looked natural, with 11 cards in the suit – and West won and continued Spades.

Now declarer had to take the Diamond finesse and when this failed, he had to lose one trick in every suit. Unlucky? Well, not really, for declarer could have given himself a better chance.

Suppose that at trick two he refrains from tackling trumps and plays a Diamond immediately. If East follows with a low card, South tries the nine. As the cards lie, West has to win with the King – and now dummy's losing Spade goes away on the Diamond winners.

And if West is able to win the Diamond with the

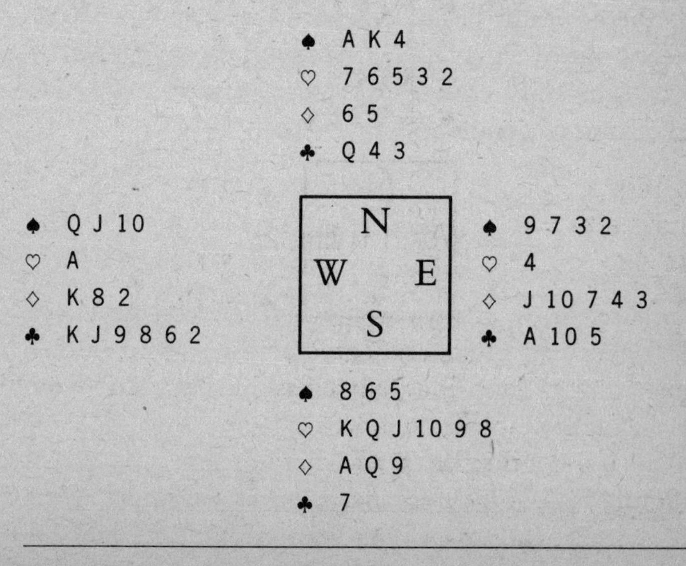

ten or Jack? Well, there is still time to try finessing the Queen.

It is true that you might manage to go two down, but an extra 50 points is a small price to pay for improving your chances of making a game. Every so often East might hold both the Jack and ten of Diamonds, as he did here.

Was It Really A Guess?

'It was a complete guess!' complained South after going down in his contract of Three No-trumps. 'If the black Aces are reversed or I lead Spades first, I make it easily.'

'Very unlucky,' agreed North, but he caught my eye (I was West) and winked.

West		East
	♠ K J 8 5 ♡ 3 ◇ K J 4 ♣ K Q J 6 2	
♠ A 10 9 3 ♡ J 9 7 6 4 ◇ 10 8 5 ♣ 4	N W E S	♠ 7 6 ♡ K 8 5 2 ◇ 9 7 2 ♣ A 10 9 3
	♠ Q 4 2 ♡ A Q 10 ◇ A Q 6 3 ♣ 8 7 5	

North dealt at game-all and opened One Club, to which South responded One Diamond. An immediate Three No-trumps would have saved time, for that is what he chose on the next round after North's rebid of One Spade. As West I had led the six of Hearts and partner's King lost to the Ace.

Without much thought declarer set about the Clubs, but East won the first round and returned a Heart. Now there was no route to more than eight tricks.

Some of South's comment was true but not the bit about it being a complete guess. He had missed a textbook avoidance play. He needed three tricks from the black suits and could not afford East getting in before these three winners were established.

The winning play, which succeeds against any distribution, is to cross to dummy's Jack of Diamonds at trick two and lead a low Spade. If East holds the Ace, he cannot play it without conceding three tricks in the suit; and if he decides not to play it, declarer switches rapidly to Clubs to establish the two extra tricks that he needs.

As the cards lie, it is West who wins the Queen with his Ace but he cannot profitably attack Hearts again from his side. Again, South has plenty of time to build up the tricks he needs in Clubs.

'One For The Road'

Competitive auctions are always the most difficult to judge. There is an old saying: 'If in doubt, bid one more' but it does not always work. This hand from an old match illustrates the point well.

South dealt with East-West vulnerable and opened One Diamond. West overcalled with Four Hearts and North, following the adage above, bid a confident Five Diamonds (on a hand that was clearly not worth it). East (also heeding the advice) decided to bid Five Hearts and North, who had certainly not left his bidding boots at home, doubled.

He led his singleton Club and the defenders took the obvious five tricks to collect 800 points.

At the other table, after the same start, East Number

	North	
	♠ J 10 7 2 ♡ K 10 4 ◇ K J 8 3 2 ♣ 8	
West ♠ none ♡ A Q J 9 7 6 2 ◇ 5 ♣ J 9 7 6 3	N W E S	**East** ♠ A K Q 8 6 3 ♡ 8 3 ◇ 7 6 ♣ K 10 4
	♠ 9 5 4 ♡ 5 ◇ A Q 10 9 4 ♣ A Q 5 2	
	South	

Two elected to take his chances in defence and doubled Five Diamonds. He was right in a sense for declarer had four top losers, but West's void in Spades proved unfortunate.

West led the Ace of Hearts and continued with the Queen. When the King held, declarer breathed a sigh of relief and discarded a losing Spade. He followed with a winning Club finesse, cashed the Ace of Clubs, ruffed a Club, came to hand with a trump and ruffed his last Club high.

He drew the last trump and now came the coup de grace. He led the ten of Hearts from the table and discarded another Spade. West, on lead, had to concede a ruff and discard and the last losing Spade went away.

What can you conclude? That North was right to bid 'one for the road' but that East was not?

If You Are Going To Bid Like This, You Should Play Better

It is a good idea, with two-suited hands, to attempt to establish the side-suit before drawing trumps . . .

South dealt at love-all and opened Two Hearts. West overcalled with Two Spades and, after two passes, South tried Three Clubs. West passed and North made the good practical bid of Five Clubs.

This, after his first round pass, suggested excellent trump support but little else. South confidently pressed on to Six Clubs and all passed. West led the King of

Spades and, after winning, declarer set to work on the Hearts. He cashed the Ace and ruffed a Heart on the table. After coming to hand with a top trump he realised there was a problem: South could not be sure that the Hearts had become established. It was too late now to try the King of Hearts in case it was ruffed.

To cater for the possibility of a 4-2 break in Hearts, he trumped another in dummy – only to find that this was unnecessary. The trumps proved to be 3-1. Although the Hearts were established, South found himself with a losing Spade and a losing Diamond at the end.

As declarer could never have coped with a 5-1 Heart division, he could have cashed both Ace and King of Hearts before ruffing a Heart.

After the third round he will know if a fourth Heart has to be trumped (when he will have to rely on a 2-2

	North	
	♠ 8 6 2 ♡ 6 ◇ J 8 5 2 ♣ K Q 10 7 6	
♠ K Q 10 9 7 4 ♡ Q 8 3 ◇ A 9 3 ♣ 3	N W E S	♠ J 5 ♡ 10 5 2 ◇ Q 10 7 6 4 ♣ 8 5 4
	♠ A 3 ♡ A K J 9 7 4 ◇ K ♣ A J 9 2	

trump break) or if the suit is established and he can cope with the actual 3-1 break in trumps.

Who Can Remember All The Pips?

This hand ended in an odd fashion. With the four players reduced to three cards each, all in the same suit, there was still considerable scope for subtlety.

At game-all South dealt and opened One No-trump. North raised to game and against Three No-trumps it was natural for West to lead the Jack of Hearts. East took his three Heart tricks and switched to a Club: declarer played off four Club winners and three top Diamonds to end in hand. This left everyone with just three Spades apiece. As the cards lie a winning play is to run **S** 10 round to East and end-play him but

West		North		East
		♠ A Q 2		
		♡ 6 4 2		
		◇ Q 10 5		
		♣ J 10 8 4		
♠ 9 8 6		N		♠ K J 4 3
♡ J 10 9 5	W		E	♡ A K Q
◇ 8 6 3 2		S		◇ 9 7 4
♣ 6 3				♣ 9 5 2
		♠ 10 7 5		
		♡ 8 7 3		
		◇ A K J		
		♣ A K Q 7		

instead South led the five. West, who could well have been excused for losing interest after parting with his solitary picture card on the first trick, stayed awake and followed with the nine. The Queen was finessed, losing to the King, and the four of Spades came back.

Can you see South's problem in the two-card ending? If East holds the Jack, the ten is the winning play. If West holds the Jack, the seven may force it and establish the ten. There would have been no story if declarer had got it right but he tried the seven and so went one off.

The key point, of course, is that if West had followed automatically to the first Spade lead with the six, South would have been left with no option but the winning play of the ten on the second round of the suit.

A Genuine 'How Could I Tell?'

When asked for an opinion, the vast majority of bridge players are only too happy to oblige. The better the player, of course, the more reliable the advice.

Sometimes it all seems to be a complete guess and, when consulted about East's defensive problem on the following hand, I have to admit that I got it wrong. Embarrassing I dare say, but I still cannot see how East could have been sure.

North dealt at love-all and opened One Heart, South responded Two Diamonds and North raised to Three Diamonds. South might have tried Three No-trumps now (which would not have been a success) but he explored with Three Spades and North had little choice but to revert to Diamonds.

South went on to Five Diamonds and West led a trump. Winning with dummy's Ace, declarer immediately led a low Heart from the table.

Put yourself in East's position – what do you do?

Is it possible that South has started with **S** A K 8 3 **H** J 2 **D** Q J 10 9 8 **C** K ? Then it is vital to go in at once with the King of Hearts and push through the Queen of Clubs.

This was the plan that East followed, but you can see what happened. Declarer ruffed the King of Hearts, trumped a Spade high in dummy and threw two Clubs on the Ace and Queen of Hearts. Now a Heart ruff and another Spade ruff gave South 11 tricks.

Yes, East got it wrong but perhaps we should give due credit to South.

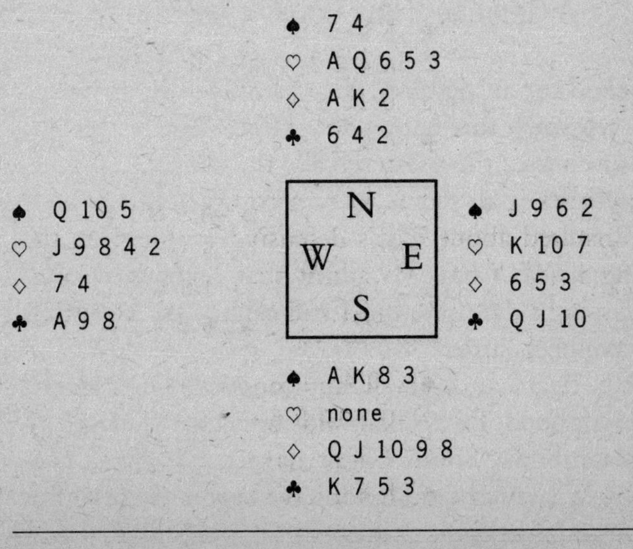

Would you have thought of the idea of leading a low Heart from dummy at trick two with a view to setting East problems?

A Weaker Dummy Would Have Helped!

'That was annoying,' remarked South after failing to make his game. 'I can get home with a better guess in Diamonds.' That was true, but he had missed a sure play that he would have spotted if dummy had been weaker.

At love-all North opened One Diamond and raised his partner's response of One Heart to Three. South went on to game. West led the Jack of Clubs against Four Hearts.

Reasonably enough, South won in hand and led the

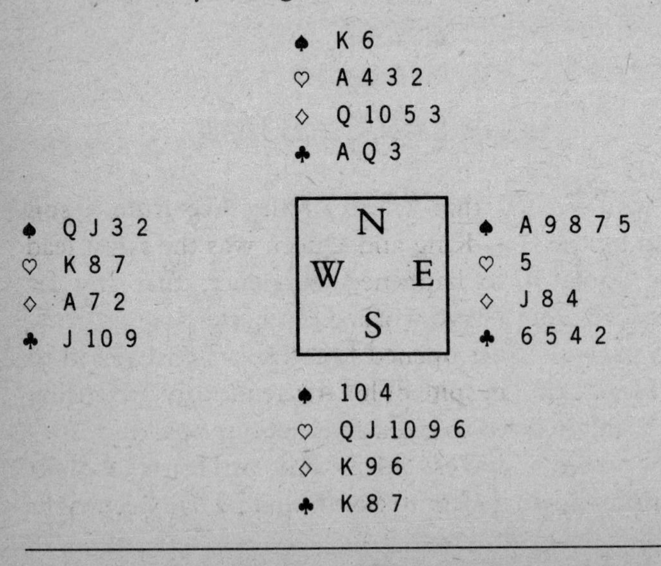

Queen of trumps. West did not cover and two more rounds of trumps left the lead in dummy.

To prepare for a possible end-play, declarer cashed the Ace and Queen of Clubs and attempted to enter his hand with the King of Diamonds. West took his Ace and switched to the Queen of Spades. The King lost to the Ace, a Spade came back and a Diamond return left declarer with a fourth loser.

While an early finesse of the nine of Diamonds would have worked, South missed a chance. After cashing the Ace and Queen of Clubs, he should simply lead a low Spade from dummy. The defenders can take two Spade tricks, but then have to open the Diamonds or concede a ruff and discard.

Can you see how a weaker dummy facilitates the play? If dummy had only two low Spades, declarer would have had no qualms about leading the suit from the table and ensuring his contract.

Not As Safe As You Think

You would think that a lead of the Ace from a suit headed by the Ace, King and Queen was the safest lead in the book. It so happened, however, that any far riskier lead would have worked out better.

At love-all West opened One Heart, East raised to Two Hearts, and in spite of his tremendously promising hand South decided to bid a simple Four Spades.

All passed and West led the Ace of Hearts. A sight of dummy made it clear to South that he had been right to bid conservatively – indeed, there were only nine obvious tricks. He was quick, however, to spot the potentialities of the Heart suit created by the opening lead.

He ruffed in hand with the seven of Spades, crossed to dummy by overtaking the eight of Spades with the ten and then led the Jack of Hearts on which he discarded a Club.

West won and switched to a Club; but declarer won, re-entered dummy by leading the nine of Spades to the Jack, and threw his last Club on the ten of Hearts.

West won but the nine of Hearts was now established and declarer was able to reach it with the six of Spades to make his tenth trick.

It seems odd, looking at West's hand, that any lead other than a Heart leaves South a trick short.

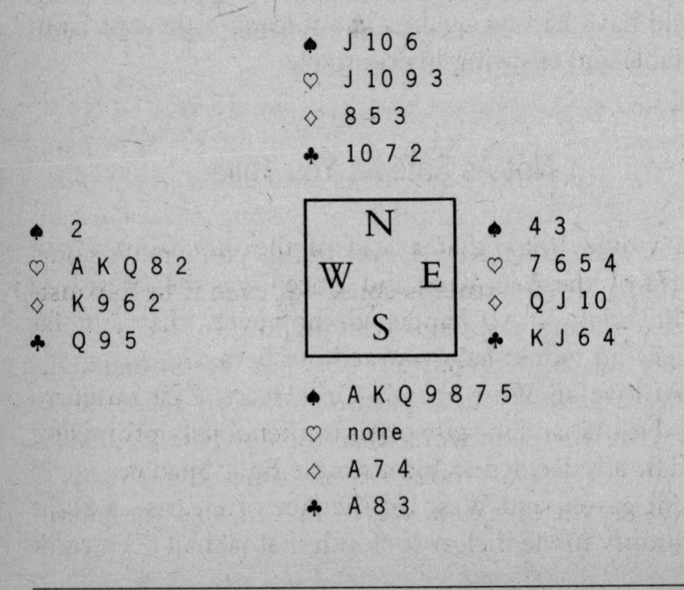

CHAPTER EIGHT

Remarks at the Table

Many of the remarks heard at the bridge table are totally unmemorable. Wherever you play, you will always find opponents (or, worse still, partners!) who complain about everything. Usually the criticisms are unjustified. I am sure that you have noticed (with a few exceptions) that the most persistent offenders tend to be the weaker players. The corollary is not true – I do not mean to suggest that, if you never say anything, your play will improve, but one thing is absolutely certain. If you refrain from bawling out your partner, his play will improve or, at least, not deteriorate.

The classic advice is that you should restrict your comments to 'Well done!' and 'Bad luck!' You can, after all, fit in quite a wealth of expression in the way you say 'Bad luck!' Another nice thing to say to an unsuccessful declarer is: 'Never mind, you gave it your best shot.' Now partner is consoled, even if he has just missed a glaringly obvious winning line.

One of my favourite, but not recommended, overheard remarks to a partner followed these lines: 'Every day you play worse than the day before. Today you are playing as though it is tomorrow already.' Fortunately the comment was neither meant, nor taken, seriously.

Another nice story was of two world class players linked in an unfamiliar partnership. North forgot that they had agreed to play Texas and, after opening One No-trump, absent-mindedly passed his partner's response of Four Hearts. Long before dummy appeared declarer started to splutter with rage – Four Spades would have been an easy contract but here they were playing in a 2-1 trump fit. 'Don't say a word!' cautioned dummy. 'You will facilitate the defence!' With ten trumps between them the defence did not really need facilitating . . .

The First Word

Seeing that dummy was bursting to comment unfavourably on his play, South got in the first word. 'I am

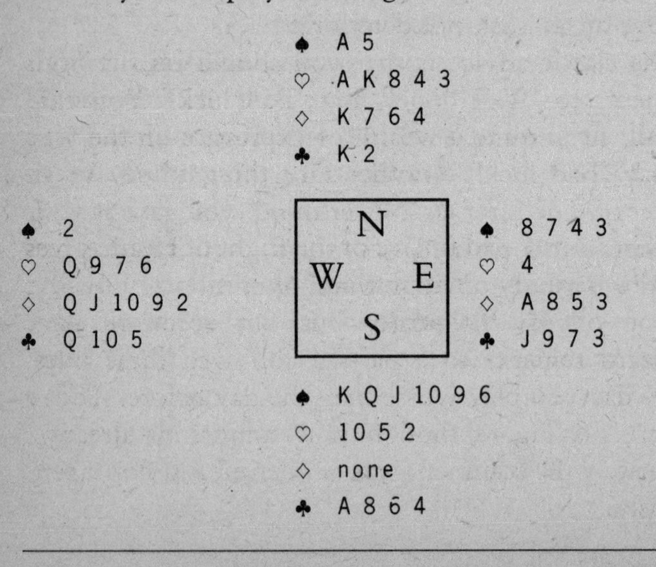

sorry,' he said, 'I thought that there might be a prize for making the first 11 tricks quickly.'

As he had just lost the contract it was a very good idea to lighten things.

At game-all it is not certain that everyone would rate the South hand an opening bid. The player at the table did. North became excited and the partnership ended in Six Spades – by no means an impossible contract.

West led the Queen of Diamonds and, as there was sure to be a Heart loser, declarer decided to ruff two losing Clubs on the table.

He ruffed the Diamond and followed with the King, Ace and another Club which he ruffed in dummy. A second Diamond ruff allowed the last Club to be ruffed, but the only way back to hand was with yet another Diamond ruff. With only three trumps left, the 4-1 break meant East won the last two tricks.

A better plan would have been to establish dummy's Hearts. After ruffing the opening lead, declarer should draw trumps and play the Ace of Hearts. When East's Jack falls, South plays a Heart to the ten and West's Queen.

Now the marked finesse of the Eight of Hearts gives South four tricks in the suit and his contract. Equally, if the adverse Hearts had divided 3-2, there would have been no problem.

'I Would Have Gone Off!'

'That was lucky!' exclaimed dummy after declarer had made his slam on this deal. 'If I had been playing the hand, I would have played to the odds. True, I would have gone down . . .'

At love-all, South opened One Spade and North raised to Four Spades. Blackwood revealed a missing Ace and a disappointed South settled for the small slam.

The lead of the King of Clubs, however, showed that even Six Spades was no certainty. With the Ace of trumps missing, the problem was to avoid the loss of a Club as well.

After winning the Club lead, declarer made the play that so upset his partner. He led the Queen of Diamonds

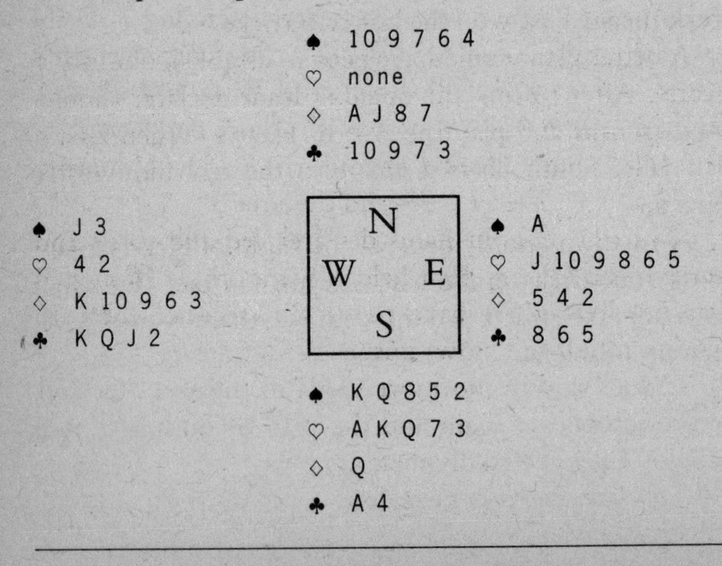

and, when it was covered by the King and Ace, took a Club discard on the Jack of Diamonds . . .

Dummy would have preferred to go down by cashing the Ace, King, Queen of Hearts, planning to throw his three losing Clubs. Fine if the Hearts broke 4-4 or 5-3, but it fails as the cards lie, when West ruffs with the Jack of Spades.

The point that dummy overlooked was that declarer had not the slightest intention of taking the Diamond finesse until West covered with his King.

Had West played low without a tremor, declarer would have put on dummy's Ace, ruffed a Diamond and tried the Hearts.

Holding Up

Holding up an Ace when you are defending is fairly routine – often it can seriously interfere with declarer's communications. Holding up with King and another can work in the same way, but it is more dangerous.

In this rubber East tried it out – he held K 2, dummy A Q J 10 9 8, West 7 6 5 4 and declarer 3.

With the lead in hand declarer led the three and finessed the Queen. East held off smoothly. He hoped that declarer might have to use up another entry to hand to repeat the (now) unsuccessful finesse.

Unlucky! With no more cards in the suit, declarer could not finesse again and the play of dummy's Ace brought unexpected dividends.

This was the very next deal.

South was the dealer at game-all and his partnership bid to Six Spades (Six Hearts would have been more comfortable).

West led the Ace of Diamonds and declarer ruffed on the table. It seemed obvious to run the ten of Spades.

If it lost, he argued to himself, declarer would still be in complete control and would have more winners than he needed.

This was equally clear to West, however, and in spite of his partner's little setback on the previous deal, he ducked the Spade.

'I hope that you are not trying one of your partner's tricks!' chuckled South as he confidently repeated the Spade finesse, catering for East holding four trumps.

'I am afraid that I am,' replied West, producing the Queen of Spades and the King of Diamonds in quick

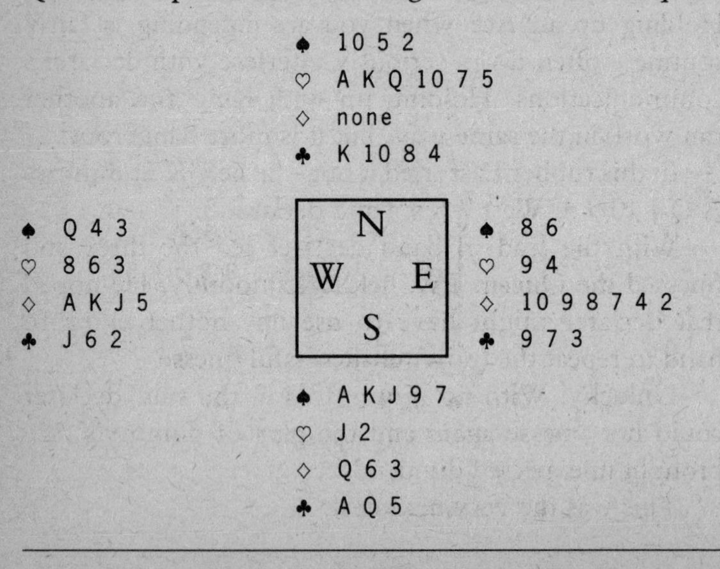

succession. To give South his due, he good humouredly joined in the general amusement.

'Hold Your Cards Up!'

'You really must learn to hold your cards up higher!' complained East, with mock severity, to his partner.

South, as declarer, had no sense of humour and insisted on explaining (at great length) the essential logic of his play. The winning line was based on an idea that you may well have seen before, but which still appeals to me.

South dealt at love-all and the bidding was dramatic. He opened Two Clubs and North responded Four Diamonds.

(Two Diamonds would have been the conventional

	North	
	♠ 7 3 2 ♡ 7 ◇ A K Q 10 7 5 4 ♣ Q 5	
West ♠ 10 9 8 6 ♡ K ◇ J 8 6 2 ♣ 10 8 3 2	N W E S	**East** ♠ J 5 4 ♡ 9 8 5 4 3 ◇ 9 ♣ J 9 7 6
	♠ A K Q ♡ A Q J 10 6 2 ◇ 3 ♣ A K 4	

negative, Three Diamonds a natural positive but Four Diamonds showed both a positive and a solid suit.)

Without wasting time, South jumped to Seven No-trumps and all passed.

West led the ten of Spades, and it was clear that if the Diamonds behaved there would be ample tricks.

As a tiny precaution (and, be honest, would you have thought of it if you had not met the theme before?) declarer played off his six black suit winners before testing the Diamonds.

When the bad break was revealed he cashed the third top Diamond and, after a little thought, led a Heart on which he played the Ace, dropping West's singleton King.

Why had South found such an apparently odds-against play, and prompted East's comment?

Well, he knew that West had started with four Diamonds and at least three cards in both black suits.

He could not hold four Hearts as well and the only distribution where a Heart finesse would land the contract (finding East with exactly **H** K x) could not exist.

What was left, then, but the remote and yet successful chance of finding the King of Hearts singleton?

'I Found A Fifth'

'There were about four ways of playing Clubs,' explained South to a disappointed partner after the deal below. 'But I managed to find a fifth.'

South opened One Spade at game-all, and North raised to Two Spades. South invited game in Spades with Three Clubs, and North accepted by bidding Four Spades.

The defence started with three rounds of Diamonds and declarer ruffed the third. He drew trumps in two rounds, eliminating the Hearts by playing off the Ace and King and turned his attention to the Club suit in which he needed three tricks.

South's actual play of finessing the Queen successfully and then cashing the Ace proved disastrous, for now East came to two tricks in the suit.

After the Queen had held, a low Club from hand would have catered for all possible distributions. If West follows low, the nine from dummy either wins or (if it loses) the suit is breaking 3-2.

If, as the cards lie, West shows out, then either the

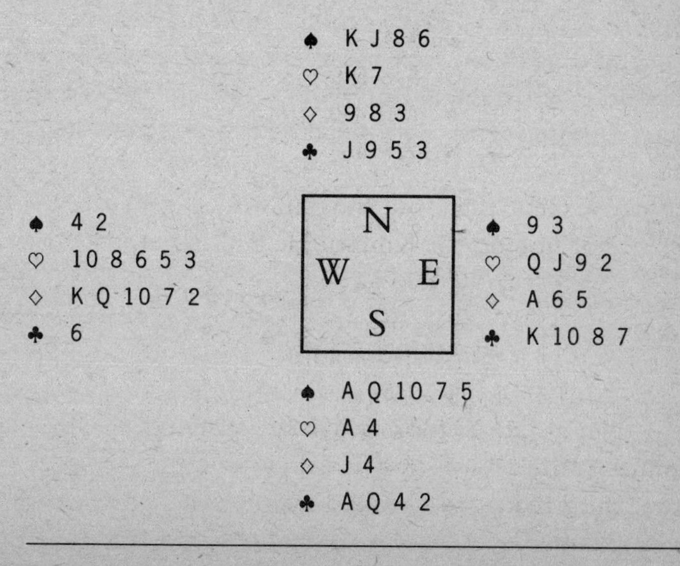

Jack or the nine from dummy will do for after winning East is end-played. He has either to lead away from his remaining honour or concede a ruff and discard.

It is worth noting that declarer is home and dry even if his Queen loses to a singleton King, for now West is end-played. Even the Jack from dummy on the first round of the suit would have guaranteed three tricks!

Out Of The Blue

Depressed by a long series of uninteresting hands, West tried an out-of-the-blue lead on this deal. It worked out well for his side in a way that he could not possibly have foreseen.

South opened One Heart and North responded Two

	North	
	♠ A 4 ♡ A 8 6 5 ◇ A Q 4 3 ♣ 7 6 4	
West ♠ K 10 9 ♡ J 9 2 ◇ J 9 ♣ K 10 8 3 2	N W E S	**East** ♠ Q 8 7 6 3 2 ♡ Q ◇ 10 7 6 5 ♣ J 9
	♠ J 5 ♡ K 10 7 4 3 ◇ K 8 2 ♣ A Q 5	
	South	

Diamonds before supporting his partner's suit, and the final contract was Four Hearts.

For no particular reason, West led the King of Spades and this had far-reaching results. Declarer won, drew two rounds of trumps, then played off three rounds of Diamonds, West discarding a Club. Then he played another trump to give West the lead.

'You can take your Queen of Spades,' declarer explained benevolently.

'But then you have to lead a Club round to my tenace.'

Ignoring this little speech, West won with his Jack of trumps and put his partner in with the Queen of Spades. Now the return of the Jack of Clubs left declarer with only nine tricks.

If he had not been prepared to rely on West holding the Queen of Spades, declarer could have got home by playing a Spade before the third trump.

East wins and returns the Jack of Clubs. South takes his Ace and now exits with a trump, end-playing West.

A Little Learning . . .

'Have you been reading too many bridge books?' demanded dummy at the end of this deal. South looked sheepish – it was true he had copied the tactics of a successful declarer in a recently publicised hand. But he had overlooked the fact that the overall position was not the same.

South dealt at game-all and opened One No-trump

(15-17 points). North raised to Three No-trumps and West led the three of Spades, which went to the Queen and King. Now the Spade position was very much as though declarer had started with A x x facing K x x in dummy when it might well have been right to duck the first trick.

Accordingly, the well-read declarer did just that. Unfortunately East could judge that there was no future for the defence in the Spade suit and, with a trick in the bag, he switched to Clubs.

Now there was no way to prevent East, with two entries, establishing his Clubs and defeating the contract.

In view of the danger of the Club switch, declarer should simply win the first trick and play a Heart. If this is allowed to win, he attacks Diamonds and makes at least nine tricks.

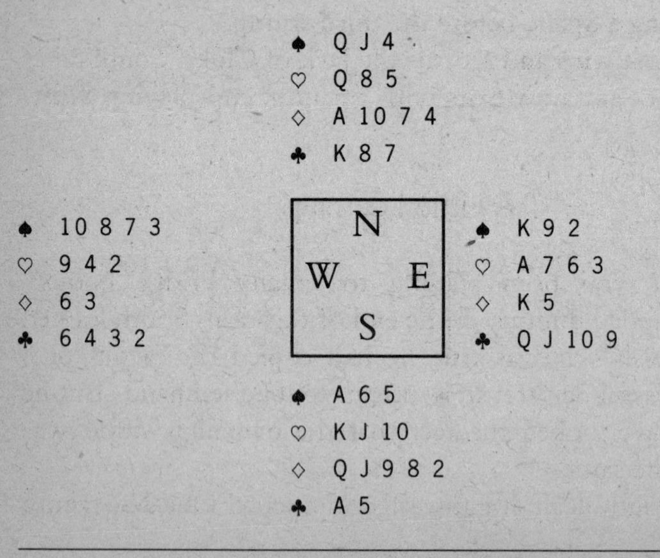

If a defender wins with the Ace of Hearts and perseveres with Spades, declarer ducks, wins a Spade continuation, comes to hand with a Club and can finesse in Diamonds. This is into the safe hand and again ensures the contract.

Curate's Egg

'Curate's egg!' remarked the solitary spectator after the hand below. We looked at him. 'Good in parts,' he explained. 'Excellent bidding, accurate defence, but declarer could have done better.' He was right, too.

North opened One Club. East overcalled with One Heart and South showed his Spades. North raised to Two Spades, South tried for game with Three Clubs and North, with extra values but only Three Spades and

West		East
	♠ A 5 2 ♡ 8 4 ◇ A 9 5 ♣ A Q J 10 3	
♠ J 10 7 3 ♡ K 3 2 ◇ Q 7 4 3 ♣ 7 4	N W E S	♠ 9 8 ♡ A Q J 10 9 ◇ J 10 6 ♣ 8 6 2
	♠ K Q 6 4 ♡ 7 6 5 ◇ K 8 2 ♣ K 9 5	

no guard in Hearts, expressed interest with Three Diamonds. South went on to Four Spades and all passed.

West led the two of Hearts and, after winning with the Ace, East intelligently switched to the Jack of Diamonds. (If he had continued Hearts, declarer would have had an easy run.)

South won in hand and played three rounds of trumps to discover the 4-2 break. He turned his attention to Clubs, but it was West who had the doubleton. He ruffed the third Club and the defenders cashed two more Heart tricks.

Rather than try for an unnecessary overtrick, South should tackle trumps by playing low from both hands on the first round, catering for a possible 4-2 break.

Dummy still controls the Hearts and, whatever the defence tries, declarer can draw the remaining trumps and claim his contract.

The Last Word

There were several points of interest on this deal, but most of them did not come to light until the discussion after the play.

At love-all West opened One Heart, North doubled (One No-trump would have been a good alternative), East raised pre-emptively to Three Hearts and South ventured Three Spades. West bid Four Hearts. North went on to Four Spades and West ended matters by doubling.

Now against Four Spades doubled West led the Queen of Diamonds, and South was quick to see that – as there was no hope of avoiding a Diamond loser – there was no reason to win the first trick.

West switched to the Ace of Clubs at trick two; but after South's hold-up in Diamonds, there was no way of gaining access to his partner's hand to take a Club ruff. South was able to drive out the Ace of Spades and make ten tricks.

'If I start with the Ace of Clubs and then switch to a Diamond, I can get a ruff,' remarked West.

'Wait a moment,' said South. 'Can't I win with the Ace of Diamonds, lead the King of Hearts and discard my other Diamond? Then you can't put East in.'

East had the last word. 'Why didn't you bid Five Hearts?' he asked his partner. 'They cannot defeat that.'

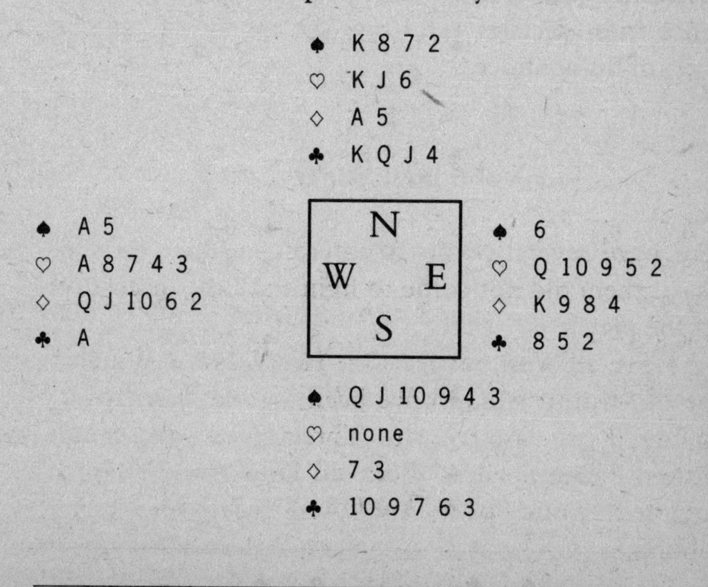

'Nothing I Could Do!'

'There was nothing that I could do about that,' claimed declarer after this deal. 'They found the best defence.'

It all sounded convincing and yet (as dummy) I harboured suspicions. Sure enough, when we looked at the hand later, an important factor came to light.

South dealt at game-all and opened One Spade. North raised to Four Spades, all passed, and West led the eight of Hearts.

The play was soon over. The King of Hearts lost to the Ace and East switched to the Jack of Clubs. The finesse failed and West returned a Club. Although declarer was able to discard one Club on an established Heart, it all led to four losers.

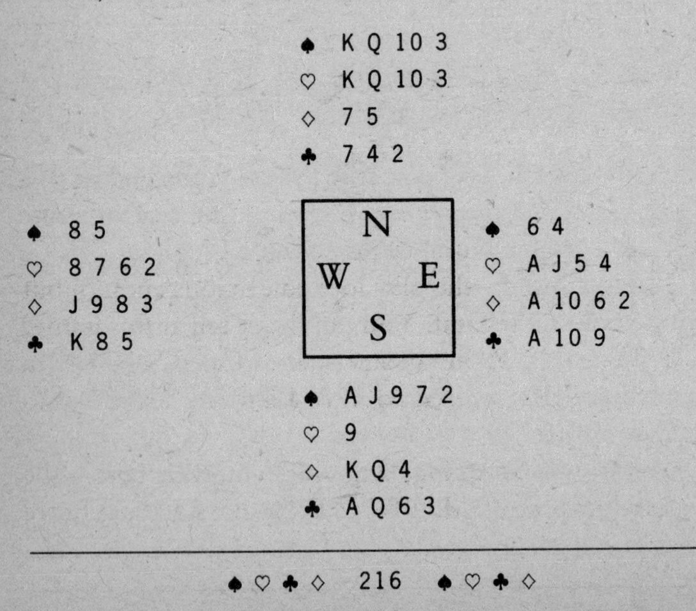

Clearly, South was unlucky – West might easily have struck an alternative opening lead – and the cards lay very kindly for the defenders.

Declarer, however, overlooked the usefulness of his nine of Hearts.

The position in the Heart suit should have been clear enough after the opening lead – so suppose that he tried the effect of the three of Hearts from dummy at trick one?

East wins with the Jack of Hearts and, as before, returns a Club. The finesse loses and the defence continues Clubs. But the difference is now that, while drawing trumps, declarer can use dummy's **H** K Q 10 for a ruffing finesse against East's Ace.

Now he can achieve two club discards and loses only three tricks.

A Double Can Be Trouble

'I don't understand it,' remarked West at the end of this hand. 'Drawing two of their trumps for one of mine looked the most natural thing possible.'

I sympathised – the play looked obvious enough but it turned out to be fatal. You can never tell at this game.

West dealt at game-all and opened One Club. North doubled and East raised to Two Clubs to leave South with a problem.

Technically speaking, a double would be best – the so-called responsive double – but South's actual choice of Two Spades proved a happy one. West competed with Three Clubs and North optimistically raised to Four Spades, which became the final contract.

West led the King of Clubs and declarer won in order to play off the Ace and another trump and leave West on lead.

Without a care in the world West drew a third round of trumps, but now the defence was finished. After ruffing the next Club lead in dummy, declarer forced out the Ace of Hearts and soon had ten tricks.

Just suppose that, instead of drawing a third round of trumps, West switches to Diamonds. Declarer wins on the table and drives out the Ace of Hearts, but East continues with another Diamond.

Now West is able to trump a Heart and cash a Diamond before declarer can get rid of his loser.

It really does not look right, does it, wasting a

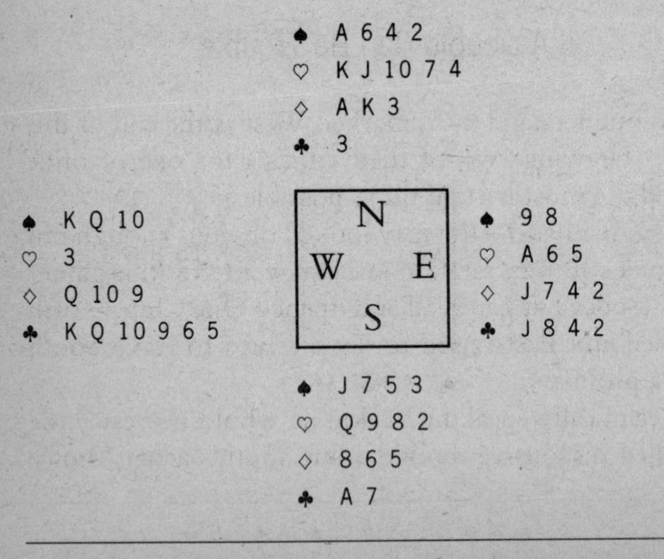

master trump to kill a side-suit winner rather than draw two adverse trumps? But it works – and that is the acid test.

The Unsafe Safety Play

'I wish that I had never bought that book on safety plays!' commented South mournfully after a disaster on this deal. There was nothing wrong with his safety play in Clubs, as such, but he should have found out whether or not he could afford it before tackling the suit.

South dealt at love-all and opened Two No-trumps. North tried Four Clubs (Gerber) and, finding that South held three Aces, plunged to Six No-trumps.

West led the Queen of Spades and declarer took stock – two Spades, one Heart, four Diamonds.

West		East
	♠ 2 ♡ 9 7 ◇ 8 7 6 4 ♣ A K J 9 3 2	
♠ Q J 10 8 ♡ Q 6 ◇ J 9 5 3 ♣ Q 7 5	N W E S	♠ 9 6 5 4 ♡ K 10 8 5 3 2 ◇ 2 ♣ 10 8
	♠ A K 7 3 ♡ A J 4 ◇ A K Q 10 ♣ 6 4	

He needed only five tricks from the Club suit and could afford to take precautions. After winning the Spade lead, South led a Club and West shrewdly played the Queen. It had the earmarks of a singleton, which would mean East held four Clubs headed by the ten, so declarer played low from the table and let the Queen hold.

He won the next Spade lead and ran the Clubs, smiling ruefully when the true position came to light. Worse was to follow, for his Diamonds provided only three tricks and the slam failed.

Declarer made a bad mistake in not testing the Diamonds first. Two rounds of the suit reveal the bad news and he now knows that he must play the Club suit for all six tricks and that no sort of safety play will be appropriate.

Every Cloud Has A Silver Lining

'Look on the bright side!' remarked South unrepentantly after failing to shine on this deal. 'If I am going to do two bad things, surely it is best if I can fit them both in on the same hand?'

It was impossible to be cross with him for long.

East, with North-South vulnerable and perhaps bored with a long succession of bad hands, elected to open One Diamond.

The bidding now got out of control. At one stage West sacrificed in Five Diamonds over South's Four Spades and North doubled, expecting to retire on the proceeds. South made his first error when he removed his partner's double to Five Spades and all passed.

West led the Queen of Clubs, clearly a singleton and, after winning on the table, declarer started on trumps. This proved fatal when West won, put his partner in with the Ace of Diamonds and collected a Club ruff to defeat the contract.

Instead of leading trumps, declarer should have played the Ace and King of Hearts, discarding a Diamond. Then he leads the Jack of Hearts and, when East is unable to cover, discards a second Diamond.

In this way, he exchanges one loser for another but leaves West with no chance of putting his partner in and so the impending Club ruff is averted.

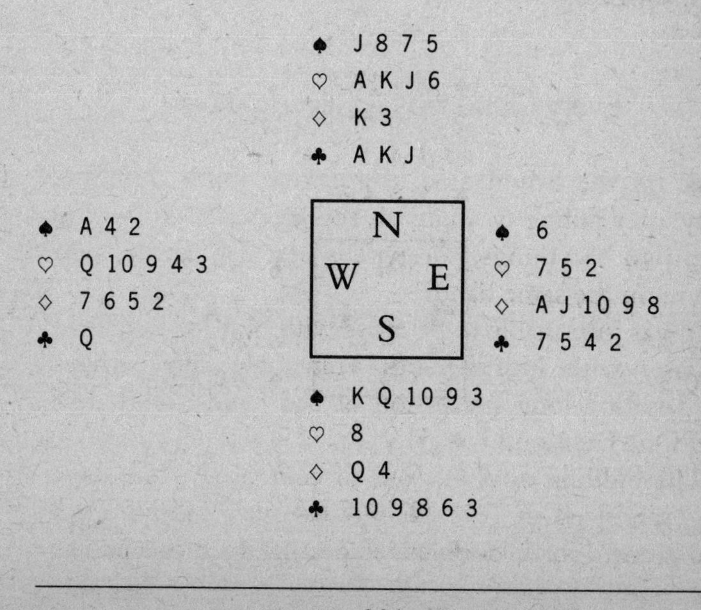

Bridge Players Are Like That

'How do you play a suit of A J 7 2 facing K 5 4 3?' demanded a friend the other day. It would have been nice if he had said 'Hello' first, but some bridge players are like that.

Wisely I asked for the full hand before venturing an opinion but had to be satisfied (for the moment) with just the North-South cards.

I was told that South had ended in Six Clubs and that West (my interrogator) had led the Jack of Hearts. After winning with the Ace, South had crossed to the King of trumps, studied the fall of the nine closely and, when East followed with the eight on the next trump lead, went up with the Ace to drop West's Queen.

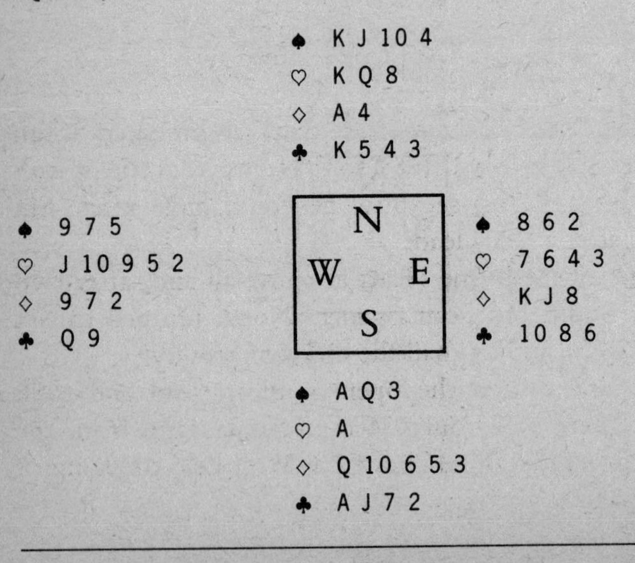

Now the play was easy and all that declarer lost at the end was a Diamond.

West felt aggrieved about declarer's play of the trump suit. Surely it would have been correct, he argued, that as a Diamond loser seemed inescapable, South should have taken the percentage play of finessing the Jack of Clubs on the second round.

I was forced to say that I thought declarer's play quite intelligent. If the trumps break 4–1 there is little hope, and playing for the drop of the Queen certainly worked well in practice.

Suppose, though, that West had followed with the ten? Then declarer can play off all his major suit winners before conceding a trump trick. Whoever wins will have the choice of conceding a ruff and discard, or leading a Diamond and giving declarer a free guess in the suit.

'I Don't See How'

'I feel that I should have made that,' commented South after the deal below. 'But I don't see how.' True, it isn't easy, but can you see how he could have made Six Spades after a heart lead?

West opened One Heart at game-all and, after two passes, South bid Four Spades. North jumped to Six Spades – the auction had the merit of brevity!

Declarer ruffed the opening Heart lead and took stock. There were only 11 top winners and from the opening bid it seemed likely that West held the King of Diamonds.

Often in these positions there is the choice between a squeeze and a throw-in, but here declarer could not cash all his black suit winners and still get to dummy without using his Ace of Diamonds.

Trying instead for a squeeze, he played off five rounds of trumps and Three Clubs. It did not quite work – on his last trump, West came down to **H** K **D** K J and duly made two tricks.

South's timing was astray – he needed to rectify the count before a squeeze could take effect.

Try discarding a Diamond on the opening lead. Now, after ruffing two Hearts in hand (just in case East held the Queen), the black suit winners finish West. When the last trump is played, he has to discard from **H** K **D** K J in front of dummy's **H** J **D** A 8 and has to surrender.

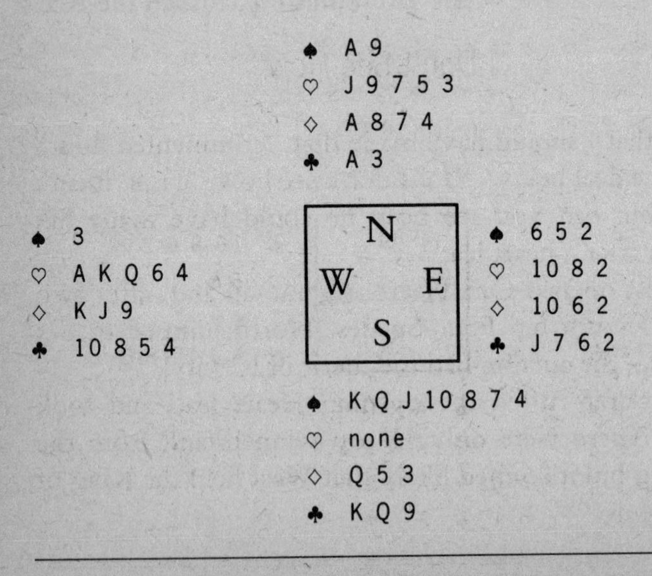

The Perfectionist

You can be too much of a perfectionist at this game. South was very cross with himself for missing the obvious way to play his slam on this hand and adopting a markedly inferior line. The fact that his play worked and that the more normal line would have failed seemed irrelevant.

South dealt at game-all and opened One Heart, North raised to Four Hearts and, after using Blackwood, South ended in Six Hearts. With little to go on West led a trump. Declarer saw that one way to make his contract was to find either defender with the Ace of Clubs and at most two Diamonds.

He drew trumps in two rounds, played off his Spade winners to throw a Club from dummy, cashed the Ace

West		East
	♠ J 7 4 ♡ A J 10 2 ◇ K 8 7 4 ♣ K 2	
♠ 8 3 ♡ 7 3 ◇ Q 10 3 2 ♣ Q 9 7 5 4	N W E S	♠ 10 8 6 2 ♡ 6 5 ◇ J 9 ♣ A J 10 8 6
	♠ A K Q 5 ♡ K Q 9 8 4 ◇ A 6 5 ♣ 3	

and King of Diamonds and exited with a Club. East took his Ace but with no Diamonds left was forced to concede a ruff and discard and give South his 12th trick.

'I'm sorry, partner,' commented South afterwards. 'My play had only about a 25 per cent chance of success. I should just have led a Club to the King after drawing trumps – that gives me a straightforward 50 per cent chance.'

'But it doesn't work!' exclaimed North. 'I can't help that,' was the reply.

Giving Up Bidding Slams

'I really will have to give up bidding slams!' exclaimed South after playing the deal below. 'I tried everything – it was an 84 per cent chance.'

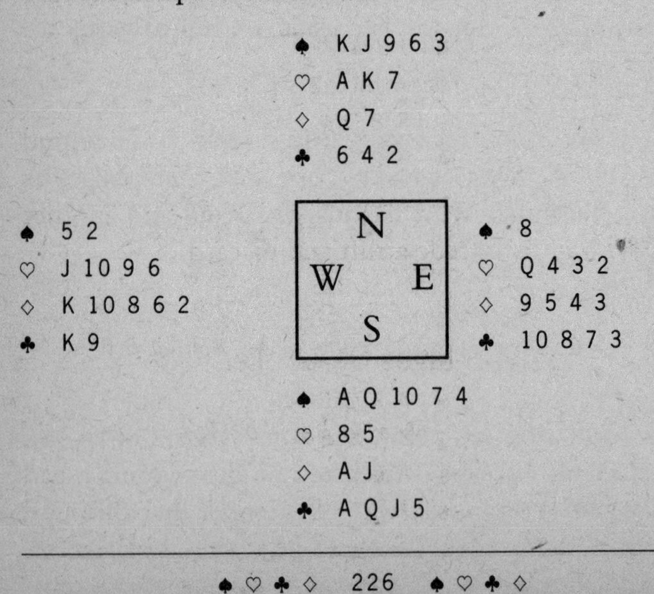

I agreed with his arithmetic, for his line of play offered just that chance, but forebore from suggesting one that would have succeeded.

South opened One Spade and North responded Four Diamonds. This was explained as a good raise to Four Spades but with no good side suit. South lost little time in contracting for Six Spades.

West led the Jack of Hearts and, after drawing trumps, declarer first tried the Club finesse. No joy, and next he tested the Clubs hoping for a 3–3 break. Still no joy and he finally fell back on the Diamond finesse. When that failed, it was all over.

Can you spot the improvement in South's play that would have helped?

After just one round of trumps he should play off the other top Heart and ruff a Heart, eliminating the suit. Then he cashes Ace of Clubs, draws the last trump with the King of Spades and leads a Club towards his Queen.

He will have given up none of his chances (King of Clubs with East, an even Club break, a Diamond finesse) but now has an extra one that materialises as the cards lie – that West has just the King and another Club and has to concede a ruff and discard.

The Advantages Of A Poker Face

It may seem a simple point, but contracts are often lost when declarer displays displeasure on discovering a bad break in suit. You must always remember that although one opponent is aware that you have met bad news, the other one is not necessarily in on the secret.

Here is a good example:

South opened One Spade at love-all, North raised to Three Spades and South plunged directly to Six Spades. West led the Jack of Clubs and declarer won. He followed with a Spade to the King and came back to the Ace before leading his singleton Heart.

You can see West's dilemma – if declarer had started with say, **S** A Q 9 8 6 5 **H** 4 3 **D** K Q J **C** A K, it would be right to play low smoothly and leave him with a guess in Hearts – which he might well get wrong and end by losing two tricks in the suit.

At the table, however, West had little difficulty in going in with his Ace. Why?

South had given a grunt of annoyance when West had showed out on the second trump. Had he continued

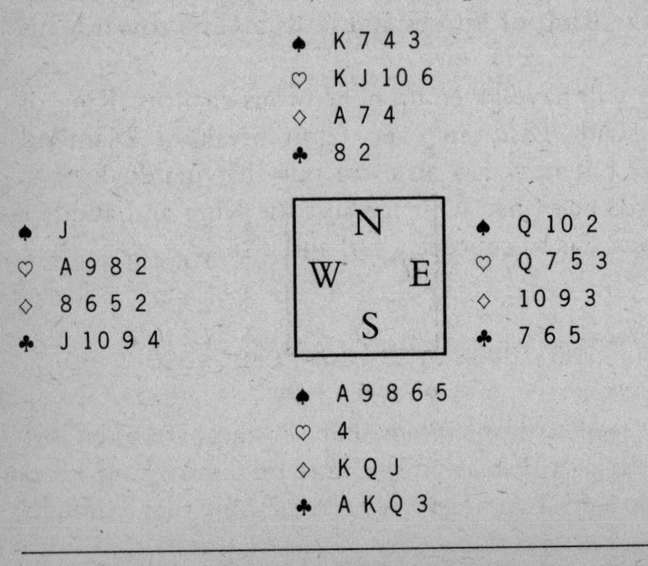

impassively, West would still not know whether it was right for him to rush in with the Ace of Hearts or not.

Incidentally, if South had held the alternative suggested hand, it would have been downright unethical – akin to cheating! – to simulate displeasure after drawing the last trump.

There Is No Justice

Anybody who expects justice in this game is due for continual disappointment. West, regarding his best hand of a depressing evening, found himself with no defence against an opposing game contract and recorded yet another minus score.

'At least I didn't double!' he remarked proudly. Indeed, the temptation must have been strong.

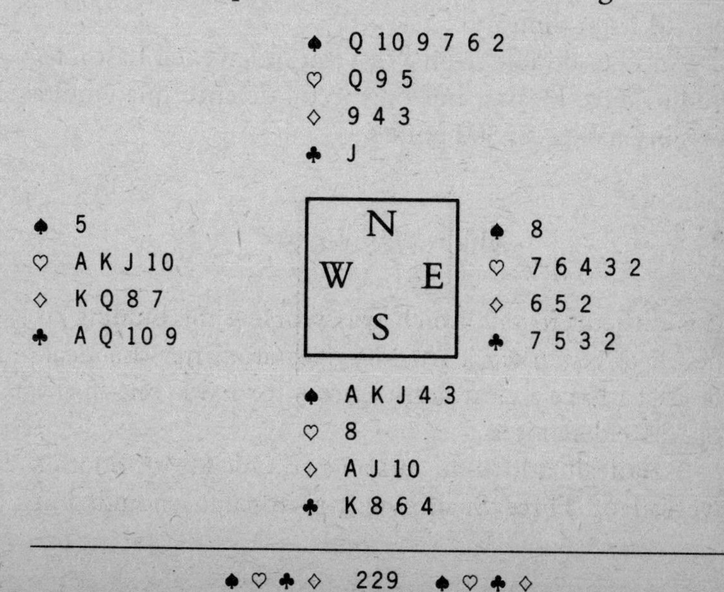

South dealt at love-all and opened One Spade. West doubled and North raised pre-emptively to Four Spades, which was passed out.

West led the Ace of Hearts and switched to his singleton trump. It would have been all too easy for declarer to rely on two finesses in Diamonds – clearly an unsuccessful line – but he spotted a much sounder alternative.

He won the trump with dummy's nine, ruffed a Heart in hand, crossed to dummy with a second trump and ruffed another Heart to eliminate the suit.

Entering dummy with a third trump, he now took a finesse in Diamonds. West won but any return he made would be to declarer's advantage.

A Diamond lead would be into South's tenace, a Heart would concede a ruff and discard, and finally the Club Ace would establish South's King for a Diamond discard from dummy.

Another double from West might have led East into bidding Five Hearts, but on careful defence this would possibly have cost 500 points.

Which Was Worse?

'It is difficult to say which was worse – the bidding or the play!' remarked a friendly spectator after this deal. At least I have a clear conscience – for I was one of the fortunate defenders.

East dealt at love-all and opened One Heart. South's overcall of Three Spades was reasonable enough but

North's effort of Three No-trumps, without any real prospect of using his partner's long suit, was ill-advised – he should have simply raised to Four Spades.

South had the last word when he went back to Four Spades. He had described his hand well on the first round and should have trusted his partner.

The play was soon over. West led the two of Hearts to dummy's Ace. East won the first round of trumps with his Ace and led the King of Hearts.

Declarer ruffed with the nine, West over-ruffed with the ten and put his partner in with the Ace of Diamonds. Now another Heart lead promoted the setting trick for West's eight of Spades.

I hope you can see the improvement in South's play noted by the spectator. Instead of ruffing the King of Hearts, he should discard his losing Diamond. This loser-on-loser play cuts the defenders' communications

West		East
	♠ K ♡ A J 10 9 5 ◇ K Q 8 5 ♣ A Q 10	
♠ 10 8 3 2 ♡ 2 ◇ 9 7 6 3 2 ♣ 9 7 6	N W E S	♠ A ♡ K Q 8 7 6 4 ◇ A 10 4 ♣ 8 4 2
	♠ Q J 9 7 6 5 4 ♡ 3 ◇ J ♣ K J 5 3	

and they come to only two tricks in the trump suit, instead of three.

'I've Been In Worse Slams!'

'I've been in worse slams!' remarked South cheerfully as he inspected dummy after receiving a favourable lead. His optimism wilted as the play progressed and, missing a not-too-difficult point, he ended by going down in his game contract.

Three No-trumps would have been easy enough, but after a long and complicated auction South ended in Five Clubs.

It all looked straightforward after the lead of the Jack of Diamonds – if either the Clubs divided 3-2 or the Spade finesse was right, there would be 12 tricks.

West	North / South	East
	♠ A K 8 2 ♡ A J 6 ◇ 7 6 4 3 ♣ Q 3	
♠ 4 3 ♡ K 9 7 ◇ J 10 9 8 ♣ J 9 7 2	N W E S	♠ Q 7 6 5 ♡ Q 8 5 3 2 ◇ K 5 2 ♣ 5
	♠ J 10 9 ♡ 10 4 ◇ A Q ♣ A K 10 8 6 4	

After winning the Diamond lead, however, the Queen and Ace of trumps revealed the bad break. Declarer drew a third round with his King, then essayed a Spade finesse.

East won and switched to a Heart. West's King went to the Ace and South played on Spades, hoping to discard his losing Heart before West could ruff. Alas, West trumped the third round of Spades and the defenders took their Heart trick.

After three rounds of trumps, declarer should not have finessed in Spades but played Ace, King and the two. East wins with the Queen, but the eight of Spades is established for a Heart discard. This line ensures success whenever West holds at least two Spades.

'I Might Have Made One More Trick'

Some players are stern self-critics, blaming themselves for missing a possible overtrick in a contract of One Club.

My partner, as South on this deal, was much more laid-back about the outcome. 'I might have made one more trick,' was his only comment. Unfortunately we were in a grand slam . . .

At game-all, South opened One Heart and I raised to Three Hearts. It seemed an ideal hand for Blackwood and, finding that I had two Aces, South decided to take the risk of not finding me with exactly three low Diamonds.

Against Seven Hearts, West led the Jack of Clubs

and the sight of only two Diamonds on the table was reassuring.

After winning with the Ace of Clubs, declarer played off the Queen of trumps. The 3-0 break was irritating, the more so as East proved to hold only two Diamonds.

There was no escape – one Diamond could be ruffed high in dummy but either East scored with his ten of trumps or West came to a Diamond trick.

It is not easy to pinpoint South's mistake. He should have realised that there might be a problem if one defender held three trumps and only two Diamonds.

The correct play is a trump to the Ace at trick two. Then if West has the three trumps, a Diamond can be safely ruffed with the nine of Hearts; if East has the trump length, two ruffs can be taken with **H** Q and **H** J and the missing **H** 10 picked up with a marked finesse.

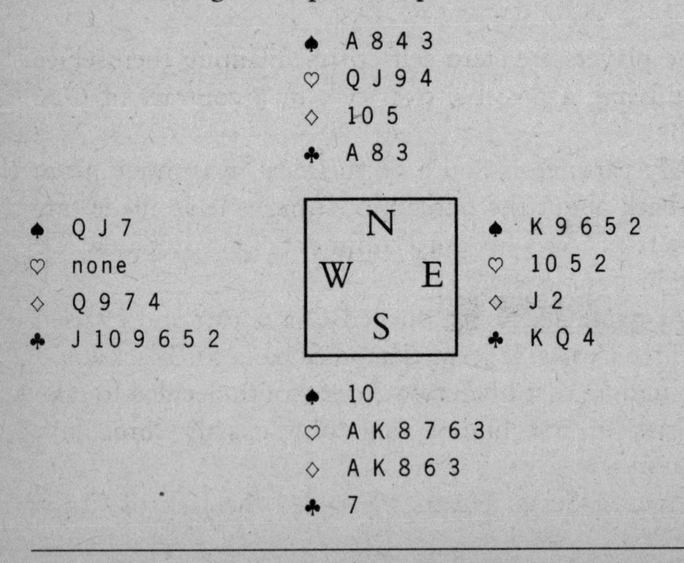

Play That Fails To Do Your Bidding

'They could have made Four Spades,' was declarer's claim after going down in his own contract of Four Hearts. He may have triumphed in the bidding, but he could certainly have done better in the play.

East dealt at love-all and opened One Club. South overcalled with Four Hearts and all passed, although it is fair to say that both East and West twitched a little first – as you can see, Four Spades would have been a good contract for them.

West led the ten of Clubs and South ruffed the Club continuation. Without a care in the world he now started on trumps, but East won the second round and forced again in Clubs.

This meant that declarer was reduced to the same

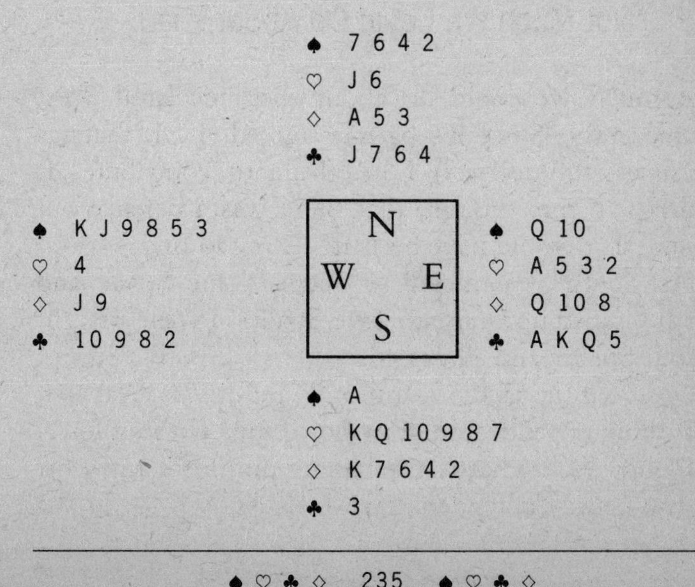

length in trumps as East, and there was no way that he could avoid the loss of two more tricks. South, of course, should have seen that he had no real chance unless the missing Diamonds divided three-two.

Rather than risk a bad trump break, he should have played three rounds of Diamonds after trumping the second Club.

East wins, but what can he do? If he plays off Ace and another trump, declarer is home and dry, for his Diamonds are established.

If instead East continues a forcing defence with a third Club, declarer accepts the force and sets out to trump both of his remaining Diamonds on the table. Whether East over-ruffs or not, he finds himself restricted to only three tricks.

'Not Much We Could Do About That!'

'Not much we could do about that!' declared West complacently. Since his partner agreed, I felt that (as the successful declarer) I had little to contribute. It occurred to me, though, that there was a defence but not one that would have been at all easy to find.

As South at game-all, I opened One Spade and North scraped up a raise to Two Spades. I went straight to Four Spades and all passed.

West led the Jack of Diamonds and it was clear that everything depended on drawing trumps without loss.

There was no harm in retaining dummy's entry for the moment – defenders have been known to do the wrong thing if they are left on lead long enough – but they persisted with Diamonds and I was forced to win on the table. A trump to the Ace revealed all, and the problem was to reach dummy twice in order to pick up East's Queen.

At trick four I tried a low Heart and dummy's Jack won. Then came a marked trump finesse and the King of Hearts lost to West's Ace. He continued Diamonds but I ruffed, trumped my winning Queen of Hearts on the table and finessed again in trumps to collect ten tricks.

Well, what could the defence have done? It looks unnatural, but suppose that West had gone in with the Ace of Hearts when I had led the two. I would have been denied a vital entry to dummy. (Equally, if I had led the King instead, West must hold off.) Then I would be bound to lose one trick in every suit.

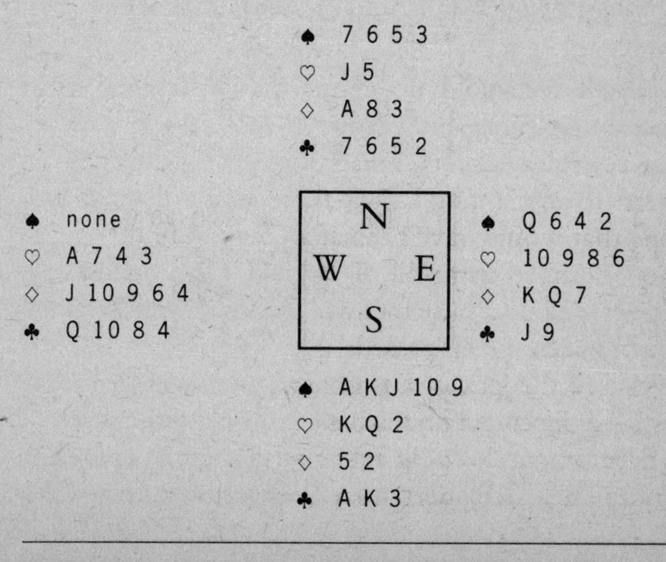

'I Was Only Dealt Three'

'I expected to find at least four Hearts in dummy,' complained South after going down in his game contract on this deal.

'I am afraid that I was only dealt three,' apologised his partner. He could have added that he had every right to expect South to have made Four Hearts, but he was too polite to say so.

East dealt at love-all and opened One Spade; South passed and West raised sportingly to Two Spades. Reluctant to be shut out, North doubled and South's jump to Four Hearts was passed out.

West led the two of Spades and declarer won East's Queen with his Ace. He started by playing on Clubs, but East unkindly ducked the first round.

West	North	East
	♠ 3 ♡ K 10 4 ◇ A Q 5 3 ♣ K J 9 6 5	
♠ J 9 4 2 ♡ 8 7 6 5 ◇ 10 8 7 ♣ 8 7	N / W E / S	♠ K Q 10 8 7 ♡ 3 2 ◇ K J 9 ♣ A 3 2
	♠ A 6 5 ♡ A Q J 9 ◇ 6 4 2 ♣ Q 10 4	

He won the second Club and gave his partner a ruff and now the ten of Diamonds set South an insoluble problem. He could ruff a Spade in dummy and draw trumps, but now the vital entry to the long Clubs had gone and he ended with only nine tricks.

There was a simple solution – South should have let East win the first trick. Now if, for example, East returns a Spade, declarer can ruff in dummy, draw trumps in four rounds and establish the Clubs at leisure: for he still retains the Ace of Spades to look after another lead in the suit.

It would have been a neat example of keeping control while playing in a 4–3 trump fit.

CHAPTER NINE

That Rarity – 'It was My Fault, Partner'

At all times it is important, especially at rubber bridge when you frequently find yourself partnered (opposed?) by an unknown quantity, to keep your partner happy. A pleasing palliative, after a particularly unsuccessful defence, is to say: 'Yes, it was difficult. Perhaps I could have made it easier for you if I had . . .' Even if your suggestion is wildly improbable, partner is left with the impression that the disaster is not entirely his fault. And, if the blame for what has gone wrong can be laid fairly and squarely at your door, admit it before partner has a chance to comment. And yet . . . things like that happen only in an ideal world.

A delightful apology came along when two top-ranking Canadian players were partnering each other in defence. East had bid Spades; a Spade lead would have defeated the contract, but for some reason West chose a Diamond for his opening salvo and declarer was home and dry. 'It was my fault,' observed East. 'Perhaps if I had bid Diamonds you might have led a Spade.'

'Did I Do A Bad Thing?'

South made his contract on this deal although he should not have done so. I had to be tactful about it for it was East, an unsuccessful defender, who asked me: 'Did I really do a bad thing? Or did declarer just play it well?' Between you and me, the answer to both questions was Yes.

East dealt at love-all and opened One Heart, South overcalled with Two Spades, West passed and North raised to game. West led the Jack of Hearts against Four Spades and declarer ruffed the Heart continuation.

It looked an irritating hand – there was the problem of avoiding three Diamond losers. There were several possibilities – East might hold only two Diamonds headed by an honour, East might hold both the Ace

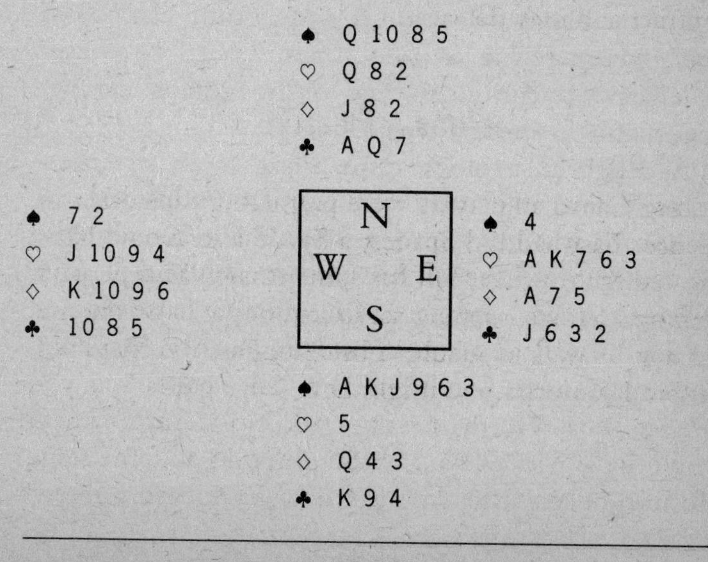

and King of Diamonds and, finally, East might get the defence wrong.

South drew trumps in two rounds, ending in dummy, and followed with the Jack of Diamonds. It looked to East as though declarer was planning a finesse, so he played low. Disaster.

West won with the King, but a later lead towards the Queen established the tenth trick. As you can see, looking at all four hands, if East had won the Jack with his Ace, the defenders would have had two more tricks to come in the suit.

East should have argued that as a Club finesse (if declarer needed it) was right, then the only chance of defeating the contract lay in taking three Diamond tricks.

You can construct a variety of hands for South, but it looks very much as though covering the Jack of Diamonds with the Ace can never give away the contract and may defeat it.

It Was A Pleasure

'I should have made that!' said South after this deal.

'No, it was my fault – I should have converted to Six No-trumps,' replied his partner. It was a pleasure to listen to them – no trace of acrimony whatsoever.

South dealt at game-all and the auction was long and complicated. South ended in Six Spades and you can see what North meant – Six No-trumps, which would have been played by South (who at some stage had introduced Blackwood) would have been impregnable. West led the Ace of Diamonds and switched to a Heart. After winning on the table, declarer led the nine of Spades to the two, four and eight.

He repeated the finesse successfully, but when West showed out East still had the guarded King. There was no way in which this could be picked up and the slam failed.

South's mistake came when he played the four of Spades under dummy's nine.

Suppose that he had followed with the seven? When the eight falls from West the position is clear and he can now run dummy's six, following with the four from hand.

The difference now is that the lead is still in dummy. Declarer ruffs a Diamond, returns to a Heart and ruffs another Diamond before crossing to dummy with the Ace of Clubs.

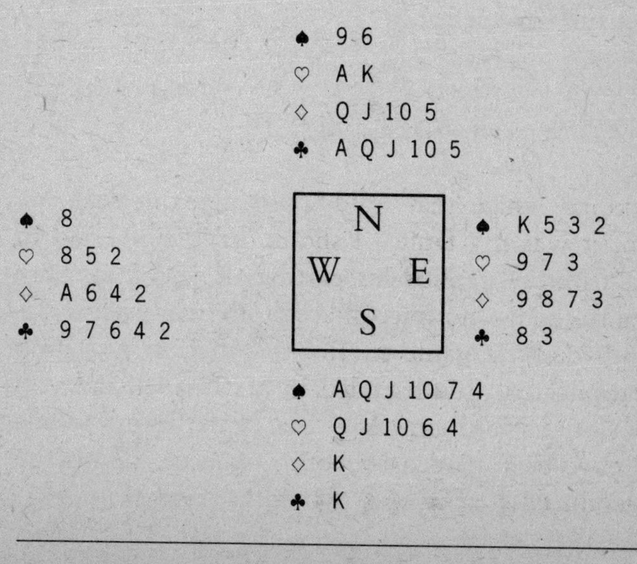

South now has the same number of trumps as East and can lead winners from dummy until East chooses to ruff.

It Seems Natural . . .

When your partner makes a good lead and you can win and return his suit, a feeling of euphoria sets in. There is an almost irresistible temptation, when you gain the lead again, to continue the suit. For example:

South dealt at love-all with a 30 partscore. He opened One No-trump and West (who might profitably have contested) passed.

He missed his chance. For North raised to Two No-trumps and the three level seemed too high to take action. West led the four of Hearts and East was allowed

West		East
	♠ 8 ♡ A 8 ◇ 9 8 7 6 3 ♣ A 7 5 3 2	
♠ K 4 ♡ K Q 6 4 3 ◇ K 5 4 2 ♣ 10 9	N W E S	♠ 10 9 7 6 5 2 ♡ J 10 9 ◇ J 10 ♣ K J
	♠ A Q J 3 ♡ 7 5 2 ◇ A Q ♣ Q 8 6 4	

to win with the nine. Naturally enough, he returned the Jack to clear the suit.

After winning with dummy's Ace, declarer played the Ace and another Club to leave East on lead again. Without really thinking about the matter, East played back the ten of Hearts and with even less regard for the consequences, West overtook to cash his Heart winners.

You can see the sequel – South discarded two Spades and, with West on lead, claimed his contract. Either a Spade or a Diamond would give him his eighth trick.

Who was more at fault? East for not playing either a Spade or a Diamond when he was in with the King of Clubs, or West for not leaving his partner on lead with the Jack of Hearts and so forcing him to do the right thing? They are still arguing about it.

It Still Seemed Natural

Hands seem to come in pairs. I wrote about the dangers of automatically returning partner's original lead without too much thought to the consequences. Believe it or not, the rubber concluded with East-West duplicating their misjudgement on the very next hand.

After three passes South opened Two No-trumps which North, rather sportingly, raised to Three No-trumps, perhaps on the strength of his good intermediate cards.

West led the two of Hearts to the ten and King and, after winning with the Ace, declarer started on Clubs.

West held off for two rounds but then won and continued Hearts.

Dummy won the third round of the suit, leaving West with a winner in the suit. After cashing his Club winner, declarer turned his attention to the Spades.

Perhaps unwisely, East hastened to take his Ace immediately – it could hardly have done any harm to wait – and even more unwisely returned his last Heart.

I felt sorry for West. With nothing else to do, for the second time in the rubber, he was reduced to leading away from his King of Diamonds to concede the vital trick. Perhaps if West had not been so vocal about the previous deal his partner might have got this one right.

West		East
	North ♠ J 10 7 ♡ Q 10 4 ♢ 10 9 3 ♣ J 9 8 3	
♠ 6 ♡ J 9 8 2 ♢ K J 8 7 ♣ A 6 4 2	N / W E / S	♠ A 9 8 4 3 2 ♡ K 7 6 5 ♢ 5 4 ♣ 7
	South ♠ K Q 5 ♡ A 3 ♢ A Q 6 2 ♣ K Q 10 5	

If In Doubt, Bid On

When a deal is highly competitive and it seems that both sides have a good fit in one or two suits, there is always a good case for bidding on. Take this deal:

East dealt at love-all and chose One Spade. South overcalled with Two Hearts, West – rather feebly – passed, and North raised to game.

Rather than raise the level, East fought on with Four Spades. But when South's next bid of Five Hearts came round to him, it seemed a little late to introduce the Diamonds.

As you can see, Five Spades (on best defence) would have gone two off, costing 300 points at most – but Six Diamonds would have failed by only one trick.

What about South's prospects in Five Hearts after a

North:
♠ K 5
♡ K 9 8 5 2
◇ A 8 6
♣ A 9 3

West:
♠ 7 6 4
♡ 6 4
◇ J 7 5 4 3
♣ K Q 5

East:
♠ A Q 10 9 8 3 2
♡ none
◇ K Q 10 9 2
♣ J

South:
♠ J
♡ A Q J 10 7 3
◇ none
♣ 10 8 7 6 4 2

Spade lead and continuation? It looks as though it will all depend on a 2-2 break in Clubs – but declarer found a neat way to improve his chances.

He ruffed the second Spade, crossed to dummy with a trump and played Ace and another Diamond which he ruffed. Then he drew the last trump and ruffed dummy's third Diamond. Finally, he led a low Club from hand and when West played low, put in dummy's nine.

East won, but whatever he returned allowed declarer to ruff in hand and discard dummy's losing Club.

The moral, on this hand at any rate, is as I suggested – if in doubt, bid 'one for the road'.

You Be The Judge

'The play was perfectly correct!' insisted one partner after this deal.

'No, there was an obviously better line – a beginner should have seen it.'

It sounded like one of those arguments that we all overhear from time to time, but there was an odd twist. It was dummy who was defending his partner's play and declarer who was apologising.

North dealt at love-all and opened One Club, East overcalled with One Spade and South bid Two Hearts. North tried Three Diamonds, South bid Three No-trumps and all passed. It was not a very elegant auction but these things happen.

West led the six of Spades to the two, ten and King. This gave declarer eight top winners and he started by leading the Jack of Diamonds, planning to run it to East – the safe hand, for if he got in he could not advantageously continue Spades. West covered with the Queen of Diamonds, however, gained the lead with his King and was able to play a killing second Spade.

The point that South overlooked was that it was essential to find the Ace of Hearts with East – if West held it, the contract was bound to fall no matter how the Diamonds behaved.

Having made this necessary assumption, the winning play is clear. Declarer leads the King of Hearts at the second trick to establish his ninth winner. This makes the contract whenever success is possible.

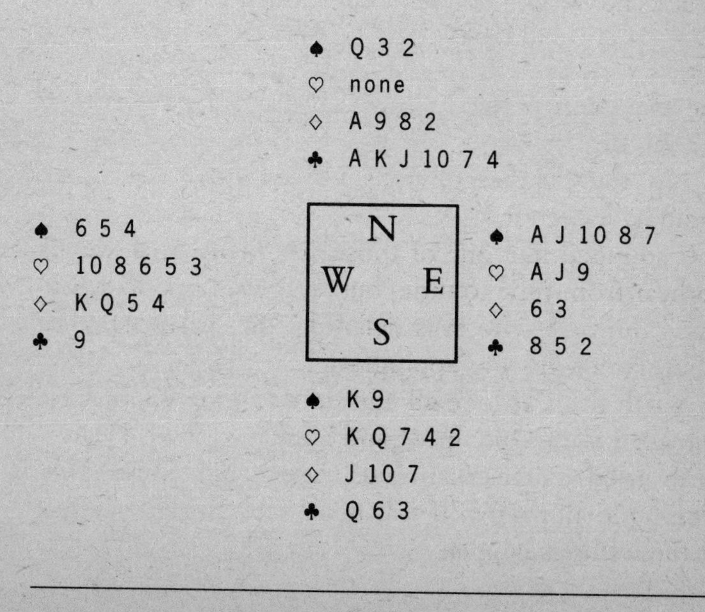

At Least They Both Agreed, Even If It Was A Disaster!

'Sorry, partner. I thought that we had caught them on the hop there,' apologised West after he had doubled his opponents unsuccessfully.

'Don't worry, I would have done just the same,' replied his partner sympathetically. Indeed, most players would.

North dealt at game-all and opened One Heart; South responded One Spade and North rebid his Hearts. South explored with Three Clubs but when his partner bid Hearts for a third time, jumped to Four Spades. To West it sounded very much as though they

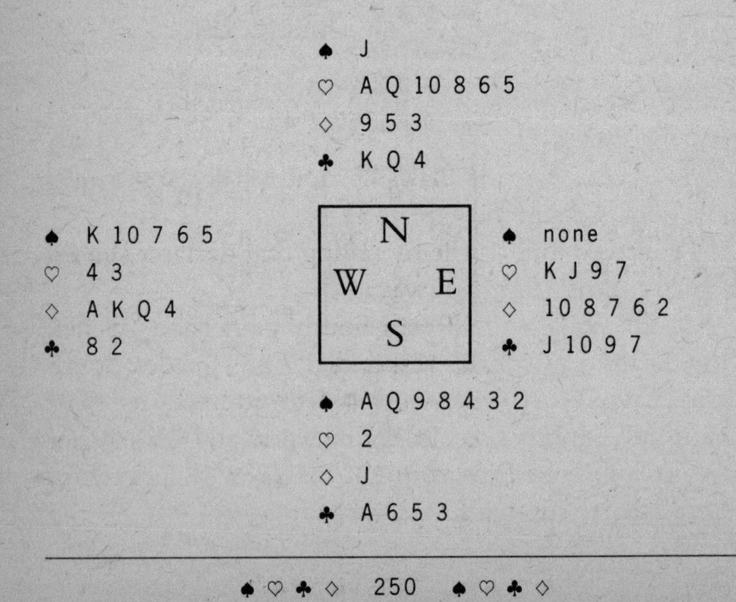

were out of their depth on a misfit and he doubled. He started with two top Diamonds and declarer ruffed.

A low trump to the Jack was allowed to win and South saw the futility of trying to draw trumps. Instead he ruffed another Diamond in hand, crossed to the Ace of Hearts and ruffed a Heart.

At this point declarer was down to three trumps, while West still held four. Three top Clubs followed and West ruffed and got off lead with his last Diamond.

Declarer trumped and exited with his losing Club but, with nothing but Spades left, West was forced to trump and concede the last two tricks to South's Ace and Queen.

It had become very clear that sometimes too many trumps can be a source of embarrassment to a defender.

Perhaps It Was A Silly Double, But . . .

At the end of play on this hand, my partner (East) was very apologetic.

'If I had not made that silly double, declarer might have gone wrong!' he explained.

I consoled him a little by saying that declarer should have got things right anyway.

South dealt with North-South game and opened One Diamond. North responded One Spade, South rebid Two No-trumps and North jumped to Four Diamonds. South cue-bid Four Hearts and his partner (just in case Four Spades might be taken as an attempt to play there) cue-bid Five Clubs.

South, with nothing in Spades, went back to Five Diamonds but North made another effort with Five Spades. East doubled this to suggest a Spade lead, but South still bid Seven Diamonds.

I dutifully led a Spade but, not unnaturally, declarer did not finesse. He won with dummy's Ace and, coming to hand with top trumps, ruffed his losing Hearts. Then came his remaining trumps, and the Ace of Hearts on which the rest of dummy's Spades were thrown. At the end East was squeezed and had to part with either the King of Hearts or his guard in Clubs.

Would declarer have finessed in Spades without East's double? I doubt it – it would only have been a 50 per cent bet. The chances of finding the Clubs 3-3 or the defender with the King of Spades holding four or more Clubs would always have looked a better bet.

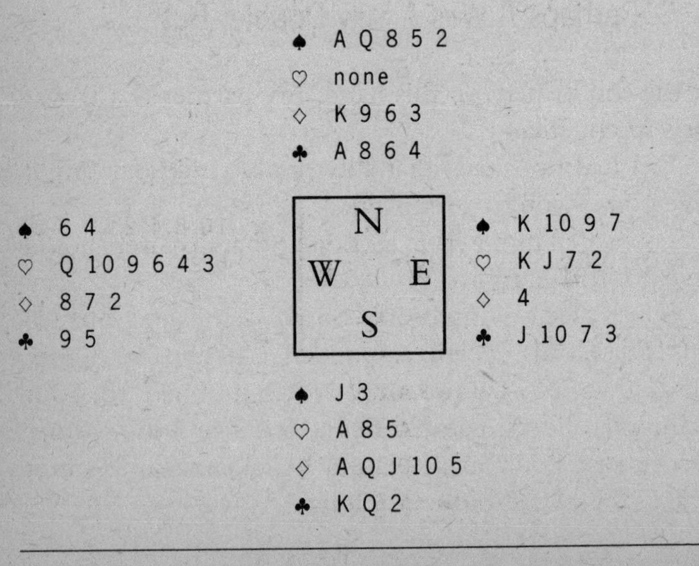

If Only We Had Discussed Our Signalling Methods

There is more than one school of thought about signalling in defence. Some players automatically show their length in the suit that their partner has led, some try only to suggest encouragement or discouragement, while a third group (confusingly) does different things in different situations.

Perhaps East–West were not sure of their methods on this deal, but the real credit must go to declarer.

South, after dealing at game-all, opened One Diamond. West overcalled with One Heart, North raised to Two Diamonds, South went on to Three No-trumps and all passed.

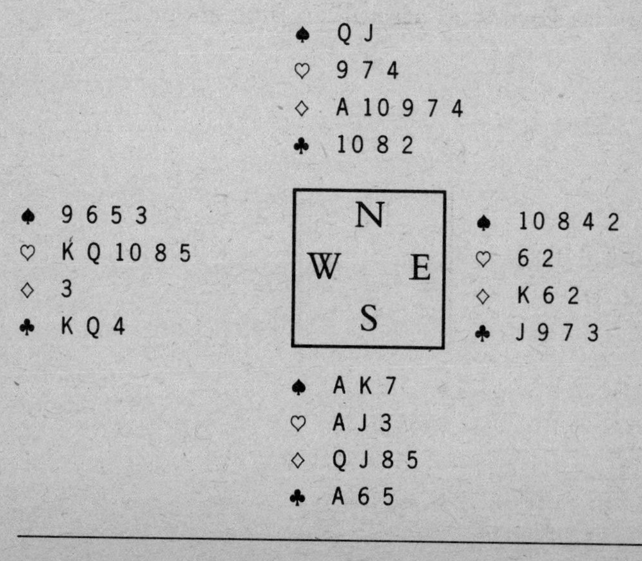

Naturally enough West led the King of Hearts and East (presumably to show lack of interest) followed with the two. It looked automatic for declarer to play low as well, guarding against a further Heart lead, but he appreciated that this might lead to a damaging Club switch.

It was equally dangerous to win the Heart lead – for if the Diamond finesse proved to be wrong, the defenders could run their Hearts.

South found a neat play – he followed to King of Hearts with the Jack! This left West with the clear impression that his partner's two was simply showing three cards in the suit and he continued with the Queen rather than look for a switch. South won and now, after the Diamond finesse had failed, East had no Heart left to return.

This play gave South a great deal of satisfaction, especially as East-West are still arguing about it!

CHAPTER TEN

Optimism

Optimism in bridge takes many guises. Some players overbid wildly – often good players, who subsequently justify their enthusiasm by playing the cards well and landing near-impossible contracts but, equally often, indifferent players who are determined to become declarer at all costs. The good rubber-bridge psychologist knows his customers. He only doubles the first group if he is on very firm ground indeed but he often doubles the second on the sound of the bidding and the (rarely misplaced) expectation that they will misplay the hand.

On balance, optimism (controlled aggression?) pays, especially when your side has a known fit and can judge that the cards lie well. The times when it is costly occur when there is no fit between the partners' hands and the opponents can judge that you are out of your depth.

There is a very real distinction between rubber bridge and match-pointed pairs. Suppose that, in defence, the only way to defeat the opponent's game contract is to find your partner with the Ace of Hearts. It is unlikely that he holds it but just possible. The trouble is that a Heart lead, if partner does not hold the Ace, will almost certainly cost an unnecessary overtrick.

Fatal at pairs, but of little consequence in the rubber game.

Again, as declarer, you can judge that only a miraculous lie of the cards will get you home in a contract, likely to be reached at most other tables, which seems doomed to one down after routine play. The problem is that, if the hoped-for distribution does not materialise, you will end up two or three down. In a pairs competition you should settle for your average but in the rubber game the loss of an extra 50 points does not matter too much and you should be more inclined to take the optimistic line.

I can always remember watching an extremely talented player at work in Four Spades. He was an incurable pessimist. He played the hand beautifully – if the missing trumps had broken 5-0 he would have been home and dry. Unfortunately, they divided 3-2 and he went two off in a contract that any beginner would have made.

I think that I will give my vote to the optimists!

'150 For Honours!'

To score points for holding honours always strikes me as unfair – if you are lucky enough to be dealt all four Aces, for example, why should you be given an extra 150 points as well?

Mind you, an obsession with honours can lead you to the wrong contract. I watched this hand recently.

South dealt at love-all and opened One Diamond.

North raised to Three Diamonds and South plunged to Six No-trumps to end the bidding.

With the King of Spades well placed the slam in Diamonds would have been a fair proposition but Six No-trumps, with only nine sure winners, was a highly speculative affair.

West did well to lead a Diamond, giving nothing away and declarer won in hand. He started by leading a low Heart to the Queen and King.

Hoping to put South to an immediate guess, East led a Spade and declarer finessed the Queen successfully. It is true that further finesses, in Clubs and Hearts, might have led to twelve tricks – but South rightly decided that that would be pushing his luck too far. Instead, he played off the Ace of Hearts and followed with four more rounds of Diamonds.

West had to keep the Jack of Hearts and all four of

	♠ 7 4 ♡ Q 3 ◇ K Q 9 8 4 ♣ K J 7 2	
♠ J 9 3 ♡ J 9 8 4 ◇ 6 3 ♣ Q 8 6 3	N W E S	♠ K 10 8 2 ♡ K 7 6 2 ◇ 10 5 ♣ 10 9 5
	♠ A Q 6 5 ♡ A 10 5 ◇ A J 7 2 ♣ A 4	

his Clubs for his last five cards. You can see what happens if South plays off his Ace of Spades – West has to discard a Club and then the Ace followed by a finesse of the Jack brings in four Club tricks.

South's play was on a par with his bidding, however, for he played on Clubs first. Now West was in no trouble for discards and the slam failed.

Said South brightly: '150 for honours!'

Too Busy!

Bidding without the necessary qualifications always has mixed results. Everyone was all at sea on this deal – but South recovered in the play.

West dealt at love-all and opened One Diamond.

	North	
	♠ A 8 5 ♡ 10 4 3 2 ◇ A 6 3 ♣ 7 4 2	
West	N W E S	**East**
♠ J 9 6 3 ♡ 9 ◇ K Q J 10 5 ♣ K J 9		♠ 10 7 4 ♡ J 8 6 5 ◇ 9 7 ♣ Q 10 8 5
	South	
	♠ K Q 2 ♡ A K Q 7 ◇ 8 4 2 ♣ A 6 3	

North passed and East busily responded One Heart, thinking that a show of strength might be psychologically right.

Certainly the bidding left South with a problem, which he decided to solve by overcalling One No-trump in spite of his lack of a Diamond guard. North pushed to the limit with No-trumps and all passed.

West led the King of Diamonds and declarer considered the problem. It was clear that at least one of his opponents did not have their bid. East, however, had bid Hearts – and about the only chance of a ninth trick lay in finding West with the singleton Jack of Hearts or (twice as likely) the singleton nine or eight.

The problem was that there were only two entries to dummy and one had to be used immediately.

Can you see how declarer tackled the Hearts? He won the third Diamond on the table and led the ten of Hearts. East covered and the nine fell under the Queen. Now the Spade entry to dummy allowed South to finesse **H** 7 for his ninth trick.

And if East-West had not been so busy in the bidding? Then almost certainly South would have gone one off in Three No-trumps or two off in Four Hearts . . .

Poker Face

It is a splendid asset at this game to own a poker face. You may feel what you like about your partner's activities, but you must keep your emotions bottled up. And, of course, if your partner tends to twitch a little you must not take advantage.

I found myself sitting behind dummy when this hand was played and although I could not see declarer's hand, I could see his face . . .

North-South overbid merrily to Six Spades. West considered his lead at length and South looked apprehensive – he knew that he had done too much in the bidding.

Eventually West made the poor choice of his singleton Heart, and the combination of the lead and a sight of dummy caused South's expression to brighten up considerably. Declarer won the King of Hearts with his Ace and attempted to cash the Queen. But West ruffed, played back a trump and declarer still had a Heart to lose at the end.

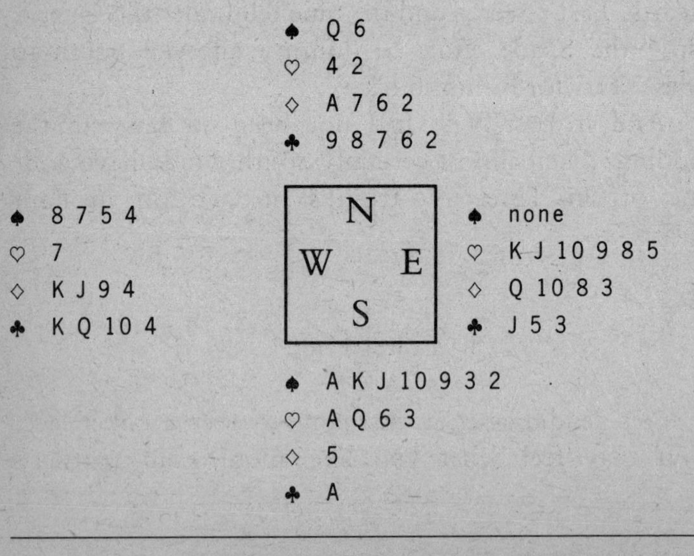

Perhaps it was something about the way that both dummy and I looked that made him ask: 'Could I have made it?'

Yes, you can see the winning line. At trick two South must play a low Heart from hand. Later he ruffs his remaining Heart loser with the Queen of trumps, draws the outstanding trumps and makes his Queen of Hearts at the end.

Silence Is Golden

West's overcall on this hand was unfortunate. Had he passed, his opponents may have ended in a doomed Three No-trumps.

South dealt and opened One Diamond. West over-called with One Heart, North bid Two Clubs and East

	North	
	♠ 10 7 3	
	♡ 5	
	♢ A Q 7	
	♣ K Q J 9 4 3	
West		**East**
♠ 9 6 2	N	♠ Q J 8 4
♡ K J 10 9 3	W E	♡ Q 8 6 2
♢ J 6	S	♢ 4 3 2
♣ A 7 6		♣ 10 5
	South	
	♠ A K 5	
	♡ A 7 4	
	♢ K 10 9 8 5	
	♣ 8 2	

raised to Two Hearts. Instead of trying Two No-trumps with his single Heart, South passed but North raised and the final contract was Six Diamonds.

West led the Jack of Hearts to the Ace and declarer immediately led a Club. West ducked but won the second Club, then led a Heart, forcing dummy to ruff and it looked as though the long suit was shut out. But a top Club from the table followed and East had a choice – if he ruffed, declarer could over-ruff and two rounds of trumps would have brought the Clubs back to life. So he discarded.

Declarer threw his Spade loser away, came to hand with the Ace, ruffed his last Heart with a Queen and cashed that Ace, then came back with the King of Spades and trumps, dropping West's Jack.

A Switch In Time . . .

It looked the most natural thing in the world for East to establish his partner's long suit but, as the play developed, it left declarer with little option other than find the winning line.

South opened One Diamond, North responded One Heart, and South rebid One No-trump. In an optimistic mood, North raised to Three No-trumps and all passed.

West led the six of Clubs to his partner's Queen. East returned the ten of Clubs and again declarer held off but was forced to win the Club continuation. The Heart finesse lost and East switched to the nine of Diamonds.

There was no real guess involved here, for West was marked with two winning Clubs. If he held the Ace of Diamonds as well, the contract was doomed; so South took his only chance and went up with the King of Diamonds.

The winning Hearts followed and, when declarer took another good view by playing West for the Queen of Spades, he was home.

East missed a difficult chance. After his ten of Clubs had held, a Diamond switch would have led to five tricks for the defence, no matter how declarer guessed in Diamonds.

It is always a thought to be borne in mind – that after taking two tricks in a suit against No-trumps, you might consider switching to another.

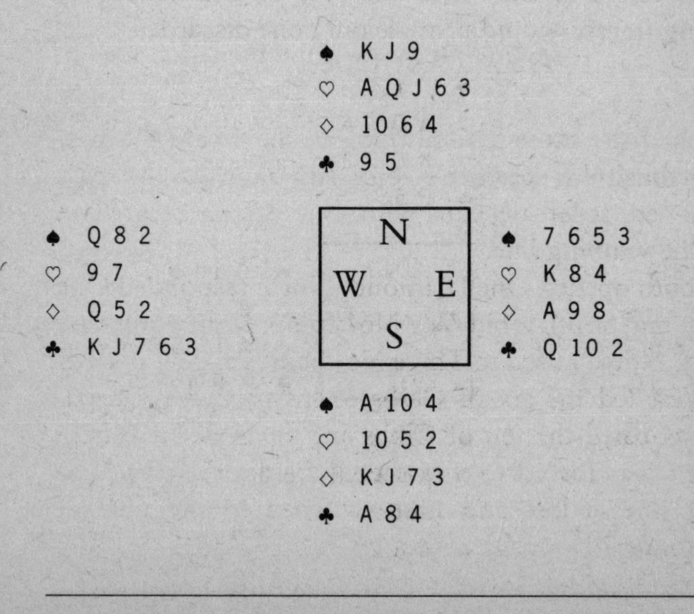

'You Can't Catch Me Like That!'

There is an old bridge saying that suggests that, if you bid badly, you have to play the cards well to compensate.

South's bidding on this hand was wild and he ended in what seemed to be an impossible contract. Halfway through the third trick, however, he spotted his only chance and found the cards lying just as he hoped.

South dealt at love-all and opened One Heart. North raised to Four Hearts and South intemperately jumped to Six Hearts.

West led the Queen of Clubs, and a brief inspection of dummy revealed to declarer that there were two losers. Even if East held the Ace of Diamonds, the ruffing finesse would provide only one discard.

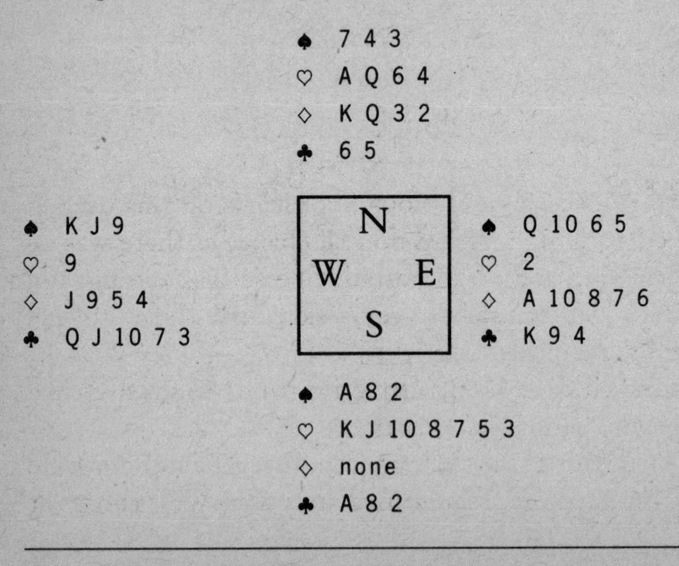

Inspiration came quickly. Declarer won the lead, crossed to dummy with the Ace of trumps and led the two of Diamonds. This caught East completely off balance. Was declarer leading towards the singleton Jack in his own hand? Then the defenders could take two tricks.

'You can't catch me like that!' remarked East as he played his Ace – it was a chatty game. But South spread his hand, explaining that he was ruffing and would throw two Spades on the top Diamonds and concede a Club.

Could East have known? A possible clue was that with a singleton Diamond Jack, South might have tried Blackwood on the way – a useless manoeuvre with a void.

As I explained, however, South was a bad bidder and perhaps not too much reliance could be placed on this.

It Looked Impossible, But . . .

South reached an ambitious Six Hearts on this deal. It looked as though he had no real chance as there was an Ace missing and an important finesse was wrong; but declarer demonstrated, very elegantly, how to get round these difficulties.

Carried away by his attractive hand, South stretched slightly to end in Six Hearts.

The lead of the Ace and another Diamond would have defeated the slam immediately, but West chose the

Jack of Spades and declarer was in with a chance. He made his first good play when he played low from dummy and ruffed in hand. In this way he did not have to commit himself as to what to throw on dummy's Spade winner.

Trumps were drawn in two rounds ending in hand. Then came the five of Diamonds. If West had taken his Ace, declarer would have been able to discard three Clubs from hand (two on Diamonds, one on a Spade with a ruffing finesse). Instead, West played low on the Diamond lead and dummy's King won.

Next came a top Spade, covered and ruffed and, after entering dummy with a trump, South discarded his losing Diamond on the Spade winner.

Finally came a Club from the table and the last good play – instead of finessing the Queen, which would have led to failure, South inserted the Nine.

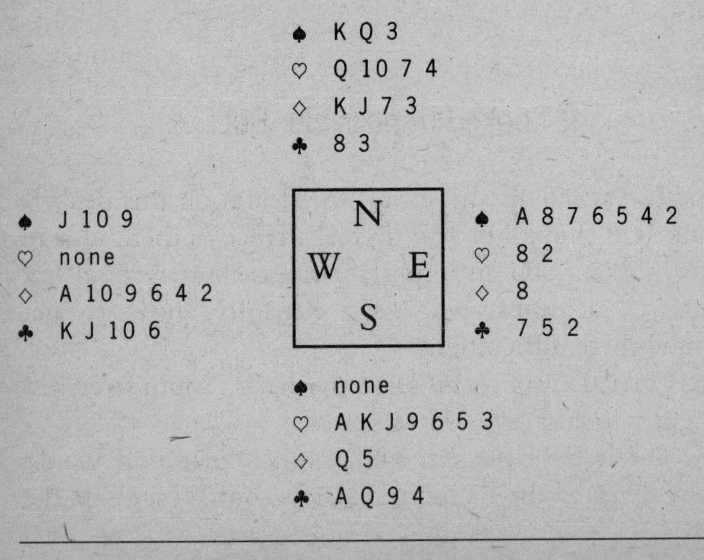

On lead, West was end-played – a Club lead would be into South's tenace and a Diamond lead allowed dummy's Jack to become the 12th trick.

Judgement Above All

Relying purely on points to value your hand works well most of the time, especially on balanced hands, and it is certainly nearer the mark than some of the other methods of hand valuation that have been suggested.

But what do you think of South's judgement/arithmetic on this deal? One thing was certain – he did not worry too much about his point-count or the textbooks.

At game-all South opened One No-trump (15-17 points) and, in the modern style, North responded Two

West		North / South		East
		North		
		♠ A Q 9 7 3		
		♡ 9 8 2		
		◇ Q 6 5		
		♣ 6 4		
♠ K 4 2		N		♠ 6 5
♡ K Q J 10		W E		♡ 7 5
◇ 9 4 2		S		◇ J 10 8 3
♣ 7 5 3				♣ A K 10 8 2
		South		
		♠ J 10 8		
		♡ A 6 4 3		
		◇ A K 7		
		♣ Q J 9		

Hearts – a transfer to Spades. Now, take a care, it may be routine at duplicate, but don't try it with a strange partner at the rubber-bridge table – you may well find yourself laying in some very odd Two Heart contracts!

South, awaiting his partner's intentions, dutifully rebid Two Spades and now North bid Two No-trumps. The message was clear – he held the values to raise One No-trump to Two, he held five Spades, and that he held no other suit.

This left South with a textbook decision – with a maximum No-trump he would choose between Four Spades (with at least three-card support) or Three No-trumps. With a minimum he would either pass or go back to Three Spades.

In practice South had a minimum (15 points) and support for Spades. A shrewd, practical player he bid Three No-trumps.

As you can see, this contract depended simply on a successful Spade finesse (a reasonable bet) and there was no possible play for Four Spades.

Could not South count? (Either his Spades or his points?) I prefer to think that he used judgement.

CHAPTER ELEVEN

Safety Plays

Safety plays are curious things. They are usually defined as 'the play of a suit in such a manner as to protect against an abnormal or bad break in that suit, thereby either eliminating or reducing the danger of losing the contract'.

Aye, there's the rub! There is a very real distinction between rubber bridge (or teams play) and duplicate pairs. A safety play, even if it guarantees the contract, may well sacrifice a vital overtrick. Who cares about the odd overtrick in a small slam contract at rubber bridge, with some thousand points at stake? But in pairs play, if even the worst pairs in the room are going to make an overtrick by poppa-momma play, can you afford the indignity (and the match points) of making one less trick than the field?

In principle the solution is simple. At rubber bridge or teams play you should make every effort to ensure your contract. In pairs play a new and important factor has to be taken into consideration. Have you ended in a good contract which is unlikely to be reached by the rest of the field? If so, a safety play to guarantee your contract, even at the expense of a possible overtrick, is warranted. If however the same contract is sure to be reached by Mr and Mrs Bloggs you cannot afford luxuries and have to try for the maximum.

Finally, alas, there are the 'safety plays' that turn out to be anything but safe. They may cater perfectly for the distribution that you fear but fall foul of another distribution that was just as likely. As I said, safety plays are curious things.

It Hurts When A Good Play Is Described As Lucky

You can accuse a bridge player of many things – infidelity, theft and so on – but the ultimate insult is when you tell him that he was lucky to make a contract

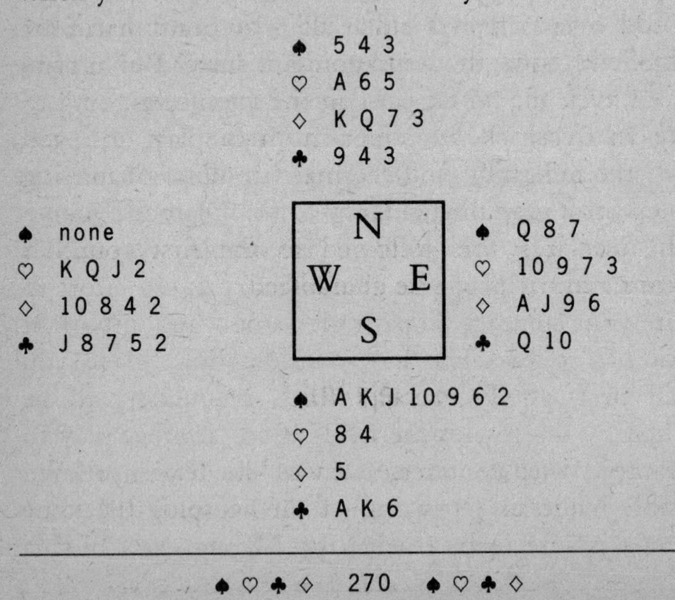

that he had played rather well. South was the aggrieved party on this deal.

South dealt game-all and opened Two Spades. With trump support and an outside Ace North raised to Three Spades; South cue-bid Four Clubs and North showed his Ace of Hearts but South's next bid of Four Spades ended the auction.

West led the King of Hearts and this proved annoying for South, driving out dummy's certain entry before a trick could be established in Diamonds.

Even so, it looked a straightforward affair for, provided that the missing trumps broke 2-1, there was still at least ten tricks. Nevertheless declarer started by winning the Heart lead on the table and immediately finessing the Jack of Spades. When it won South was home and dry.

East felt aggrieved and asked why South had taken this 'lucky' view in the trump suit instead of playing the Ace and hoping for the drop of the Queen.

I hope that you can see why. If the Jack of Spades loses unnecessarily to the Queen in West's hand, the five of Spades will be an entry to the Diamond winner and, once East has followed to the first round of trumps, ten tricks will be guaranteed.

'Déjà Vu'

Somebody used the phrase, 'It was like déjà vu, all over again.' While disapproving of the tautology, I knew exactly what they meant when this deal came up at rubber bridge.

South dealt at game-all and, without any great conviction, ended in Three No-trumps. He certainly took the Clubs on trust for his partner had not suggested any values in the suit.

Declarer was off to a good start, however, when West led the seven of Clubs to the three, ten and Queen. There were at least ten tricks if the missing Diamonds broke 3-2; but, with only one side entry to dummy, there was a problem if they divided 4-1.

South found a neat solution. At trick two, he cashed the King of Diamonds and continued with the Queen, overtaking on the table when West followed suit.

If the Diamonds had divided 3-2, he planned to give up a trick in the suit (unnecessarily) but ensure his

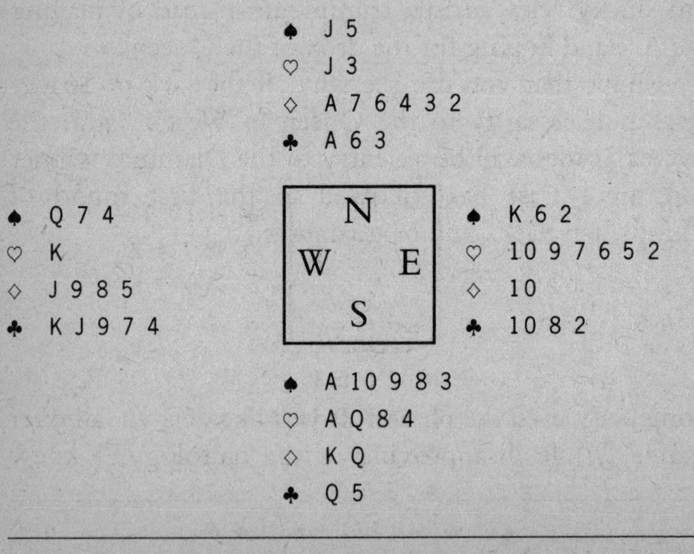

contract. When East showed out, though, he abandoned the Diamonds and turned his attention to Spades.

He ran the Jack unsuccessfully but, when he won the next Club lead on the table, took a second Spade finesse to give him four tricks in the suit and his contract. There was a little bonus to come as well for the King of Hearts proved to be singleton.

Where had we seen the theme before? The deal was very similar to one that had won the 1977 Charles Solomon Award for the Hand of the Year.

An Odd Way To Turn The Tables

After two attempts to be too clever on the same hand, South ended with a highly unsatisfactory minus score on this deal from a pairs' competition.

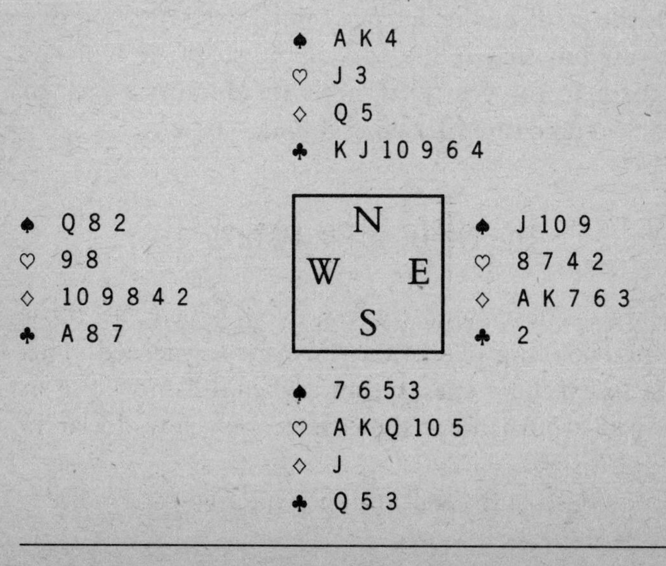

North dealt at game-all and after several rounds of bidding during which South had stressed his good Hearts, the partnership settled in Four Hearts.

A contract of Five Clubs would have been easy but the lure of +620 rather than +600 proved too much for South.

West led the 10 of Diamonds to his partner's King and East continued with the Ace. In an attempt to keep control against the (likely) 4–2 trump break, declarer discarded a losing Spade.

East was quick to take advantage – he switched to his singleton Club and an immediate ruff gave the defenders the first four tricks.

South was right to be worried about a possible 4–2 trump break – if he ruffs the second Diamond and draws trumps the roof falls in. What he missed was the simple idea of ruffing and playing on Clubs himself.

As the cards lie the defence can take the Ace and one Club ruff but that is the end of the story. It will not help them to force in Diamonds for dummy's Jack of Hearts can take care of a third round.

The Off-Beat Play Works

I am always fascinated by hands on which the most unnatural-looking play is the only one to succeed. This deal is an excellent example and when it came along in a big pairs tournament there were very few declarers who got it right.

South dealt at love-all and, playing five-card majors,

opened One Heart. West overcalled with Two No-trumps (unusual, showing length in the minor suits), North raised to Three Hearts and South went on to game.

West led the ten of Spades and the play usually started with the Jack, Queen and Ace. Declarer drew trumps in four rounds and led another Spade but now East had two entries in the suit.

When he won with the eight he pushed through a Diamond and later, when he got in with the King of Spades, the defenders had two tricks to take in the minor suits.

The successful declarers (and there were not many of them!) allowed West's opening lead of the ten of Spades to win. East could not overtake without sacrificing one of his side's tricks in the suit and now there was no way for the defence to get to their Diamond trick.

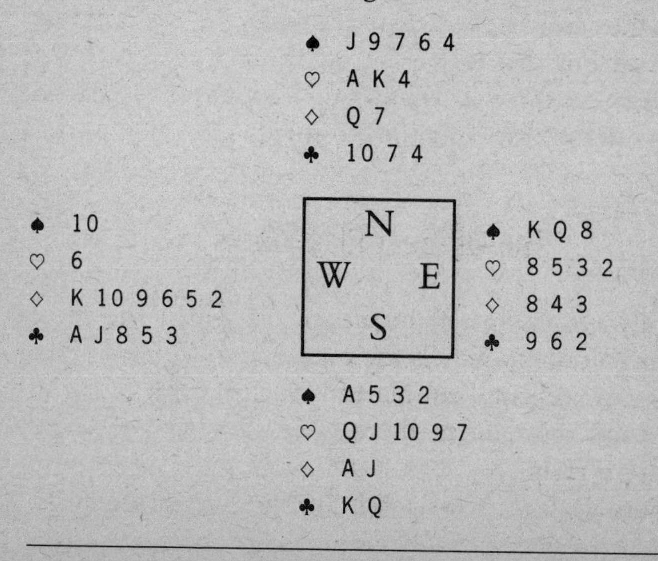

In practice West, left on lead, tried the Ace and another Club but South won, drew trumps and cleared the Spades. Then there was time for him to throw his potentially losing Diamond on dummy's long Spade.

Yes, In A Pairs Competition, Anyone Would Play Like That . . .

How should you play this hand in Three No-trumps against the lead of a low Spade?

First you need to know what game you are playing. In a pairs competition, with overtricks vital, it would be sensible to play low from dummy in the hope West had led away from the King. But at rubber bridge?

West		East
	North ♠ A 10 5 ♡ A K 5 ◇ 10 7 4 3 ♣ 10 8 6	
♠ J 8 7 4 3 ♡ 10 8 6 4 3 ◇ none ♣ Q 7 2	N / W E / S	♠ K 2 ♡ J 9 ◇ Q J 8 5 ♣ K J 9 5 3
	South ♠ Q 9 6 ♡ Q 7 3 ◇ A K 9 6 2 ♣ A 4	

South opened One Diamond at game-all and rebid Three No-trumps over his partner's Three Diamonds. West led the four of Spades and declarer greedily played low from dummy. He hoped East would produce the Jack and, with an even Diamond break, he might well win 12 tricks.

Disaster! East won with the King and switched to a low Club. South won the second round and tried the Ace of Diamonds, but West showed out and he ended with only eight tricks.

I know that if declarer cashes his major suit winners, East can be squeezed out of one of his winners. But South was so rattled that this possibility escaped him.

Unless East is void in Diamonds, the safe way to ensure the contract is to win the opening lead with the Ace, lead a low Diamond and cover whatever East plays. West is welcome to win, if he can, for now at least four Diamond tricks are assured, and with West on lead the Queen of Spades is invulnerable.

There Was Something Exotic About This Safety Play

If, like me, you have a flair for getting 50-50 finesses wrong, you will be better advised to look for a line of play that is 100 per cent safe. And sometimes it is not too difficult to spot.

There was a pleasantly simple answer to this hand,

for instance. Cover up the East-West hands and imagine that you, as South, are declarer in Four Hearts after East has opened One Club.

West leads the eight of Clubs, East wins with the Jack and continues with the Ace and King. Make your decision.

The lead may well be from a doubleton and, if you ruff the third Club low, there is the danger of West scoring with a singleton King of trumps, exiting with a Diamond and leaving you with an infuriating two-way finesse in Spades to guess.

And so to that 100 per cent safe answer. Ruff the third Club with the Ace of trumps! You follow with the Ace of Diamonds and a Diamond ruff in hand, before exiting with a trump.

No matter which opponent wins with the King, they will be left with the choice of conceding a ruff and

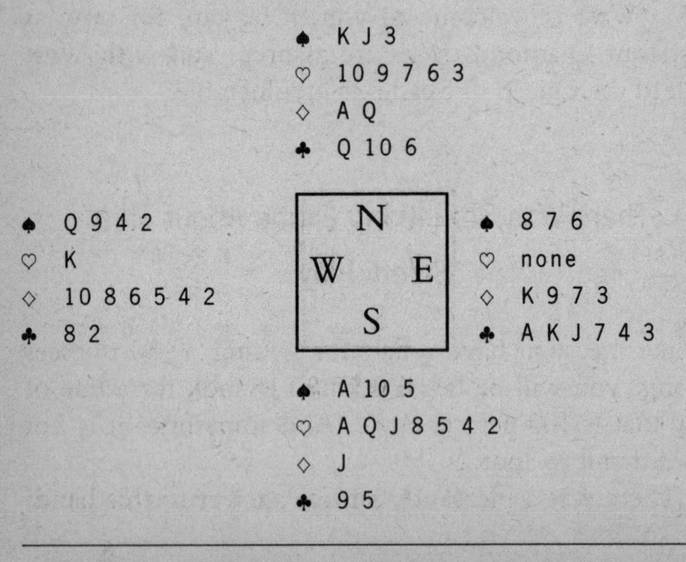

discard or leading a Spade and taking away all your worries.

Very neat and a practical idea too.

Are You Bridge Literate?

Some winning plays by declarer look unnatural and it is usually that they are missed by players who refuse to read any of the literature of the game.

I am not saying that you will achieve perfection if you study my columns, but I am sure it helps. On this deal I suffered when it became clear that partner had not seen the situation before.

At love-all I passed as North, East opened One Club and South overcalled with Four Spades to end the auction. West led the eight of Clubs and declarer won

West		East
	♠ A J ♡ 8 5 3 2 ◇ Q 10 8 7 2 ♣ 6 2	
♠ 7 6 5 2 ♡ J 9 7 6 ◇ K 6 4 3 ♣ 8	N W E S	♠ 3 ♡ K Q 10 ◇ A J 9 ♣ K J 9 7 6 4
	♠ K Q 10 9 8 4 ♡ A 4 ◇ 5 ♣ A Q 10 3	

cheaply with his ten. Without a care he continued with the Ace of Clubs. West ruffed and switched to a trump.

Now, although declarer could trump one of his losing Clubs on the table, he still had to lose a Club, a Diamond and a Heart to go one off.

'It was unlucky to find West with a singleton Club,' he explained and I nodded gravely. As you can see, declarer missed a neat safety-play that would have ensured ten tricks.

Suppose, after winning with the ten of Clubs, he simply leads a low Club from hand, keeping the Ace for safer times?

Perhaps East wins this and returns a trump; but South can win in hand, ruff the Queen of Clubs on the table, come to hand with the Ace of Hearts and draw trumps. Then – and only then – he will take his Ace of Clubs.

If I Had Played, I Am Sure I Would Have Got It Right

There is plenty of top-class bridge to watch in the *Sunday Times* Invitation Pairs Championship. I was due to play with Paul Chemla in the first event but had to cancel. Paul instead played with Michel Perron and won convincingly.

All the declarers got the following hand right in this event some 20 years ago . . .

At game-all South played in Four Spades after East

had overcalled in Diamonds. (Five Diamonds doubled would have escaped for 500 points.)

West led the King and another Diamond to East's Ace and a third round of the suit followed, forcing South to ruff high.

It would have been all too easy for South to lead a top trump, but then a fourth round of Diamonds would have promoted West's nine of Spades for the setting trick.

So, instead, declarer crossed to dummy's King of Clubs before leading trumps. East had to play his Ace on thin air and declarer could afford to ruff the next Diamond lead high and draw trumps safely.

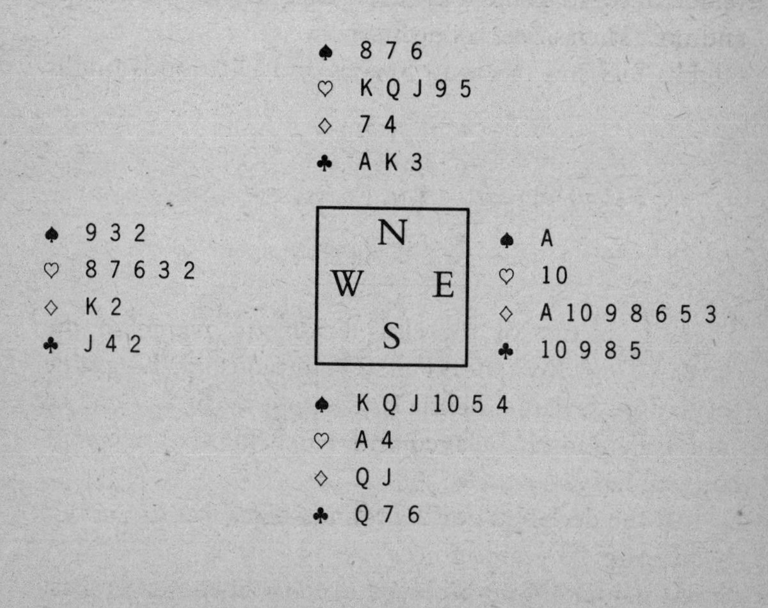

An Opinion

There were all sorts of arguments raging after this hand from rubber bridge. I was only watching and fortunately was not required to give an opinion on either the bidding (which I agree was difficult) or the play (which should not have been).

North dealt game-all and opened Two Clubs. It was true that his hand could not be classed as 'game-going' but with four first-round and four second-round controls, it is difficult to criticise.

South responded Two Diamonds (negative), North bid Two Spades and South showed his Hearts. North, reluctant to go to the four level, tried Three No-trumps and now it was South's decision.

His bits and pieces in Spades and Diamonds might

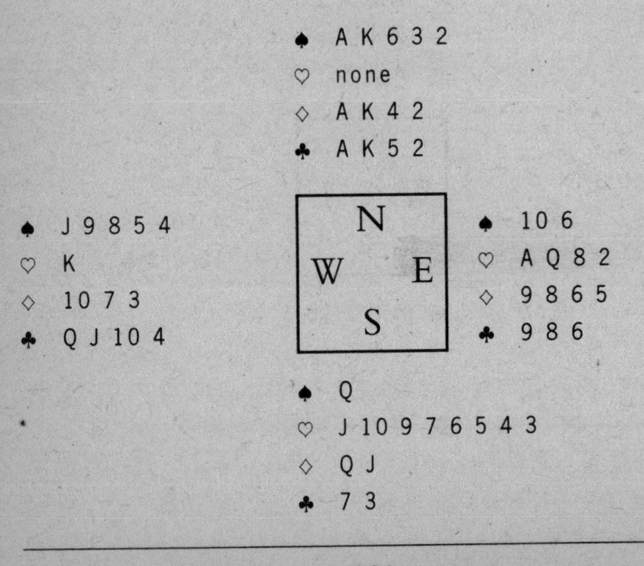

ruffing one of declarer's sure losers, West was right on the ball when he ruffed and led another trump. Now, whatever declarer tried, he found himself restricted to nine tricks.

Can you see South's mistake? After his Ace of Diamonds had held, he should have abandoned the suit and started his cross-ruff. Then he scores seven trumps separately to go with three Aces and makes his contract.

An Unlikely Top Score

It does not seem possible that the play of a suit of 8 2 facing the 10 3 dummy could be of interest, but it proved so on this deal from a pairs' event.

At practically every table South ended in Five Diamonds after East had overcalled in Clubs. At my

West	North	East
	♠ A Q 4	
	♡ K 9 8 6 3	
	◇ A 6 5	
	♣ 10 3	
♠ 9 7 6 5 2	N	♠ K 10 8
♡ Q 10 7 5	W E	♡ J 4
◇ 4	S	◇ 3 2
♣ 9 7 4		♣ A K Q J 6 5
	♠ J 3	
	♡ A 2	
	◇ K Q J 10 9 8 7	
	♣ 8 2	

table I had no problems in the play – West led the seven of Clubs (MUD – middle, up, down) and East was forced to win. He could win another Club trick, but could not profitably attack Spades from his side of the table.

Now I had the time and the entries to establish a long Heart for a Spade discard and so avoid the losing finesse.

At another table West led the nine of Clubs (top of nothing) and an absent-minded declarer played low from dummy. Now East was able to let his partner's nine win and, realising this must be for a reason, West found the punishing Spade switch. As the Diamonds in dummy gave declarer only one entry, he could no longer come to an eleventh trick.

Finally, one West again led the nine of Clubs and declarer covered with dummy's ten. East could see the dangers ahead so, after winning with the Jack, he attempted to put his partner in with the eight of Clubs by returning the six.

Unfortunately South held the eight and that is how he made an unlikely overtrick and a top score.

Weak Or Strong?

Whether you play a weak or a strong No-trump, you are sometimes dealt a hand with a long minor suit and are tempted to open One No-trump . . .

After two passes at love-all, South decided to open One No-trump (15-17 points). He preferred this to One

Diamond as it made it more difficult for the opponents to compete in either major suit.

West passed and North invited game with a raise to Two No-trumps. South went on to Three No-trumps. He felt it was the type of hand on which, if the Diamonds ran, there could be nine top tricks; if they did not, even eight tricks might prove too many.

West led the King of Spades and it was clear that declarer, having escaped a Heart lead, was in with a good chance. Playing too quickly, declarer won and led a Diamond to the Ace and returned to the King. The 4-1 break was bad news and now, with the lead in his own hand, it was too late to try for five tricks in Clubs, even if the Queen fell doubleton.

A slight change in timing would have made all the difference. Suppose that South starts the Diamonds with the King first, then the Ace.

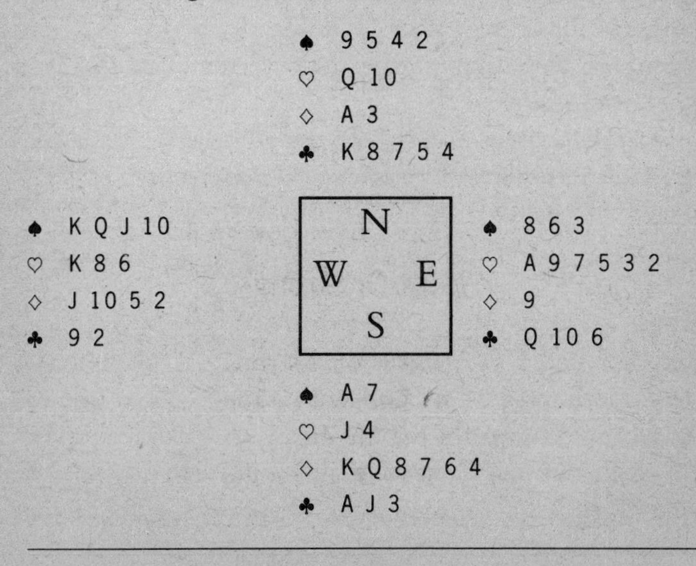

If the suit divides 3-2, the Ace of Clubs provides an entry to the rest of the Diamonds and, when the bad division emerges, the lead is in the right hand to play the Clubs for five tricks, finessing the Jack on the first round.

From Three Small?

Fashions change; the current choice of which card to lead from three small in a suit is MUD (middle, up, down). But it can be ambiguous . . .

East dealt at game-all and opened Two Clubs. South overcalled with three Spades and, after two passes, East doubled. Nobody knew if this was for take-out or penalties, but they all passed anyway.

With little to go on, West led the seven of Diamonds

West	North	East
	♠ 4 2	
	♡ 10 6 5	
	◇ 10 8 5 4 3	
	♣ 10 9 4	
♠ K	N	♠ A 8 7
♡ 8 3 2	W E	♡ A K 7
◇ 9 7 2	S	◇ A K Q J 6
♣ J 7 6 5 3 2		♣ K 8
	♠ Q J 10 9 6 5 3	
	♡ Q J 9 4	
	◇ none	
	♣ A K	

(MUD), and this went to the eight and Jack. Declarer ruffed and started on trumps, but West won the first round and continued with the nine of Diamonds, forcing South to ruff again. A top trump went to the Ace; another Diamond came back.

After drawing the last trump, South turned to Hearts. But the defence was one step ahead and, when declarer had run out of trumps, East still had a top Diamond to cash.

Just suppose that declarer had not made the completely pointless play of the eight of Diamonds on the first trick, and instead had played low.

East would have been unable to read the lead accurately (it might equally have been from the 7 2 doubleton) and would have been sure to have played the Jack.

As before, West wins the first trump and can push through the nine of Diamonds – but now dummy covers with the ten. The difference is that East is left with the six of Diamonds.

Simple Enough?

This looked simple enough to declarer – everything hinged on his being able to make three tricks from the Spade suit. But playing too quickly, he missed the line that would have given him the best percentage chance.

At game-all, South opened One No-trump and North raised to Three No-trumps.

West led the Queen of Diamonds and a glance at dummy told declarer that, although the partnership held 28 points, there were only eight top winners. Declarer started by letting the Queen of Diamonds hold but the enthusiasm with which West continued the suit made it clear that it was not dividing 3-3.

South's first thought was that an opponent held the Queen-Jack doubleton. So after winning the second Diamond in hand, he led a low Spade and the ten lost to the Jack. But the Queen did not fall on the next round and South ended with only eight tricks.

A better way to tackle the Spades is to win the second Diamond in dummy and lead the ten of Spades, planning to let it run if it is not covered. This succeeds, not only when the suit breaks 3-3, but also when East has started with Q x, J x or that Q J doubleton.

As the cards lie, a cover by East allows South to

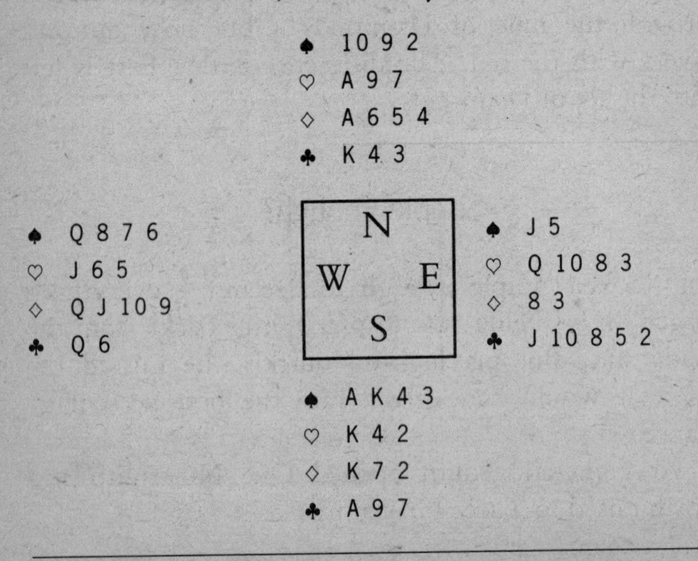

win and lead low towards the nine. If East does not cover, the Ten loses to the Queen, but the Jack falls on the next round.

An Odd Affair

The multi-coloured Two Diamonds convention is a tournament weapon that has enjoyed long, and perhaps undeserved, popularity. This adventure met with mixed success but led to an interesting point in the play.

South dealt at love-all and opened Two Diamonds – a weak Two-bid in either major or a strong three-suited hand.

North pre-empted with Five Diamonds and East, with little room for manoeuvre, could only double. South passed, perhaps with some trepidation (was it

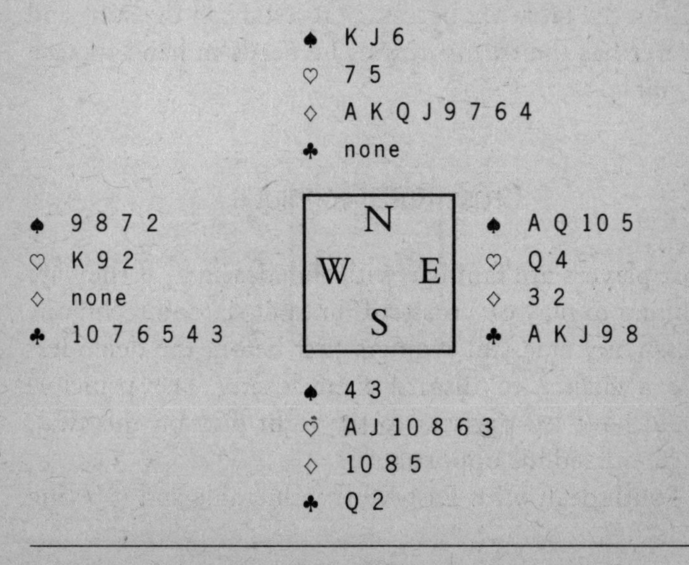

possible that partner had forgotten the convention?) and West, perhaps unwisely, also passed.

As you can see, 12 tricks might have been available (rather luckily) to East–West in either black suit.

West led a low club against Five Diamonds – remember, South was declarer and the play was soon over. After ruffing on the table declarer attempted to establish his Hearts but, when West got in with his King, a Spade switch led to two more tricks for the defence.

So East–West at least collected 100 points as a substitute for their game or possible slam, but their loss should have been greater.

Just suppose that declarer had discarded a low Heart from dummy at trick one instead of ruffing. East wins but, unless he cashes his Ace of Spades immediately, it will run away. Now only two Heart ruffs on the table are necessary to establish the suit, and declarer has the trump entries he needs in hand to cash the suit.

Cross-Ruff Technique

Most players are familiar with the idea that, if they are planning to play on cross-ruff lines, it is good technique to cash any side-suit winners first before the defenders have a chance to discard their losers. The principle should have led declarer to the right play on this deal, but he missed his opportunity.

South dealt with East–West vulnerable and (playing

five-card majors) opened One Diamond. West contented himself with an overcall of One Spade, although more aggressive action would undoubtedly have set North-South further problems, and South ended in Five Diamonds.

West led two top Spades and declarer ruffed. He planned to ruff another Spade in hand before drawing trumps and so make four tricks in Hearts and six in trumps to go with his Ace of Clubs.

It looked safest to start by crossing to dummy with a trump but, when the next Spade was ruffed, East discarded his singleton Heart. South followed by cashing the Ace of trumps but when he attempted to cross to dummy with a Heart, East ruffed and declarer was left with an inescapable Club loser.

If declarer uses dummy's Heart entry first before taking his second Spade ruff, there is nothing that the

West		East
	♠ 8 6 3 2 ♡ K J 5 ◇ K Q J 8 ♣ 10 2	
♠ A K Q J 7 4 ♡ 10 8 7 4 2 ◇ 3 ♣ 3	N W E S	♠ 9 5 ♡ 9 ◇ 10 9 5 4 ♣ K Q 9 8 6 5
	♠ 10 ♡ A Q 6 3 ◇ A 7 6 2 ♣ A J 7 4	

defenders can do. Trumps can be drawn after the Ace and a low one to dummy and 11 tricks roll in.

Percentages . . .

Sometimes you read that one line of play is 'about 3.4 per cent better than the alternative line of . . .' Who cares, except the mathematicians?

But when one play offers twice the chance of success as an alternative, it really matters.

South dealt at love-all and, with a difficult opening bid, selected One Diamond. North responded One Heart, East overcalled with One Spade and South showed his strength with a bid of Two Spades – the opponents' suit. Eventually South ended in Five Diamonds and West led the two of Spades.

West		North / South		East
		♠ A 7 5		
		♡ J 7 6 4		
		◇ 5 4 2		
		♣ J 10 4		
♠ J 8 6 2		N		♠ K Q 10 9 4
♡ 10 9 8 2		W E		♡ 5 3
◇ K		S		◇ A 10 6
♣ 8 6 5 3				♣ 9 7 2
		♠ 3		
		♡ A K Q		
		◇ Q J 9 8 7 3		
		♣ A K Q		

Clearly everything hinged on the trump suit and, after winning the lead, declarer led a low Diamond from the table. East followed with the six, South tried the Queen and lost to West's King.

There were still two more trump tricks to lose and the contract failed by one trick. There would have been three sure losers in diamonds if the suit had divided 4–0, while, if it had broken 2–2, any play would have succeeded.

The only chance of winning against a 3–1 break (after East had followed with the six) was to find West with a singleton.

To play the Queen is only right if West holds the singleton ten, but to finesse the nine gains if he has either the singleton King or Ace. Even to a non-mathematician like myself, that looks like 2–1!

True, And False

'I can make Three No-trumps but I can't possibly make Four Hearts on that lead,' claimed South after this deal. I agreed with the first part of his statement but not the second.

West opened One Spade at love-all and a confused auction left North with the choice of passing his partner's bid of Three No-trumps or converting to Four Hearts – a suit in which he knew South held at least five cards. He chose the latter, but (as the cards lie) Three No-trumps would have been easy.

West led the King of Diamonds and matters did not

look hopeful to South – there were three minor suit losers and very likely one trump. South won and, with no clear idea, exited with a Diamond.

West won, cashed the Ace of Clubs and – in spite of his partner's encouragement – persisted with Diamonds. Things looked better; for surely West had held the singleton Ace of Clubs.

In an attempt to take advantage, declarer cashed the Ace of trumps and followed with three rounds of Spades. If East had followed, another trump would have put West in and forced him to concede a ruff and discard.

Unlucky! East ruffed and there was still a trump to lose.

Can you see the winning line, unlikely though it may seem? Ruff the Queen of Spades with the Queen

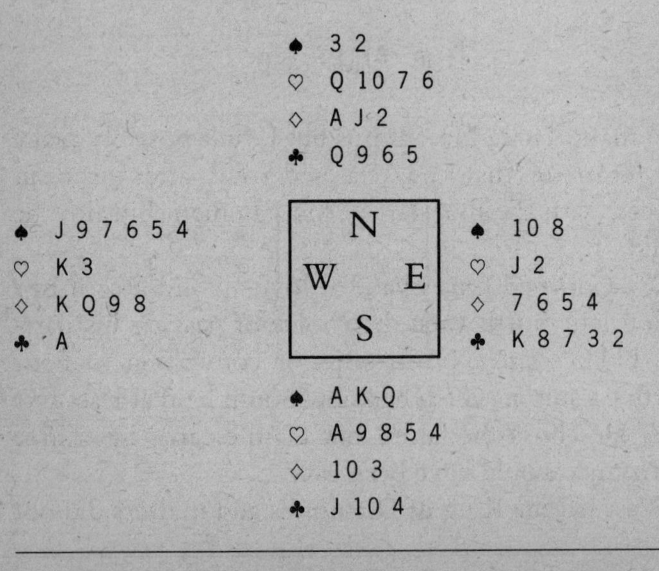

of trumps and then play a trump. Now West is end-played.

It Really Does Not Matter

I am often asked whether I think it is better to play a weak No-trump (12–14 points) rather than a strong No-trump (15–17 points). Usually I prefer the latter but, just to show my impartiality, here is a triumph for the other camp.

South dealt at love-all and, playing weak, started with One No-trump. West passed and North, judging correctly that nine tricks in No-trumps might be an easier proposition than the 11 tricks needed for game in Diamonds, raised to Three No-trumps.

There was no real reason for West to lead a Heart.

West		East
	♠ A K ♡ 6 3 ◇ K 10 8 7 6 3 ♣ Q 5 2	
♠ Q J 10 ♡ Q 5 2 ◇ 9 5 4 ♣ K 8 7 4	N W E S	♠ 9 8 7 6 ♡ K J 10 9 8 ◇ A ♣ 9 6 3
	♠ 5 4 3 2 ♡ A 7 4 ◇ Q J 2 ♣ A J 10	

Some Wests chose the Queen of Spades; some chose a low Club and South had an easy run to nine or ten tricks.

The strong No-trumpers did not have such an easy ride. Either South passed and North opened One Diamond, or South opened One Club and North responded One Diamond.

In either case East was able to overcall with One Heart, suggesting a lead, and there was no longer any chance of the No-trump game succeeding.

True, that Five Diamonds depended only on the (unsuccessful) Club finesse, but that's poor consolation for the advocates of the strong No-trump.

A Good Start

After starting with what looked to be an effective (if lucky) defence, West found himself with a new and difficult problem at the third trick. Even seeing all four hands, the winning continuation is not at all obvious.

With East-West game South opened One Spade and West overcalled Two Clubs. In view of the vulnerability North gave some thought to a penalty double but wisely, in view of his length in his partner's suit, settled for a raise to Three Spades. South went on to game and West decided not to risk any further enterprise. He led the Two of Diamonds and was pleasantly surprised when he collected a ruff with his singleton trump after East had returned the Jack of Diamonds.

Now, however, West found himself end-played. A Heart at this stage would give declarer two tricks in the suit and dummy's third Heart would go away on the King of Diamonds later on.

In practice West led the Ace of Clubs but South ruffed and, after losing a trump trick, was able to dispose of his losing Hearts on dummy's Clubs.

It would have been an almost impossible play to find at the table, but try the effect of the Jack of Clubs at trick three. Now declarer gets only one discard from hand and still has a Spade and, eventually, a Heart to lose.

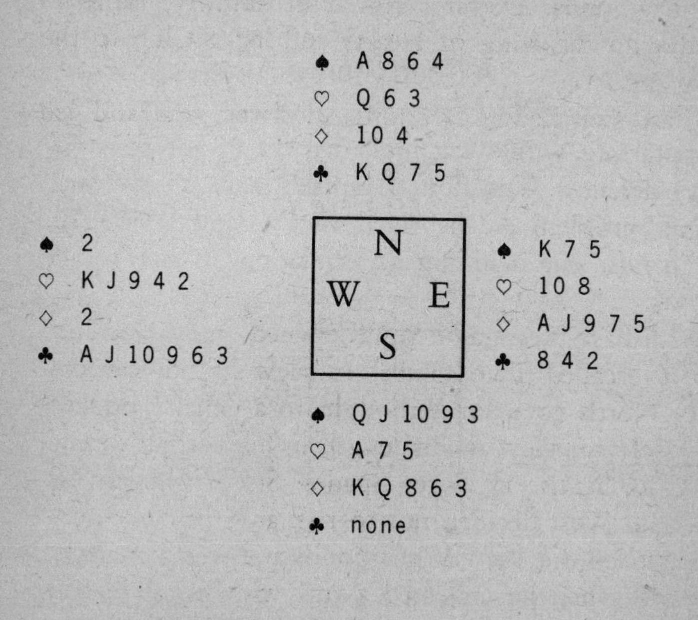

Everybody Else Got It Right

'There was nothing that I could do against that defence,' claimed declarer at the end of this deal. But his partner, both defenders and the three spectators all good-heartedly disagreed – and they were right.

East opened One Diamond at game-all and South ended in Three Spades ('150 for honours, partner!')

West led with the nine of Diamonds, and it looked like nine easy tricks for declarer – with six trumps, the Ace and King of Hearts, and one ruff in dummy. East won the lead, however, and continued with two more top Diamonds. Declarer ruffed in dummy, came to hand with the King of Hearts and led a Club to the King and Ace.

East switched to a trump, declarer won and led

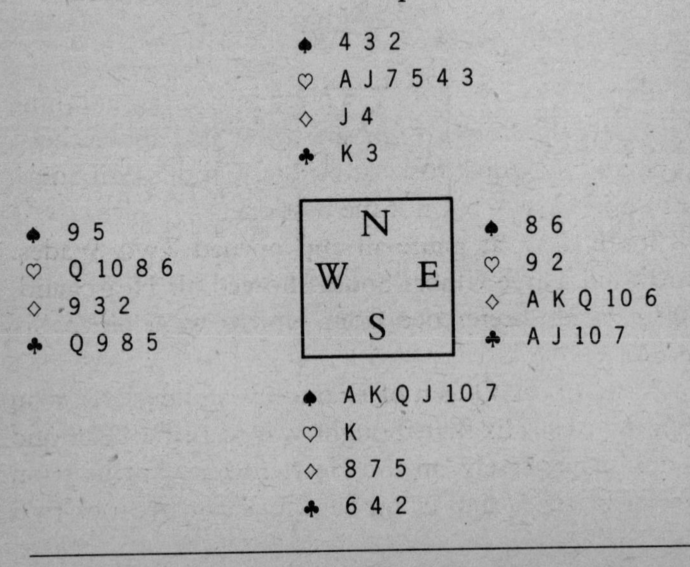

another Club, but the defenders came back with a second trump. There was now no way of getting to the Ace of Hearts, and declarer lost three Clubs and two Diamonds.

From East's opening bid it was extremely likely that the Ace of Clubs was wrong and that South would gain nothing by leading towards the King.

Declarer does better to refuse to ruff the third Diamond lead, discarding a Club from dummy instead.

If East switches to a trump, South wins, unblocks the King of Hearts and leads a Club. Now declarer can ruff a Club on the table and get to the Ace of Hearts for his ninth trick.

Chess Does Have Considerable Value At Bridge

'When you have thought of a good move, try and think of a better one,' was, I am sure, first said about chess. It applies with equal force at bridge. On this deal South had a good idea – but not the best one.

South dealt at game-all and opened Two Spades. North bid Three Clubs, South showed his Hearts and, after a Spade preference from North, went on to Six Spades.

West led the Queen of Diamonds and declarer won with the Ace. His first thought was to ruff a Diamond in dummy and rely on the Heart finesse, but he soon had the better idea of using dummy's suit. At trick two he carefully led the nine of trumps to dummy's Queen. Then came the King of Clubs and, when East failed to cover, a Heart discard from hand.

It all looked too simple. With the Spades breaking no worse than 3–1, declarer planned to draw trumps ending in dummy and take four more discards on the long Clubs.

Disaster! On winning with his Ace of Clubs, West forced dummy with another Diamond and now South could take only two more discards on the Clubs before West was able to ruff.

It was a fair plan but (clearly) not quite good enough. Try discarding the five of Diamonds on the King of Clubs.

Now dummy's trumps cannot be shortened and all four losing Hearts can be thrown away at leisure after drawing trumps.

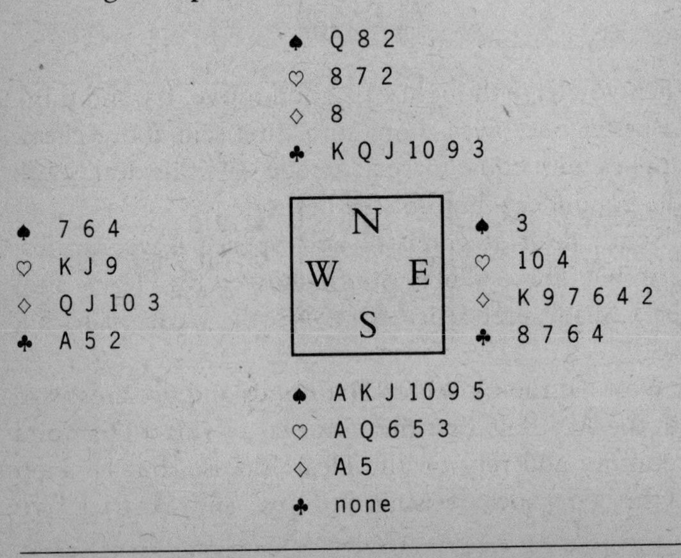

Good Bidding, But . . .

The bidding was intelligent on this deal, but declarer missed a not-too-difficult opportunity in the play.

After two passes, West opened One Spade at game all, choosing the major suit in the hope of hampering North-South.

North might have overcalled with One No-trump but he decided to double, firstly because his partner might fit in Hearts and, secondly, because it might be better for his partner to be declarer in No-trumps if he had a bolster in Spades. South did indeed have a guard in Spades and ended in Three No-trumps, against which West led a low Club to the three, ten and Queen.

On the assumption that the Spade finesse was right, declarer had eight tricks. There seemed no chance of a

West	North / South	East
	♠ A 3 2	
	♡ A Q 7 4	
	◇ A 10 5	
	♣ J 5 3	
♠ K 10 8 7 5	N	♠ 9 6
♡ J	W E	♡ 10 9 8 6 5 3
◇ Q 2	S	◇ J 9 6
♣ A K 7 6 2		♣ 10 8
	♠ Q J 4	
	♡ K 2	
	◇ K 8 7 4 3	
	♣ Q 9 4	

ninth without bringing in the Diamonds, so South played on the suit immediately.

He hoped that West had led from a four-card suit and that the defence could take only three Clubs and one Diamond.

However, East won the third Diamond and returned a Club to defeat the contract. South missed his chance. He should return a Club at trick two.

If West proves to have only three Club tricks, there will be time to develop the Diamonds. If West has four Club tricks but refuses to take them, declarer can arrange to lose a Diamond trick safely to East.

Finally, if West cashes four Club tricks, South can follow with two Spade winners – then East has to unguard one of the red suits – and gives South his ninth trick.